HODOS
LEADERSHIP

Leadership matters! But to describe leadership, and especially good and transformative leadership, is notoriously difficult. Anyone can find words to warn against wrong and destructive leadership, but it is more challenging to train and empower leaders who lead in transformative love. Alexander Negrov's timely and inspiring text achieves this difficult task. Not only does this well-written text clearly define Christ-centered leadership in a thoroughly robust Biblical and theological way, but it also maps out a way forward to train the next generation of leaders who could bring godly transformation to their world. I expect this book to become a standard text for those who seek to embody transformative leadership.

- **Dr. Corné J. Bekker,** *Professor and Dean, School of Divinity, Regent University*

Upon initially starting this book, my reaction was tinged with skepticism: "Oh, not another book on leadership!" Yet this skepticism was quickly dispelled as the unique nature of the text revealed itself. This book delves into an intricate tapestry of spiritual, ethical, and practical leadership dimensions, enriched with theological insight, social research, and an innovative mix of personal and collective leadership strategies. Dr. Negrov intersperses thought-provoking questions throughout, enhancing the book's relevance and applicability for young adults who seek to forge their path in leadership. Life, as we know it, is a journey (*hodos*), and it is often said that the value of a journey lies not only in its end but also in those who accompany us along the way. In the realm of leadership, this book stands out as a sage companion for such a journey.

- **Dr. Riad Kassis,** *International Director, Langham Partnership International, Lebanon*

I am honored to recommend *Hodos Leadership* by internationally respected university president, Hodos Institute founder/CEO, and visionary, Alexander Negrov. Young Christian professionals have been the focus of Dr. Negrov's ministry endeavors for decades and now this volume provides the culmination of his experiences, knowledge, and wisdom. May this leadership manual bless all who read it.

- **Dr. Ronald L. Ellis,** *President, California Baptist University*

In his well-sourced and research-informed book, Dr. Alexander Negrov provides a beautifully trenchant pathway for becoming theocentric leaders. Spiritual intelligence and ethical wellbeing combine for mature Christ followers on the leadership journey. Dr. Negrov embodies what he teaches in the U.S., Ukraine, and around the world. *Hodos Leadership* invites you to a Trinitarian odyssey. Leadership coaches, be sure to explore the "Pro 7" Leadership Formation Model!

- **Dr. Thomas F. Tumblin,** *Professor, Asbury Theological Seminary*

I have come to know Dr. Alexander Negrov and his family quite closely over the last couple of years. Negrov's lifelong commitment to learning, observation, and practical application shines through everything he does. This book offers a vision for leadership that is spiritual, ethical, and effective. No matter your field of work, the compelling truths in *Hodos Leadership* will help you become a healthier and better leader.

- **Russell Korets,** *Pastor, Woodmark Church, Kirkland, Washington*

Hodos Leadership is an excellent guide and resource for Christians who wish to be formed as leaders. Alexander Negrov serves as an instructor and coach towards the reader's development in spiritual, ethical, and effective leadership. In each chapter, he provides stories, research, teaching, and most importantly, reflective questions for the reader to consider and assess themselves. Academically rich, *Hodos Leadership* taken a section at a time for reflection will be life changing.

- **Dr. Keith Webb,** *Founder and President, Creative Results Management*

As a pastor and seminary president, I have been teaching leadership courses for years. I have read numerous books on leadership and regret it is only now that I have read this book. Once you begin reading Dr. Negrov's book, you won't want to put it down. It is not just another book on leadership in the conventional sense. Instead, it is a book that goes far beyond mere knowledge transmission. In *Hodos Leadership*, Dr. Negrov shares his extensive knowledge and invaluable experience. The greatest strength, and simultaneously the most significant contribution of this book, lies in its ability to pose the right questions about leadership. Those who engage seriously with these questions will be able to develop their own concepts of leadership. The theological depth, practical insights, personal experiences of the author, and helpful explanations are a treasure trove I would not want to do without. "Hodos" translates to "path," and Dr. Negrov wants the reader to understand leadership as a life path. Every chapter and every topic is conceived from this fundamental idea. I am convinced that this book will become a standard work and will be required reading at theological seminaries and universities in the field of leadership around the world.

- **Dr. Heinrich Derksen,** *President, Bible Seminary Bonn (BSB), Bonn, Germany*

I highly recommend *Hodos Leadership*. A healthy leader cultivates healthy families, churches, communities, and nations. True transformation begins from within, and this book provides invaluable tools for every leader to analyze, develop, and enhance their personal leadership. This is a must-read book for those committed to making a lasting impact.

- **Vadym Dashkevych,** *Pastor of SOL Church, Sacramento, California*

My colleague, Dr. Negrov, has carefully and with great wisdom crafted this "Leadership Handbook," which will empower and equip young professionals on a journey of developing high-impact leadership. These pages contain valuable insights, among which are those for character building and spiritual growth, as well as those for crafting personal visions for their futures. Within *Hodos Leadership* is a "strategy for HOPE" that I highly recommend!

- **Dr. Gregory L. Jantz,** *Founder and President, The Center • A Place of HOPE, bestselling author*

Amid the multitude of leadership books, Dr. Alexander Negrov's work shines through with its unique perspective. He compellingly argues that the dynamic nature of organizational structures, cultural norms, and social challenges necessitate a fresh leadership approach—one that's contemporary yet firmly grounded in timeless biblical truth. *Hodos Leadership* masterfully weaves together academic knowledge with real-world applications. Negrov's profound comprehension, personal journey, and receptiveness to novel concepts beckon us to view leadership as an ethical odyssey—a calling—and a shared pilgrimage with others and, ultimately, with Christ. Its perceptive analysis equips leaders to navigate complexity without compromising their principles. Whether it's for a pastor leading his congregation through a time of change, a nonprofit director dealing with new funding, or an educator preparing the next generation of Christian leaders, Negrov's work is a guiding light. It leads us toward leadership based on ethical integrity, outward focus, and transformative effectiveness.

- **Dr. Roman Soloviy,** *Professor and President, Eastern European Institute of Theology, Lviv, Ukraine*

Hodos Leadership is an excellent and professional guide for those on the leadership journey. Alexander Negrov guides with insightful questions and helpful reflections, avoiding simplistic one-size-fits-all prescriptions. This is a must read for value-based business leaders on a mission.

- **Mats Tunehag,** *Chairman, Business as Mission (BAM) Global Movement*

The story of the Exodus of the people of Israel from Egypt shows that while leaders changed, the ultimate goal remained the same. *Hodos Leadership* is a wonderful book for emerging leaders. Dr. Negrov equips readers to navigate life with purpose and wisdom, ensuring a lasting personal legacy that reaches far beyond the present moment.

- **Vasiliy Papirnik,** *Pastor, Seattle Bethany Church, Seattle, Washington*

In *Hodos Leadership*, Dr. Alexander Negrov has written a very insightful and valuable book, one which I believe will be an asset for young leaders just starting out and for experienced leaders seeking new ideas on leadership. The book is a reflection and synthesis of Dr. Negrov's journey as a leader and teacher of many. I've known him for nearly thirty years and his life of vision, leadership, and integrity is one that is reflected here.

- **Dr. Kent L. Eby,** *Professor, Bethel University*

I sincerely recommend *Hodos Leadership*! Drawing on biblical narratives, personal leadership experience, and a rich Eastern European heritage, Dr. Negrov introduces the innovative Hodos Leadership model. Integrating faith with everyday leadership, Dr. Negrov offers readers a unique perspective on leadership through the lens of inner transformation, character development, reflection, and the practical application of biblical teachings. Addressing contemporary challenges within the Christian community, this book advocates for authentic leadership that bridges Sunday faith with Monday life, tackles ethical issues, and fosters effective leadership across different sectors. With a focus on continuous growth, community engagement, and self-awareness, the Hodos Leadership model presents a transformative and practical roadmap for today's Christian leaders.

- **Dr. Yaroslav Pyzh,** *President, Ukrainian Baptist Theological Seminary (UBTS), Lviv, Ukraine*

Leaders are made, not born. Unique among leadership programs is Dr. Alexander Negrov's compelling approach to developing spiritual, ethical, and effective leaders. Such leaders, he emphasizes, are crucial in both Christian and secular fields everywhere. The Bible and *Hodos Leadership* are essential books for nurturing today's young leaders. They will change people's lives!

- **Dr. Michael M. Whyte,** *CEO, Global Academy for Transformational Leadership*

Hodos Leadership is a worthy read for all of us interested in the much-needed integration of faith and work. Pressing for such an integration has been a longstanding ministry of mine within a congregation consisting mostly of professionals. How I have longed for church members to live out a deeper sense of calling in their differing vocations! Dr. Alexander Negrov asks soul-searching questions throughout his book, daring and showing us how to bring our Christian faith and values to our work and life beyond the church.

- **Dr. Ross Goodman,** *Pastor, Saint Paul Lutheran Church, Arlington, Massachusetts*

A lack of morally courageous leadership is one of the defining issues of our day. We desperately need it in politics, in economics, and in society as a whole. Morally courageous leadership is what separates those willing to take on responsibility from those desiring nothing but power for personal gain. The former are those who combine genuine ability with humility in a lifelong seeking for wisdom; the latter are those who combine genuine ability with a sense of self-importance in aspiring to power and influence. Morally courageous leadership requires a very solid foundation – and for me that foundation must be built on deep spiritual roots. In *Hodos Leadership*, Alexander Negrov leads his readers on a journey, posing a series of provocative questions as he explores many different aspects of leadership. And in doing so, he challenges the readers to think through their understanding not only of leadership in general but also of Christian leadership in particular. Such a task is not easy. But Dr. Negrov's exploration of biblical leadership and spirituality, and the distinction to be made between them and a secular understanding of leadership, are fundamental to developing sound ethical leadership. This book demands attention, offers practical advice, and should be approached with honesty and humility.

- **Major General Tim Cross CBE, (Retired),** *Ex-Commander of one of three Divisions of the United Kingdom Field Army, Licensed Lay Minister, Church of England, Surrey, United Kingdom*

Hodos Leadership provides for us a framework that is grounded in God and undergirded in faith in Jesus Christ. By commending space for reflection and inquiry, Dr. Negrov helps us realize a leadership practice that is spiritual, ethical, and effective. His book is a guide that if used diligently, serves as a conversation partner and coach to help readers find an enlivened way and mindset of a type of leadership made possible and enriched by a personal relationship with Christ. Focusing on formation and a cultivated inner spiritual life that prioritizes service to others, Dr. Negrov provides a model of leadership which fosters active and responsible communities that are characterized by compassion, trust, and mutual respect.

- **Dr. Debora Jackson,** *Dean and Professor, Worcester Polytechnic Institute Business School*

Hodos Leadership is a transformative guide tailored for young and middle-aged Christians eager to deepen their leadership impact across various life spheres. Within these pages, Alexander Negrov offers an insightful and engaging path to leadership development, enriching the roles of leaders within the family, organization, and community. Dr. Negrov captivates readers, fostering self-reflection and growth in Christian maturity and leadership skills. This book prepares prospective and experienced leaders alike to integrate essential elements into an effective leadership model, aiming to positively influence individuals, teams, and the broader society. It is my belief that *Hodos Leadership* will soon not only reach American leaders but also inspire Latin American young professionals to cultivate genuine, ethical, and exemplary leadership.

- **Dr. Jorge F. Salcedo Mireles,** *Professor, School of Business, University of Monterrey, Mexico*

Hodos Leadership serves as a guide of inspiration for young leaders navigating the complexities of today's business world. Whether you're just a budding novice or already a seasoned executive in your field, this book provides invaluable insights for cultivating a soulful approach to leadership that goes beyond conventional management practices.

- **Beryl Basham,** *Co-founder, One Earth Rising, founder of Beryl Basham Fine Art*

Alexander Negrov's lifelong commitment to leadership and his framing of leadership as a journey connects deeply to the felt needs of Christians as they serve in their places of work. Dr. Negrov offers a well-informed understanding of the social, spiritual, biblical, and theological challenges that confront today's leader. *Hodos Leadership* is an excellent guide for readers making their way along the path of leadership development. The book is an invitation to grow in theological depth, in understanding leadership theory and practice, and in ethical wisdom and courage. These qualities and knowledge are to be developed in intimate connection with the leader's personal spirituality. All said, this book will prove to be a blessing to many who desire to impact their world as they participate in God's mission.

- **Dr. Jack Barentsen,** *Professor, Evangelische Theologische Faculteit and Institute of Leadership and Social Ethics, Leuven, Belgium*

When I pick up a book, my first question is whether the author has the knowledge and experience to credibly address the subject. Any book on leadership by Dr. Alexander Negrov immediately has my attention because of his many years of outstanding leadership, his extensive knowledge, and his personal integrity. But Negrov is not just another clever and knowledgeable leader. He is a wise leader. This wisdom makes it possible for him to address the topic of ethical leadership with keen insight and sound counsel. Sadly, many churches, businesses, educational institutions, and non-profit organizations today suffer from unethical and toxic leadership. I highly recommend *Hodos Leadership* for younger leaders who long to lead like Jesus leads.

- **Dr. Daryl McCarthy,** *CEO, The Leadership Anvil*

Hodos Leadership, as presented by Alexander Negrov, provides a fresh, biblically grounded framework for Christ-centered leadership. Its holistic integration of faith, ethics, and effective leadership practices distinguishes it from countless models focused solely on profits or enriching organizational elites to the detriment of society and the environment. By placing Christ-like love and servanthood at its core, *Hodos Leadership* argues powerfully that true leadership is not merely about guiding others but about embodying spiritual maturity and ethical integrity. This Christocentric model invites leaders to align their professional and personal lives with Christian values, making it particularly relevant for those striving to lead within the constraints of secular leadership models that often lack a moral compass. Reflecting selfless love, ethical decision-making, and transformative service, *Hodos Leadership* offers a compelling pathway for leaders seeking to create lasting impact in their organizations and communities.

- **Dr. Louis (Jody) Fry,** *Regents Professor of Leadership, Texas A&M University-Central Texas; Founder, International Institute for Spiritual Leadership*

Much has been written about leadership in the past century, yet there is surprisingly little from non-western authors. Considering his background and expertise, Dr. Negrov's contribution to the global debate is a very welcome addition. *Hodos Leadership* marvelously applies timeless Biblical principles to the realities and challenges of leadership throughout the world. I am particularly impressed by Dr. Negrov's insight into the theology of work, considering the Eastern European entrenched legacy of a sacred – secular divide. I highly recommend *Hodos Leadership*! I am convinced that this book will contribute to a better understanding of the biblical perspective on work and the invaluable contributions Christians can make through their professions.

- **Dr. Sebastian Văduva,** *IT Executive, Professor of Entrepreneurship, Emanuel University of Oradea, Romania*

As a top organizational executive in the areas of education and science, I have always sought new approaches to management and leadership. *Hodos Leadership* turned out to be exactly the resource I was looking for. Thanks to Dr. Negrov, I am enriched by the concept of "hodos leadership," which has not only fascinated me, but it has also forced me to rethink my own approach to leadership. *Hodos Leadership* prudently interrelates spirituality, ethics, and effectiveness—a fine achievement highly relevant to me as a Christian leader. I highly recommend this book to all—educators, students, researchers, practitioners, leaders, team members—who want to become better leaders. *Hodos Leadership* will be a reliable guide in your journey of leadership and personal growth.
- **Dr. Lyudmila Shtanko,** *Rector, The Ukrainian Institute of Arts and Sciences, Bucha/Kyiv, Ukraine*

We need books that can, in Dr. Alexander Negrov's words, help us "reflect on and advance spiritual, ethical, and effective leadership"! I very much appreciate *Hodos Leadership* and the holistic model of leadership development which he advances within the book. The book is practical in content and contains excellent inquiries for reflections. It offers tremendous help to those who are willing to take the time to focus on their leadership careers with the intent of improving their effectiveness. Dr. Negrov does not offer simple recipes for leadership development, but instead, leads his readers to deeper reflections on their own leadership proficiencies. I highly recommend this book. It deserves a broad audience and would make an excellent resource for churches, Christian-led organizations and businesses, and non-profits, looking to strengthen their Christian leadership training. and institutions as well as for training Christian leaders in civil society and business.
- **Øivind Augland,** *Founder and President, M4 and Exponential Europe, Kristiansand, Agder, Norway*

ALEXANDER NEGROV

HODOS
LEADERSHIP

An Invitation to
Young Christian Professionals to Reflect
and Advance in the
Paths of **Spiritual, Ethical, and Effective Leadership**

© 2025 by Alexander I Negrov

Published by Hodos Institute

www.hodosinstitute.com

Printed in the United States of America

Library of Congress Control Number (LCCN): 2024945943

ISBN: 978-1-7353774-5-2 (paperback)

Negrov, Alexander I, 1966- author. *Hodos Leadership: An Invitation to Young Christian Professionals to Reflect and Advance in the Paths of Spiritual, Ethical, and Effective Leadership.* Seattle: Hodos Institute, 2025. | Includes index.

LC record available at https://lccn.loc.gov/2024945943

All rights reserved. No part of this publication may be reproduced, stored in a retrieval system, or transmitted in any form or by any means-for example, electronic, photocopy, recording— without the prior written permission of the publisher. The only exception is brief quotations in printed reviews

All Scripture quotations, unless otherwise indicated, are taken from the Holy Bible, New International Version®, NIV®. Copyright ©1973, 1978, 1984, 2011 by Biblica, Inc.™ Used by permission of Zondervan. All rights reserved worldwide. www.zondervan.com The "NIV" and "New International Version" are trademarks registered in the United States Patent and Trademark Office by Biblica, Inc.™

Scripture quotations marked NASB are taken from the (NASB®) New American Standard Bible®, Copyright © 1960, 1971, 1977, 1995, 2020 by The Lockman Foundation. Used by permission. All rights reserved. lockman.org.

Scripture quotations marked ESV are from The ESV® Bible (The Holy Bible, English Standard Version®), © 2001 by Crossway, a publishing ministry of Good News Publishers. Used by permission. All rights reserved.

Cover design by Kendal Marsh

To the Holy Trinity who saves us and shows us the way, and to those who faithfully seek God to love him with all their heart, follow him with all their strength, and bring others to him through selfless love and service.

In these years of continued war in Ukraine, I also dedicate this book to the Ukrainians who have exemplified spiritual, ethical, and effective leadership, and to those who have steadfastly supported the Ukrainian people.

TABLE OF CONTENTS

BIBLE BOOK ABBREVIATIONS	XVII
PREFACE	XIX
FRAMING THE LEADERSHIP MAP	XXIII

CHAPTER 1. EMBARKING ON A JOURNEY OF LEADERSHIP — 1
1. Quests for Growth — 2
2. Starting Questions — 5
3. Self-Inquiry Prompts — 8
4. Probing the Nature of Leadership — 11
5. Exploring Followership — 14
6. Exploring Leadership Growth — 17

CHAPTER 2. THE WAY: METAPHOR IN HODOS LEADERSHIP — 23
1. Leadership Defined — 23
2. Leadership Metaphors — 27
3. Hodos Leadership Language — 33
4. Hodos Terminology — 44

CHAPTER 3. THE 3M HODOS LEADERSHIP FRAMEWORK — 55
1. Mindset in Leadership — 55
2. Model in Leadership — 58
3. Maturity in Leadership — 62

CHAPTER 4. THE CONFLUENCE OF FAITH AND LEADERSHIP — 77
1. Theological Bearings on Leadership — 78
2. Why Theological Inquiry? — 80
3. Theocentric Approach — 84
4. Plan for a Theological Journey — 88
5. Leadership in the Bible — 95
6. Christian Worldview and Leadership — 100

CHAPTER 5. SPIRITUALITY AND LEADERSHIP	**107**
1. Spirituality and Religion	107
2. Christian Spirituality Framework	111
3. Trinitarian Guidance	115
4. Spiritual Direction and Companionship	120
5. Spiritual Intelligence in Leadership	124
6. Spirituality and Personal Leadership	131
7. Spirituality and Marketplace Leadership	135
8. Toxic Religious Leadership	137
CHAPTER 6. HODOS LEADERSHIP AT WORK	**145**
1. Missional Leadership	145
2. Revamping A Work Mindset	149
3. Navigating Workplace Realities	156
CHAPTER 7. ETHICAL LEADERSHIP	**165**
1. What Defines Ethical Leadership?	165
2. The Way of Ethical Leadership	169
3. Ethical vs. Unethical Leadership in Teams	173
4. Deepening Ethical Leadership	176
5. Professional Ethics	180
6. Ethical Leadership and Workplace Spirituality	184
7. Ethical Leadership Checklists	187
CHAPTER 8. EFFECTIVE LEADERSHIP	**199**
1. Defining effective leadership	199
2. The Complexity of Effective Leadership	203
3. Effective Leading and Following	206
4. Communication, Listening, and Feedback	208
5. Leadership Styles for Effectiveness	211

CHAPTER 9. LEADERSHIP FORMATION AND LEADERSHIP DEVELOPMENT — 251

1. Illuminating the Path — 251
2. The Key Elements — 255
3. Climbing Leadership Mountain — 262
4. A Multigenerational Approach — 266
5. Leadership Formation and Youth — 277
6. Leadership Development and Organizational Culture — 282
7. Leadership Development in Nonprofit Organizations — 285
8. Showing the Way: The Role of Mentoring and Coaching — 293

CHAPTER 10. THE NOW AND THE NEXT — 301

ABOUT THE AUTHOR — 310

ACKNOWLEDGMENTS — 312

INDEX — 316

NOTES — 328

BIBLE BOOK ABBREVIATIONS

(According to Collins, Billie Jean, et al. *The SBL Handbook of Style: For Biblical Studies and Related Disciplines*. 2n. ed., SBL Press, 2014.)

Old Testament

Gen - Genesis
Exod - Exodus
Lev - Leviticus
Num - Numbers
Deut - Deuteronomy
Josh - Joshua
Judg - Judges
Ruth - Ruth
1Sam - 1Samuel
2Sam - 2Samuel
1Kgs - 1Kings
2Kgs - 2Kings
1Chron - 1Chronicles
2Chron - 2Chronicles
Ezra - Ezra
Neh - Nehemiah
Esth - Esther
Job - Job
Ps - Psalms
Prov - Proverbs
Eccl - Ecclesiastes
Song - Song of Solomon
Is - Isaiah
Jer - Jeremiah
Lam - Lamentations
Ezek - Ezekiel
Dan - Daniel
Hos - Hosea
Joel – Joel
Amos - Amos
Obad - Obadiah
Jon - Jonah
Mic - Micah
Nah - Nahum
Hab - Habakkuk
Zeph - Zephaniah
Hag - Haggai
Zech - Zechariah
Mal - Malachi

New Testament

Matt - Matthew
Mark - Mark
Luke - Luke
John - John
Acts – Acts
Rom - Romans
1Cor - 1Corinthians
2Cor - 2Corinthians
Gal - Galatians
Eph - Ephesians
Phil - Philippians
Col - Colossians
1Thess - 1Thessalonians
2Thess - 2Thessalonians
1Tim - 1Timothy
2Tim - 2Timothy
Titus - Titus
Phlm - Philemon
Heb - Hebrews
Jam - James
1Pet - 1Peter
2Pet - 2Peter
1Jn - 1John
2Jn - 2John
3Jn - 3John
Jude - Jude
Rev - Revelation

"I am the vine; you are the branches.
If you remain in me and I in you, you
will bear much fruit;
apart from me you can do nothing."
– Jesus Christ (John 15:5)

PREFACE

Hodos Leadership is based on a Christian theological framework, and as such is written for those who wish to grow and excel in spiritual, ethical, and effective leadership. The book is especially addressed to young and middle-aged Christians desiring to experience a fusion of spirituality with high-impact leadership in all spheres of life.

As you embark on this journey with me, I kindly ask for your thoughts once you've finished. Honest reviews on platforms like Amazon help share this message with others who may need it.

The ancient Greek word ὁδός [hodos] means "the way" or "the journey," carrying with it the notion of "development and maturity." Metaphorically, it expresses what might be described as "ways of thinking, feeling, and behaving." The leadership approach, which in this book I refer to as *Hodos Leadership*, thus employs a well-known spiritual metaphor universally referred to as *The Way or The Path*. In the following chapters, I explore different aspects of the *hodos* metaphor, with the idea of inviting my readers to reflect upon and advance good leadership in their personal or organizational capacities.

Theologically speaking, *hodos leadership* is linked to God, his kingdom, and Christ-like love. Its emphasis, accordingly, is Christocentric. In full self-disclosure, Jesus says that he is the only way to God (John 14:6). He *is* the way, and he *shows* the way, not only the way to live, but also the way to lead. Jesus says that through him, his followers belong to God and, thus through an active and abiding relationship with him, they will bear much good fruit. They can and will be salt and light in a dark world for his noble cause!

My sincere hope in putting forward this book is that you, the reader, will be taken on a journey in which you're introduced to or become acquainted with the principles of *hodos leadership*. This learning process, of course, to be successful requires exercising such attitudes and disciplines as follows.

ATTEND: This book, as I see it, serves as an invitation to engage in dialogue. As its author, I have fulfilled my role in that process by initiating the conversation. Now I invite you to accept and embrace the invitation. I believe that by participating in dialogue, your leadership will be enhanced in a positive way.

DESIRE: Adults learn effectively when they are willing to consider a new or different thought. Do you have a desire to connect your faith to a leadership role you currently hold? Is there a craving for God's guidance and blessing in your professional life? Do you wish to see Christ actively at work in every sphere of your life? Are you striving for high-impact leadership and want it to be refined by God?

SEARCH: When what is desired is known, ways to achieve that desire must be found. The desire to connect faith to work and spirituality to leadership leads us to a journey of exploration. This book can be the starting point of such a journey for you. It should be read carefully, accompanied both by reflection on what it has to say and by discernment as to what to apply to your own experience.

APPLY: Without application, acquired knowledge and skills bring little or no benefit. Progress comes only if we apply what is discovered along the way.

Exploring in depth the concept of *hodos leadership* in the pages that follow will require pauses to think more deeply about the following four questions:

1. What was new for me in the material just covered?
2. What thoughts/ideas stood out to me?
3. What is of value here applicable to me personally?
4. What can I, moving forward, apply from what I have learned? And how can I go about doing that?

It will be at your discretion on how to respond to what is proffered in this book. My sincere hope is that you will be inspired as a result of reading it carefully and thoughtfully. Attend, desire, search, and apply to bear more fruit in your life!

It's essential to define and cultivate a list of passions and desires for good leadership. However, real impact comes from a steadfast commitment to turning these aspirations into actions.

FRAMING THE LEADERSHIP MAP

WHY LEADERSHIP?

Fascination with leadership is a particular human interest that characterizes many. Chances are, if you're reading this book, you're intrigued by the leadership phenomenon.

- Why are you interested in leadership?
- What questions do you have about leadership, and why are these questions important to you?

I believe that it's God who is drawing your attention to this matter of leadership. How do you feel when you consider that God himself is inviting you to reflect on leadership and on how to advance spiritual, ethical, and effective leadership?

LEADERSHIP AND THE JOURNEY OF LIFE

Life is often said to be a journey, and I agree. Life is *hodos*, "the way." In life we each carry a personal past full of stories we remember, share, forget, and sometimes even try to hide. Although we cannot change our past, it can still equip us for good if we know how to learn from it. If attuned to life's experiences and what they mean, we can always find meaning for our present, and perhaps even for our future. Reflecting on our past from a proper perspective can make the present much more meaningful.

Right from the outset of our journey together, through this book, let me ask you three important questions:

1. **Generally speaking, what have you learned about leadership throughout your life?** The answers here could include insights you've gained from personal experience, observations you've made of others, or even lessons you've learned from studying leadership theories.

2. **From reflecting on the past, what specific lessons about leadership have you learned?** These could be lessons learned either from experiences where leadership was distinctly lacking or from times when you saw highly effective leadership in full action.

3. **Who in your life has modeled good leadership for you?** Such an individual might have been a teacher, family member, mentor, or perhaps even a public figure. What qualities or actions have such people displayed that you

found particularly inspiring or helpful in shaping your own understanding of leadership?

By actively engaging with these questions, you can identify key insights, lessons, and role models that have molded your understanding and approach to leadership. It's always important to be attentive to good, thought-provoking questions, because such questions foster your self-awareness and growth along the leadership journey.

Here are several selected memories from my own life that have significantly shaped my understanding of leadership.

Wisdom from Above

When I was still in school, I frequently visited my grandparents in the Ukrainian city of Simferopol (Crimea). My grandfather on my father's side, Pavlo Negrov, used to say, "It takes higher education to become a specialist, but then there is also education from above, namely, knowing God and learning from him. One should pursue both!" Not surprisingly, my parents echoed the same sentiment throughout their prime parenting years. This advice from my family has guided me to explore leadership from various sources. However, above all, as St. James states, "If any of you lacks wisdom, you should ask God, who gives generously to all without finding fault, and it will be given to you." (Jam. 1:5)

Knowing Goodness

My grandfather on my mother's side, Oleksii Chumak, had a remarkable life, including enduring numerous hardships, especially during World Wars I and II. Despite these challenges, he remained hopeful, generous, and hardworking until his passing at the age of 109. During a visit my children and I made many years ago to Dzhankoy in Crimea, Ukraine, he shared many of his life stories with me. When I asked him what he believed to be the most important thing in life, he thought for a moment and then responded with this powerful maxim, "To know goodness!" Those words from my grandfather have been a guiding light for me ever since, motivating me to always seek out and prioritize the good in life.

I cannot say that I fully grasp what it means to embrace goodness, but I can at least say that it probably means to possess an awareness of what is spiritually and morally right, of what is useful and beneficial both for me and others. And knowing goodness also means not only understanding who and what is good, but also realizing it involves acting on this transforming reality for advancing God's Kingdom and glory. James 4:17 underscores this by stating, "Anyone, then, who knows the good he ought to do and doesn't do it, sins." This verse highlights that true knowledge of goodness demands action.

Mission of God and Serving with Purpose

My grandmother on my mother's side, Hanna Chumak, was a compassionate and empathetic woman who left a deep impression on me. When I was a small boy, she would take me with her to visit elderly people who had been abandoned by their families and unable to care for themselves.

We would wash and clean their bodies and homes, cook meals, and feed them. My grandmother instilled in me a sense of purpose by involving me in her activities and teaching me how to serve and find joy in even the smallest tasks such as washing floors and dishes. She always reminded me that we should serve others because God loves and cares for us, and that by serving others we help God care for them too. To this day I'm grateful for my grandmother's leadership example in serving others and being committed to God's mission in the world.

The Heart of a Good Leader

During my graduate studies in Canada, I had the opportunity to study under theology professor, Dr. Henry Budd. In one of his classes, I was tasked with writing a paper on what constituted the heart of a king as described in Old Testament wisdom literature. Through this assignment I gained powerful insights on godly leadership from Proverbs, Ecclesiastes, and the Psalms. I learned that a king's focus should never be on acquiring power and wealth, perhaps the two most high-powered temptations facing kingly rule. Instead, the king's focus should be on aligning his heart with God's will and assuming such traits of character as mercy, justice, protection, and care for those under his rule. For example, Proverbs 29:4 says: "By justice a king gives a country stability, but those who are greedy for bribes tear it down." Old Testament wisdom literature everywhere stresses that deep in the heart of a wise and righteous king are to be found the virtues of love, faithfulness, justice, and self-discipline. "Love and faithfulness keep a king safe; through love his throne is made secure." (Prov. 20:28)

Attending to God's wisdom as portrayed in these biblical teachings, I'm reminded to strive more consciously to align my heart with God's will and to embody good leadership for the well-being of my family, my organization, my church community, and society in general.

At Peace with God and With the Past

As a researcher, I have conducted many interviews over the years. One interview that particularly stands out to me is a conversation I once had with the former president of a large church union. During the interview, I asked him if there was anything he would change about his past if he had the power to do so. His answer both surprised and enlightened me, for he said he would not change anything. He believed that God had allowed both good and bad experiences in his life to prepare him to serve others with compassion, especially those who are weak and crushed. This lesson in accepting and learning from one's past experiences has remained with me ever since.

Faith in God and possessing an awareness of his providential love overseeing our lives help us find peace and purpose in life's journey. Trusting in that providential care and viewing our life experiences as a journey directed towards meaningful service that is grounded in faith, hope, and love is important.

Mapping Our Passion for Leadership

I believe that leadership is one of the most crucial areas of learning and practice in all of our human endeavors. I'm enthusiastic about leadership for a very simple reason: If we explore leadership carefully and thoroughly, and if we learn to practice good leadership, I believe we will be in a much greater position to more effectively serve individuals, organizations, and communities with God's grace.

As the founder and president of the Hodos Institute, my focus has always been to inspire my team to promote spiritual, ethical, and effective leadership through a combination of theological inquiry, social research, individualized approaches, and collective collaboration. The goal is to support emerging leaders and especially young Christian professionals in recognizing their calling and developing their professional and spiritual abilities to become effective leaders in both the Church and the marketplace.

I enjoy engaging in dialogue with people about leadership. My understanding about leadership grows daily and in various settings: at home, with my family members, at work, and as I read, talk, and collaborate with others.

How can we explore and chart the underlying motivations, interests, and drives that fuel our enthusiasm for leadership? A few years ago, I created a map of reasons that form the foundation of my own personal passion for leadership. I share them with you below in the hope that they may inspire you also to develop your own list.

- **I desire to make an impact:** Improving spiritual, ethical, and effective leadership can lead to positive social and spiritual change, making a meaningful impact upon the world for good.

- **I desire to improve:** Many existing leadership approaches have proven inadequate to meet the challenges of today's world, leaving a deep need for a kind of leadership that can successfully confront those challenges.
- **I desire to expand:** Since good and bad leadership alike have far-reaching effects, expanding and promoting good leadership across all areas of life is of critical importance.
- **I desire to participate in God's mission:** Leadership formation can cultivate the personal relationship that Christian co-workers have with God, thus bridging the gap between the sacred and secular and helping individuals understand their professional activities within the context of God's Kingdom.
- **I desire to follow well:** Understanding what it means to follow is important for effective leadership, as we are all followers in relation to the lordship of Christ. Ironically, to lead well, we must first learn how to follow well.
- **I desire to research:** Conducting research on leadership can help individuals and organizations identify critical issues for concern, address gaps in performance, and find solutions to pressing problems.
- **I desire to equip others:** Proper training and guidance can equip individuals to serve effectively in God's Kingdom and to be salt and light in the world generally.
- **I desire to focus on individuality:** Effective leadership should value the unique experiences, personalities, and cultures of those under its charge and, accordingly, focus on providing personalized support and care.
- **I desire unity with God:** For me, studying or writing about leadership is just a starting point; it is not an end in itself. In my spiritual journey, I engage in various activities, including research, reflection, and writing about

leadership, but my ultimate goal is to experience God's love and grace and to attain unity with him.

It's essential to define and cultivate a list of passions and desires for good leadership. However, real impact comes from a steadfast commitment to turning these aspirations into actions.

Achieving excellent outcomes depends on having strong initial conditions or resources and executing well-designed, effectively managed processes. These elements are crucial for transforming our aspirations for leadership into meaningful and impactful results.

One of the most important hallmarks of good leadership is assuming the responsibility necessary for such a task.

CHAPTER 1
EMBARKING ON A JOURNEY OF LEADERSHIP

The purpose of this book is to assist you in a journey of reflecting upon and advancing spiritual, ethical, and effective leadership. Success in any leadership journey depends, of course, on how we embark upon it. "Embarking" carries with it the connotation of setting sail on a voyage, or heading out on an expedition, or in the language employed here in this book, setting out on a journey – a journey of exploration, discovery, and adventure! And so I invite you right from the outset of this adventure to come to it with a sense of purpose, enthusiasm, and commitment. Make a commitment to learn, self-reflect, and personally grow in the ways of leadership.

As you read this book, possibly revisiting its pages multiple times, always keep in mind and think about these two important questions:

1. Continuously ask yourself: *"How do the concepts resonate with my spiritual journey?"* My sincere desire is that I could be of encouragement to you.

2. Continuously ask yourself: *"What insights am I gaining about God's love and his wisdom?"* I would be most thrilled if what I'm writing here will help you to be more attentive to God's gracious care for your heart and soul and leadership.

This chapter will present you with your first opportunity to explore some of the various and engaging aspects connected to the fascinating world of leadership. Its content is intended to prompt reflections on your part. A 'heads-up' though! Thought-provoking questions might push you to step outside your comfort zone as you take the time to seriously think about them.

1. QUESTS FOR GROWTH

One cannot think of a "journey," at least as we're talking about it here, without also raising the idea of "quest." It is synonymous with journey; yet it's not *just* a journey. It's the medieval knight's long trek *in search of* the Holy Grail. It's John Bunyan's long and arduous pilgrimage *to arrive at* the Celestial City. It's Moses and the children of Israel fleeing Egypt and crossing the Red Sea *in pursuit of* a land God has promised. Quest characterizes life, and no less so in the desire and effort to attain effective, ethical, and spiritual leadership.

A thoughtful and probing quest can play a powerful role in fostering and developing leadership. From a Christian perspective, we can identify five such quests that together serve as a strong foundation upon which to build leadership.

1. Quest for a biblical theology of leadership
2. Quest for Christian spirituality
3. Quest for an academic theory of leadership
4. Quest for ethical and effective leadership practices
5. Quest for personal growth and development in a leadership mindset, model, and maturity.

These quests are interdependent and complementary to one another. While guiding leaders to a deeper understanding of their own roles and purposes, the quests also equip them with the knowledge and skills they need to lead effectively with integrity and authenticity.

Today, a wealth of information exists pertaining to leadership, yet there is a distinct lack of understanding of what constitutes spiritual, ethical, and effective leadership. The reason for this discrepancy is not difficult to pinpoint. The five quests mentioned above, if known, are either ignored or outrightly dismissed. If known, it's a case that being informed is not equal to being transformed. Desired changes in personal or organizational life do not occur simply because of the availability of the great body of knowledge on leadership in today's world.

It goes without saying, then, that merely having access to leadership resources and tools is not sufficient for transformation to the highest level of leadership. What is really required is a personal dedication to learning, reflection, and development. Right from the outset, it must be emphasized that one of the most important hallmarks of good leadership is assuming the responsibility necessary for such a task. Taking personal ownership for one's own growth and development is, in fact, an absolute must to achieve desired success.

To be successful, the quest or pursuit of *hodos leadership* will require you to actively engage your mind. Responding willingly to intellectual stimulation is an absolute must when embarking upon and growing into your leadership capacity. Keeping in tune with the guidance and work of God's Holy Spirit is another critical component in the leadership process. Spiritual practices and theological reflections form the foundation for spiritual, ethical, and effective leadership, thus highlighting the need for the Holy Spirit's illumination and wisdom in the process.

In keeping with our idea of embarking upon a journey towards the highest form of leadership, while embracing the five quests previously mentioned, always remember never to overlook an opportunity to engage your soul and intellect when:

- guided to reflect on the inner promptings of God's Spirit,
- involved in pondering biblical teachings that nurture the soul,
- invited to brainstorm ideas and problem-solve,
- encouraged to engage in creative thinking and innovation,
- asked to respond to reasonable questions,
- presented the opportunity to give and receive feedback,
- invited to conversations that stimulate thought and imagination, and
- encouraged to think in ways that are new.

Hodos leadership begins with learning and thoughtful contemplation. In what follows, various tests and assessments will be presented to help you broaden your perspectives, identify areas of growth, and prompt personal reflection. Sometimes a probing question is all that is necessary to jumpstart a transformation process.

Remember, engaging with challenging questions can shape your understanding of leadership, ultimately influencing your whole orientation toward it. This is true whether you happen to be leader or a follower.

2. STARTING QUESTIONS

> "Questions serve as the foundation for increasing individual, team, and organizational learning. Every question can be a potential learning opportunity. As a matter of fact, deep significant learning occurs only as a result of reflection, and reflection is not possible without a question – whether the question comes from an external or internal source." (Michael Marquardt and Bob Tiede, *Leading with Questions*)[1]

Many people believe that to become better leaders, they need good advisors, directors, or successful influencers to provide them with the right instructions on how to carry out their responsibilities. Ready-made formulas are often sought to guide leadership development. Undeniably there is untold value in wise recommendations from experienced mentors and consultants, yet the most valuable assistance does not come from answers and suggestions offered by external advisors but from asking the right questions.

Coaching expert, Dr. Keith Webb, Founder and President of Creative Results Management, a global Christian coaching training company, places a very high premium on questioning. He teaches that coaching is an intentional conversation in which the coach asks the right questions, and in so doing, empowers individuals or groups to understand God's calling and follow his direction. This is very important. Good questions stimulate and grow people both professionally and spiritually. According to Webb, coaching as an approach to Christian leadership development is exciting because it allows individuals to reflect on their personal situations while the Holy Spirit works through the coach's questions.[2]

I encourage you, as an intelligent and attentive individual, to take your time to thoughtfully consider the questions listed below. Some of the questions will resonate with you, others perhaps not so much. Yet together they represent the first step in your leadership quest. If necessary, feel free to take notes as you engage with the questions. Embrace the opportunity they provide to exercise both your heart and mind, and embrace the opportunity to experience the joy that comes with beginning an adventurous journey into personal growth and development.

Let's begin our conversation about leadership together. The following questions are intended to provoke your thoughtful reflections:

1. In what way do you understand leadership?
2. How do you characterize the potential for leadership?
3. How, in your opinion, does spirituality connect, if at all, with personal or organizational leadership?
4. How would you describe the leadership in your company/organization and/or church?

5. How would you characterize the leadership of other Christians whom you know?
6. What do you think it takes to develop leadership among Christian youth and/or adults?
7. How would you distinguish between positive and negative leaders?
8. What do you think about the idea of spiritual leadership being practiced in the church, the workplace, various platforms and spaces, such as media, online forums, and community meetings, where public opinion is formed and expressed.

Once you have thoughtfully considered these general questions regarding leadership, it's time to delve deeper. This next round of questions is intended to heighten your sense of self-awareness as to the level of leadership you currently practice.

Ask yourself these questions:

- Who and what inspires and corrects me in my leadership journey?
- How do I perceive the influence of God in shaping my leadership and my decisions?
- What specific actions can I personally take to improve my leadership?
- Are there any obstacles or challenges that might hinder my growth as a leader? If so, how can I overcome them?
- How can I encourage and support others in their leadership development?

As you reflect on these questions, consider developing an action plan that outlines concrete steps you can take to strengthen your leadership abilities. It may be beneficial to incorporate aspects of your spiritual formation into this plan. Reflect on how your awareness of God aligns with your leadership. Perhaps you can identify specific spiritual practices or disciplines that could enhance your spiritual growth.

A leadership journey integrates a process of personal and leadership development with an openness to God. It's important to approach this process with eagerness, curiosity, and a willingness to learn and grow, ensuring that your developing sense of leadership is ever aligned with your inner values and contributes to the well-being of both self and others.

3. SELF-INQUIRY PROMPTS

Practicing stillness and self-reflection are essential for spiritual growth and cultivating a deeper awareness of God. Many Christian writers point out that for spiritual transformation to occur it's important to take time to be quiet and be under the guidance of God's Holy Spirit to ponder one's life and relationship with God. Accessing a deep level of spiritual transformation into Christlikeness, this form of self-inquiry, as espoused by many Christians who have gone before us, can be considered as a way of examining one's thoughts, beliefs, emotions, and perceptions, free from the deceptive turnings of our self-centered egos.

Hodos leadership is not about busyness, being "on the run," or making daily decisions "on the fly." It's more about finding time to be quiet, to really listen, and to think deeply about the important issues of life. Most people find it tough to pause their busy lives to take a moment to stop and contemplate these things. We all know that quiet time for serious thought is hard to come by when our day is full of tasks! But it all comes down to what is important to us. If we think it matters, we'll make time for it.

Besides observing times of quietness, an effective self-reflection requires an organized approach. Here it's helpful to have a list of relevant questions or prompts to guide the process. You can develop a list yourself or glean from others.

I encourage you to include in your self-reflections at least some of the following questions. They will help guide your thoughts in the right direction.

- Who am I, really?
- Who are the authorities in my life. What influences do they exercise over me and why?
- Who or what has helped me to become the person I am today?
- What matters most in my life?
- What is my purpose in life?
- How do I experience my connection to God?
- Why am I working, serving, leading?
- Where am I on my professional journey? What are my next steps and why?
- What are my most importantly held values and how are they reflected in my attitudes and behavior?
- Am I holding on to something I need to let go of?
- How am I doing emotionally?
- What worries me most about the future?
- How can I have an anxious-free presence?
- Whom could I serve better?

Remember to take the time necessary to reflect deeply on these questions. Doing so will reward you with insights and understandings that can help you improve as a leader.

Self-Reflective Survey

Consider taking a moment for a simple self-assessment. Read each statement and indicate your agreement level. 1 is "completely disagree" and 5 is "completely agree." Honesty is the key.

- I have regular opportunities to realize my talents and gifts.
- I have people around me who care about me.
- I spend most of my time on things that hold great meaning for me.
- I feel that my life has meaning and significance.
- I have set goals for the next few years of my life.
- I feel that people understand and value me.
- When I think about God, I feel his love.

The above survey functions as an important tool for you to evaluate whether or not your most basic and foundational needs in life and work are being met. Approached thoughtfully, the survey permits you to assess your state of well-being with a relatively high degree of accuracy. To use your talents, belong to a caring community, find meaning and purpose in life, receive appreciation, and have a clear sense of future direction are the prerequisites to a rich and full life. You also need a reasonable base in order to bring your leadership to the next level.

As you answered the survey questions above, perhaps you noticed something that needs to be addressed. If this is the case, ask God for assistance as you confront these issues. Then seek help from someone outside yourself, perhaps a friend, pastor, mentor, spiritual director, or leadership coach who can further assist you in navigating this process of self-understanding, correction, growth, and maturity.

4. PROBING THE NATURE OF LEADERSHIP

If you have had experience working on a team, consider reflecting on that experience and evaluating the leadership styles that were employed. What worked well for your team? What did not work so well? What could have been improved?

Thinking about leadership in the context of your own experiences will allow you to gain a deeper understanding of its dynamics and on how to apply that knowledge to future leadership opportunities.

Below, I provide you with three survey-type questions and accompanying notes to stimulate your thinking about leadership in general.

Question 1. Choose one definition of leadership with which you most strongly agree, and choose one definition of leadership with which you least agree.
- Leadership is about influencing others.
- Leadership is about showing the way and helping or inducing others to pursue it as well.
- Leadership is about popularity, fame, and success.
- Leadership is about the cooperation between a leader and his/her followers in pursuit of a common goal.
- Leadership is about exercising power over others.
- Leadership is about serving God and others for the sake of higher goals.

Please take a moment to reflect on the following questions:

- What other options might have been listed?
- In 10-15 words, define leadership as you now understand it.
- What defines and describes your own personal brand of leadership?
- How would you want others who might assess your leadership to finish this sentence: "His/her leadership is all about..."?

Question 2. What is the role of a leader in fostering teamwork? Choose one or more of the following:

- To determine and demonstrate by personal experience the rules and standards to be practiced within the team being led.
- To formulate and communicate a clear and compelling vision to team members.
- To create the conditions necessary for team members to fulfill their tasks.
- To explain the meaning and importance of the team's common goals and actions.
- To encourage, motivate, and inspire, so that team members feel galvanized toward achieving common goals.
- To develop and implement a strategic plan for team-related projects and activities.
- To encourage and provide the environment and opportunities for the personal development of each team member.

How many answers did you choose, and why did you choose the ones you did?

If you are currently a member of a working team, whether in a church or at a job site, consider what your team leader is doing well and in what areas he/she might improve.

How would you complete the following sentence, "The ideal leader is characterized by..."?

Question 3. In your opinion, which of the following best characterizes negative (bad, toxic) leadership in teamwork? Choose one or more:
- Inability to resolve conflict
- Seeking one's interests to the detriment of the team overall
- Inability to define a common goal and strategy for the team
- Reluctance to support others
- Dishonesty or lack of fairness
- Little or no understanding of the function that roles play within a team
- Arrogance
- Distrustfulness

In my research, I have found that the answer: "Seeking one's interests to the detriment of the team" to be the one selected more commonly than any other. I think this predominance reflects a common and recognizable behavior in toxic leaders. Such behavior can harm a team's internal cohesion, morale, sense of trust, and overall performance.

Think about possible harmful and toxic leadership practices present within the team on which you currently serve or one on which you've served. How can you address these? What steps can your group take to move such leadership from bad to good, from good to great?

As you reflect on the negative behaviors of others, consider whether God is nudging you to reassess your own leadership with the purpose of identifying and correcting any such inimical behaviors.

5. EXPLORING FOLLOWERSHIP

Jesus said, "My sheep listen to my voice; I know them, and they follow me." - John 10:27

Paul wrote, "Follow my example, as I follow the example of Christ." - 1 Corinthians 11:1

In furthering our discussion on spiritual, ethical, and effective leadership, we should be careful not to overlook the matter of followership. Followership is an integral part of the leadership discussion. Here are several survey-type questions along with accompanying commentary to stimulate your thinking about followers and followership:

Question 1. *What do you think is the role of followers in relation to their team leaders?* **Choose the one statement from the list below with which you most strongly agree.**
- To follow their leader without question looking to him/her to do their thinking for them.
- To obey orders from the leader, performing required tasks unquestioningly.
- To exhibit independent thinking along with a desire to influence the leader in positive ways.

- To pursue common goals along with the leader and fellow team members.

Question 2. Select the option you consider best for each of the following questions:
- In which role do you find yourself more often?
  (a) leader (b) follower (c) both
- In which role do you feel most comfortable?
  (a) leader (b) follower (c) either
- In which role do you see yourself in the future?
  (a) leader (b) follower (c) both

The answers you have selected for the questions above could all be the same, but are they all the same? If they differ, why?

In the research I have conducted over time, I have consistently observed that respondents' answers to the above questions rarely align. In general, respondents indicate that currently they act in different roles, and that they are, for the most part, comfortable with those roles (although some do say they are not comfortable with their present situation and would like to see it change). As to the future, however, most respondents express the desire to be leaders rather than followers. People think that when they've "arrived" as a leader, they will be all done following. I don't believe this expectation is wise. Sometimes we can be of much better service when we follow good leaders or collaborate with others in a form of shared leadership. Leader-in-chief is not always all it's cracked up to be.

When it comes to the leadership/followership question, it's my opinion that for those who are concerned with the progression of spiritual, ethical, and effective leadership, entertaining such self-reflective questions is vitally important.

- Where and when am I leading, and where and when am I following?
- Why do I lead, and why do I follow?
- Whom do I follow and why?
- What motivates me to lead and/or follow?
- How do I care for those who follow me?

A Brief Description of Followership

Human leadership involves a dynamic process in which the roles of subject and object are not fixed. Think of a sports team or a work team. Typically, a designated leader assumes the role of subject, while the team members individually and collectively become the object(s) of his/her leadership. However, team members can also exert important influence upon the leader and the team's activities, and in this way the team members become both the subject and object of the team's collective action. The relation of leader to follower is never a static one and can shift, sometimes even dramatically, depending on the specific circumstances and type of leadership required.

Effective leadership requires followership. It's crucial to both leaders and followers alike to recognize that both parties must play a vital role in achieving team goals and success. Good leaders are boosted by good followers, but as Jean Lipman-Blumen rightly points out, "Toxic leadership can be enabled by toxic followership."[3] Therefore, fostering a culture of accountability for both leaders and followers is paramount for team and organizational sustainability.

In the introduction to the book, *The Art of Followership: How Great Followers Create Great Leaders and Organizations*, Warren Bennis, widely regarded as one of the pioneers in the contemporary field of leadership studies, makes a profound statement: "The moment when each of us realizes he or she is mostly a follower, not a leader, is a genuine developmental milestone."[4] Bennis' insight is very important. Within each of us is an inherent follower. Recognizing this fact that we're constantly being impacted and guided consequently helps us to transcend our ego-centric aspirations to embrace humility, collaboration, and a commitment to collective goals.

In modern day, leadership is elevated without much of any attention being paid to the importance of followership. For example, while leadership training is widely available on different levels in schools, universities, business companies, churches, and nonprofits, the focus on followership training is almost completely absent. Books on leadership outnumber those on followership. Leadership coaching and consultancy services abound, but how often do we hear of a followership coach? It's simply not glamorous to follow.

6. EXPLORING LEADERSHIP GROWTH

Our perspective on leadership development or maturity is critical, as it shapes our approach to personal growth and our efforts to support others.

- What is your perspective on leadership development? Do you believe it to be a lifelong process or something that can be achieved through acquiring a finite set of skills and knowledge?
- What has helped you to grow as a leader or follower? Have you benefited from mentors, training programs, feedback from others, or other resources?

- What areas do you feel are lacking in your own leadership development? Are there specific skills or qualities you would like to develop further?
- How can you support others in their leadership development journey? Are there individuals or groups you can mentor, provide feedback to, or otherwise assist in their growth as leaders or followers?

Please work through the three survey-type questions below and reflect accordingly.

Question 1. Which statement best characterizes your view?
- Leaders are born (some people have an innate predisposition for leadership)
- Leaders are born and made (individuals are born with leadership potential but need to be developed)

Question 2. What helps you more than anything else to develop as a leader? Choose up to 5:
- Care within the local church
- Involvement in various Christian ministries and projects in the church
- Involvement in various projects outside the church
- Educational programs, training, or seminars
- Family
- Relationship with God; spiritual growth
- Personal desire and self-discipline
- Motivation and encouragement from others
- Mentoring (personal relationships with more experienced people)
- Other (explain)

As you reflect on your leadership development, take a moment to think about the specific individuals and events that have influenced your growth. Consider expressing your gratitude to those who have supported you along the way, whether they be individuals or organizations. You could express your thanks through a personal call or visit, a handwritten note, or even a small gift. Remember that showing gratitude is a powerful way to strengthen relationships and to affirm the importance of the support you have received.

Question 3. What, more than anything else, is lacking in your development as a leader or effective team member? Choose 3 of the following:

- Involvement of the local church in my formation
- Educational programs, training, seminars
- Involvement in church ministries and projects
- Involvement in various non-church projects
- Motivation and encouragement from others
- Personal desire and self-discipline
- Relationship with God; spiritual growth
- Difficult to identify what is lacking
- Other (explain)

As you answered this question, have you become aware of anything that God has perhaps brought to your attention? What is God now inviting you to do?

As you continue to grow as a leader or follower, take time to reflect on ways you can develop and empower yourself. Consider what areas of your leadership or followership could use improvement and a plan to work on those areas. This may involve seeking out a mentor or coach, attending training or educational programs, or simply practicing self-reflection and seeking feedback from others.

Remember that growth and development are ongoing processes, and that seeking help and guidance from others can be a powerful way to accelerate your progress.

Before moving on, take some extra time to reflect on these questions:

- Where are you on your spiritual journey? What is God's desire for you?
- What leadership qualities and skills are you trying to develop in yourself?
- Who potentially can be of help to you in acquiring those qualities and skills?
- Who do you have in your life who helps you in your personal development and spiritual formation?

Endnotes

1. Marquardt, M. J., and Bob Tiede. *Leading with Questions: How Leaders Discover Powerful Answers by Knowing How and What to Ask*. 3rd. ed., John Wiley & Sons, 2023, pp. 28-30.
2. Webb, K. *The Coach Model for Christian Leaders*. Morgan James Publishing, 2019, pp. 18-19, 24.
3. Lipman-Blumen, Jean. "Following Toxic Leaders," in Riggio, Ronald E., et al. *The Art of Followership: How Great Followers Create Great Leaders and Organizations*. 1st ed. Jossey-Bass, 2008, p. 89.
4. Warren, Bennis, "Introduction," in Riggio, Ronald E., et al. *The Art of Followership: How Great Followers Create Great Leaders and Organizations*. 1st ed. Jossey-Bass, 2008, pp. xxiii-xxiv.

Leadership is fundamentally about discovering, accepting, and illuminating the path forward for oneself and others. It involves understanding and practicing the various aspects of both leading and following.

CHAPTER 2

THE WAY: METAPHOR IN HODOS LEADERSHIP

1. LEADERSHIP DEFINED

Leadership is a journey! Any leader on this journey is a pilgrim, an explorer, a wayfarer, or perhaps even a mountain climber. The explorer is commissioned to new worlds of discovery, the wayfarer and pilgrim to an extended expedition, often over unfamiliar terrain, and the mountain climber to some distant peak, an endpoint to be triumphantly and happily reached. As these metaphors illustrate, each in its own particular way, leadership at its heart is about finding, accepting, and illuminating the path forward for oneself and others. It's a coming into an understanding and practice of the multifold aspects of both leading and following. It can thus be described as a holistic journey that encompasses "showing the way" towards discovery, embodiment, guidance, accomplishment, and a host of other such traits that together define good leadership.

The phrase "showing the way" commonly appears in a variety of contexts in which leadership or guidance is involved. Who hasn't heard such expressions as:

- The CEO showed the way by implementing new policies that increased efficiency.
- In times of crisis leaders must show the way to guide their teams to safety.
- The coach showed the way, leading the team to victory.
- The experienced hiker showed the way to the mountain's summit for the first-timers.
- The mentor showed the way for her mentee to achieve success in her career.
- The priest showed the way to forgiveness, not only through his sermons but also by his life.

Roger Gill, a member of the advisory council at the Hodos Institute and a visiting professor of Leadership Studies at Durham University Business School, was the first to introduce me to the idea of leadership as "showing the way." According to Gill, a helpful way to understand leadership is to examine the etymology of the word itself. While the notion of "leadership" as understood today goes back no farther than the 19th century, the English word "leader" actually originated in the 13th century. According to Gill's research, the word "lead" is derived from various old European terms, all of which encompass the idea of guiding others along a path, showing the way, and ensuring a safe journey. Gill concludes then that the fundamental element of leadership is "showing the way." In his book *Theory and Practice of Leadership*, he says,

> "Leadership is showing the way and helping or inducing others to pursue it. This entails envisioning a desirable future, promoting a clear purpose or mission, supportive values and intelligent strategies, and empowering and engaging all those concerned.... 'Showing the way' presupposes knowing, or at least believing in, that way. And 'the way' implies the route to a destination: a vision of a desirable future position - what we want to be or where we want to be. This may be a state of being or a position or place, even more specifically a goal, an objective or a target. Knowing or believing in the way also presupposes the desirability of this known or believed-in destination."[1]

Gill argues here that effective leadership necessarily involves several kinds of behaviors that can be categorized into six core themes or practices:

1. **VISION.** Effective leaders define and communicate a valid and appealing vision of the future.

2. **MISSION.** Effective leaders also define and communicate a valid and appealing mission or purpose.

3. **VALUES.** Effective leaders identify, display, and promote shared values that inform and support the vision, purpose, and strategies employed to achieve goals.

4. **STRATEGY.** Effective leaders develop, communicate, and implement rational strategies that are informed by vision, purpose, and shared values.

5. **EMPOWERMENT.** Effective leaders empower people to be *able to do* what needs to be done. Empowerment involves equipping people with knowledge, skills, and self-confidence, as well as the opportunities, freedom, authority, and resources to manage themselves and be responsible for their performance.

6. **ENGAGEMENT.** Effective leaders engage other people by influencing, motivating, and inspiring them to *want to do* what needs to be done.[2]

I appreciate Gill's six-part framework. Its themes and practices may be considered as the hermeneutical keys to constructive and fruitful collaboration among people. Vision, mission, values, strategy, empowerment, and engagement are crucial for aligning individuals towards common goals and ensuring their well-being. This conceptualization and definition of leadership is very helpful. In unfolding the leadership phenomenon as "showing the way," Gill allows us to think of leadership as a journey. It begins with mapping out a compelling vision, purpose, and plan to move from point "A" to point "B." The principles that govern the trip are embraced by one and all who travel its steps. To be successful those same travelers are also equipped with all that they need for the trek, including a spirited enthusiasm and commitment that empowers them to reach their destination.

The concept of "showing the way" is also one that is everywhere present throughout the Bible, particularly in the Old Testament. The leadership of God depicted there can be understood as leadership exercised on behalf of the entire creation, including humanity. He is often portrayed, for example, as a shepherd who guides and protects his flock. This leadership dimension to God's relationship with humanity is put forward in the Bible as an example and model for us as the people of God to follow. The Bible stresses that God is the ultimate leader and guide for his people, a guide willing to show us the way if we seek him with a humble and sincere heart. Although countless biblical references could be cited here to highlight this divine leadership exercised by God as showing the way, I will limit the following list to just three examples, each adequately illustrating the point:

Psalm 25:4-5: "*Show me your ways*, Lord, teach me your paths. Guide me in your truth and teach me, for you are God my Savior, and my hope is in you all day long."

Psalm 143:8: "Let the morning bring me word of your unfailing love, for I have put my trust in you. *Show me the way* I should go, for to you I entrust my life."

Proverbs 3:5-6: "Trust in the Lord with all your heart and lean not on your own understanding; in all your ways submit to him, and *he will make your paths straight*."

2. LEADERSHIP METAPHORS

What is a Metaphor?

Metaphors have always been employed to convey complex ideas in a way that makes those ideas intelligible to a wide-ranging audience. Linguists categorize metaphors as figurative language, defining them as words or expressions that compare two or more generally unlike things where the comparison is implied rather than directly stated. To say that someone *is* a night owl, to cite a simple example, is different from saying that the person is *like* a night owl. In the second instance here, the comparison is signaled by the word *like*, but in the first instance, there is no such signal is present in the metaphor. The person is just simply and directly stated *to be* the night owl; the comparison is implied.

All metaphors are conceptual in nature. The cognitive aspect of a metaphor involves drawing a mental (implied) comparison between an abstract concept and an unrelated physical entity. For its part, the linguistic aspect of a metaphor, the wording in which the mental comparison is expressed, can manifest itself in one or more possible ways.

Metaphors featured in full glory are most likely to be found in works of imaginative literature. Yet they also constitute a great portion of our ordinary everyday language. If we struggle to explain a challenging concept in a way that is easy for others to understand, resorting to an apt metaphor might be the answer to our dilemma. In fact, we often aren't even aware that we're using them. So embedded are they in our ways of thinking and speaking that we practically regard them as no different from literal language. Common metaphors that we might hear on a daily basis, at least in the English-speaking world, might be *heart of stone* to describe a hard-hearted, unfeeling individual, *train wreck* to describe a failed venture, or *couch potato* to describe someone who spends the weekend sprawled out on a living room couch watching sporting events on television, scrolling through social media feeds, and gorging on chips and soda.

Two Eminent Examples

First, an example from the words of Jesus: In the Gospel of John, chapter 10, verses 11 to 18, Jesus utters one of the most profound and universally known metaphors of all time. He states, "*I am the Good Shepherd*" (v.11). Here he refers to himself in both a literal and a figurative sense. The "I," of course, is Jesus himself, quite literally; "the Good Shepherd" represents the general concept of an ideal shepherd as universally conceived. Jesus completes the metaphor by directly equating himself with that concept, not by saying that he is *like* that good shepherd, but that he is that good shepherd. It's that direct equating that makes his words a metaphor.

After stating that he's the good shepherd, Jesus moves on in the passage cited above to extend the metaphor to explain how, as this good shepherd, he differs from the hired hand in caring for the owner's sheep. When the wolf comes the hired man flees; but the good shepherd "lays down his life for the sheep" (v.11), a metaphorical expression for which Jesus himself provides the literal interpretation. In verse 15, referring directly to himself, he specifically states, "I lay down my life for the sheep." The entire passage is in fact metaphorical in nature, the references to the "hired hand," "the wolf," and "the sheep" all being what we might call implied metaphors. The hired man is the false shepherd, the wolf is the devil, and the sheep are Jesus' followers.

Second, an example from the sermons of Martin Luther King: In one of his most famous sermons, *Loving Your Enemies*, Dr. Martin Luther King Jr. says, "Returning hate for hate multiplies hate, adding deeper darkness to a night already devoid of stars. Darkness cannot drive out darkness; only light can do that. Hate cannot drive out hate; only love can do that."[3] Here, Dr. King employs two powerful metaphors to succinctly drive home the point that only love can effectively counter hate.

In his first metaphor, hate is compared to the darkness of "a night already devoid of stars." The comparison, however, is not stated outright; rather it is implied through directly *equating* hatred with darkness. The two entities are unlike each other in almost every respect but share this one similarity in common, and when that similarity is exploited as Dr. King does here it powerfully highlights the point about hatred that he is attempting to make. Hate is awful—just as awful as the blackness of a starless night.

The second metaphor in the quote operates in exactly the same manner. Love is compared to light (also suggested by the word *stars*), but nowhere in the quote are we directly told that such a comparison is intended; rather, it is again clearly implied by directly stating that love *is* light. Once that similarity is drawn, again between two entities that otherwise are dissimilar in practically every way, Dr. King is ready to move into the final two sentences of the quote.

Carrying all the imaginative and emotional clout established by the two metaphors, these two sentences come down with the force of a hammer in scoring the moral truth he is making. Had he attempted to make the same point employing only straightforward literal language, chances

> are that by the time he arrived at the final sentence, it would not in any way carry the moral authority that it should. That authority derives its weight from the cumulative effect of the two preceding metaphors now being poured into that sentence.

Leadership Depicted Through Metaphors

Allow me to pose two questions to you. Please take as much time as you need to reflect upon and respond to each one.

1. If you were to express your understanding of leadership with a metaphor, what would that metaphor be?
2. Could you summarize leadership in a single word or perhaps create a sketch to visually represent your idea of leadership?

Now that you've had the chance to reflect upon and respond to these two questions, let me explain how metaphors play a crucial role in comprehending leadership. Scholars and practitioners use various metaphors such as a map, tournament, jazz band, building, or even a machine to describe leadership. Such metaphors typically have both a literal meaning and a symbolic or comparative function. While the term or phrase employed to serve as metaphor may have a concrete definition, it is also used figuratively to represent some aspect or another of leadership.

> John Adair, a distinguished British scholar, author, and leadership consultant, utilizes Jesus's metaphor of "the

good shepherd" in the Gospel of John, for instance, as a supportive example for his Action-Centered Leadership model. Adair's model consists of three overlapping and interdependent circles that define good leadership in terms of three action-oriented focuses: Task, Team, and Individual.[4] According to Adair, effective leaders accomplish significant tasks, establish excellent teams to work on those tasks, and take care of the individuals within those teams. But, again, it is the metaphor of the good shepherd that he employs to reinforce and commend the efficacy of his model.

Max De Pree, a leadership author and former CEO of Herman Miller, is among the experts who have explored the metaphor of leadership as jazz. In his book, *Leadership Jazz*,[5] De Pree points out that while in a jazz performance, each musician brings to the fore his or her own unique style or voice. It is only in performing in concert with the other musicians that together the band as a collective is able to create something of great harmony and beauty. Similarly, leadership cannot be approached as a one-size-fits-all approach. It requires risk-taking, improvisation, and the ability to adapt to changing circumstances. Just as jazz musicians must be in tune with the rhythm and flow of the music being played around them, so too must leaders be attuned to the needs and perspectives of those working with and under them.

In my younger days, I studied music, taking seven years of piano lessons. Although today I'm not a skilled pianist, I still enjoy listening to jazz music. So, for me, the metaphor of leadership as jazz offers a unique perspective on the dynamic nature of leadership. It highlights the importance of collaboration, creativity, and adaptability in achieving success, and it emphasizes the need for active listening and communication in building strong relationships and achieving common goals. Understood in this way, the concept challenges the traditional hierarchical model of leadership, focusing on co-creation and on distributed and participatory leadership.

3. HODOS LEADERSHIP LANGUAGE

The *hodos* metaphor I've selected to explore leadership in this book belongs to a class of metaphors referred to as universal metaphors. As the term implies, these metaphors are universal in their reach, both in time and place, showing up in many different historical settings, cultures, and linguistic groups in both the past and present. It's from this backdrop that the *hodos* metaphor, "the way" or "showing the way" arises. It's embedded in the realities and experiences common to all humanity: the realities of love, beauty, family, war, sorrow, death, and other such verities of life that we often refer to as "the human condition."

Who hasn't heard or read of love being depicted as a *journey*, or life in its frailty and shortness portrayed as a *flower*, or death as a *gaping monster* that mercilessly devours its prey? Such are the metaphors that strikingly depict human existence as we know it. Transcending the here and now in their representation of what we might call the ultimate realities of lived human experience, they assume 'larger than life' proportions.

It's important to note that as a simply worded phrase, *hodos leadership* isn't to be taken literally. The terms: "the way" and "showing the way," are inherent notions within the Greek meaning of *hodos*, but are not the actual focus of our attention. Rather, it's in how we're drawing upon these phrases as universally applied metaphors to highlight the reality and significance of leadership. The concept of *hodos leadership* includes a variety of such figurative phrases as "I am the way," "discovering the way," "understanding the way," "guiding the way," and "embodying the way," among others, as means of exploring leadership's full and rich meaning. Employing the Greek hodos, "*the way*," therefore, helps us to formulate and comprehend the many different facets of leadership, whether they be good or bad, personal or organizational.

Ways of Life

It's interesting to note that throughout history, religious and moral philosophers have described life in terms of following one or the other of two diametrically opposed paths or ways.

The following list represents a sampling of many such examples that could be cited:

- the way of life versus the way of death
- the narrow way versus the broad way
- the way of the wise versus the way of the foolish
- the way of freedom versus the way of enslavement
- the way of sight versus the way of blindness
- the way of truth versus the way of the lie
- the way of righteousness versus the way of wickedness
- the way of the godly versus the way of sinners
- the way of love versus the way of hatred
- the way of unity versus the way of division

- the way of forgiveness versus the way of resentment
- the way of hope versus the way of despair
- the way of courage versus the way of fear
- the way of integrity versus the way of dishonesty
- the way of healing versus the way of injury
- the way of resilience versus the way of capitulation
- the way of empathy versus the way of indifference
- the way of collaboration versus the way of competitiveness
- the way of excellence versus the way of mediocrity
- the way of innovation versus the way of stagnation

From this list, we can see that in some sense, life can ultimately be defined in terms of **choice**. But we cannot choose the ideal unless its opposite also exists as a possible option. Otherwise "the way" or "the path" as a positive notion is left meaningless, as is the metaphor "showing the way." Understanding these metaphors in this way has huge implications for leadership.

The Way in the Old Testament

The ancient Hebrew term, *derekh* [דֶּרֶךְ], frequently rendered as "path," carries a dual connotation of a physical road on the one hand, and a symbolic journey on the other, a journey representing the course or direction followed in one's lifestyle.[6] This path in life is characterized and determined by the daily decisions that shape its trajectory.

If *darekh* signifies "path" or "way," the Hebrew word *madríkh* translates as "guide" or "leader." To highlight its meaning, I'd like to cite here Isaiah 48:17 as rendered in three English translations:

> "This is what the Lord says— your Redeemer, the Holy One of Israel: "I am the Lord your God, who teaches you what is best for you, who directs you in the way you should go."
>
> "The Eternal One, who rescued you, the Holy One of Israel declares, Eternal One: I am the Eternal One your God. I have given you My instruction for living well and right, leading you in how you should be and do." (Voice)
>
> "Thus saith Hashem, thy Go'el, the Kadosh Yisroel; I am Hashem Eloheicha thy Melamed (Teacher) of doing that which profiteth, thy Madrikh (Guide, Instructor) in the Derech that thou shouldest go." (Orthodox Jewish Bible)

Isaiah 48:17 teaches that God shows us the way as Guide. He leads his people by "walking" with them as they traverse the path. The idea of "showing the way" is highlighted through various teachings and narratives that we find in the first five books of the Hebrew Bible (Genesis, Exodus, Leviticus, Numbers, and Deuteronomy). In Genesis 12:1-3, for example, God calls Abram (later known as Abraham) to leave his country and go to a land that God will show him. During the Israelites' journey out of Egypt, God guides them by a pillar of cloud by day and a pillar of fire by night (Exod. 13:21-22). Moses urges the Israelites to walk in God's ways, to love him, and to serve him with all their heart and soul, and to keep the commandments of the LORD (Deut. 10:12-13). Moses expresses gratitude to God for his nearness to the Israelites and for providing commandments to the nation. He says, "What other nation is so great as to have their gods near them the way the Lord our God is near us whenever we pray to him? And what other nation is so great as to have such righteous decrees and laws...?" (Deut. 4:7-8)

On another occasion, we see Moses' father-in-law, Jethro, instructing Moses on how to effectively govern and lead God's people. He tells him, "Teach them his decrees and instructions, and show them the way they are to live and how they are to behave" (Exod. 18:20). Showing the way is also spotlighted in the Old Testament in its strong emphasis upon transmitting wisdom from one generation to the next. From early times, God had established that it was the responsibility of the adults in Israel to impart religious and moral teachings to the younger generations, thus ensuring the continuity of spiritual values and practices.

The Old Testament poetic books (Psalms, Proverbs, Job, Ecclesiastes, and Song of Solomon) provide a wealth of wisdom, reflection, and expressions of faith. They emphasize the importance of trusting in God's guidance, seeking His ways, and living in accordance with his truths. Psalm 25:4-5 says, "Show me your ways, LORD, teach me your paths. Guide me in your truth and teach me, for you are God my Savior, and my hope is in you all day long." The book of Proverbs, known for its practical wisdom, teaches, "Trust in the LORD with all your heart and lean not on your own understanding; in all your ways submit to him, and he will make your paths straight." (Prov. 3:5-6)

During the era of the prophets, the Israelites consistently strayed from following God and, as a result, consistently experienced the consequences of their disobedience. They disregarded God's instructions and guidance; in turn, their indifference and often outright rebellion led to them experiencing severe discipline at the hand of God. The prophet Jeremiah, for instance, confronted the people of Judah and called upon them to return to God and follow his ways.

He says, "This is what the LORD says: 'Stand at the crossroads and look; ask for the ancient paths, ask where the good way is, and walk in it, and you will find rest for your souls.'" (Jer. 6:16). Years earlier, the prophet Isaiah had also commanded God's wayward people to correct their errant path. The commandment was accompanied by the promise that prompt obedience would result in their existence being overseen by God's continual guidance. "Whether you turn to the right or to the left, your ears will hear a voice behind you, saying, 'This is the way; walk in it.'" (Is. 30:21)

These and other Old Testament texts highlight that God not only directs his people (shows the way) but also accompanies them on every step of the way, offering his constant presence and guidance. God's provision encompasses physical sustenance, emotional solace, and spiritual nourishment, as well as equipping us to meet every challenge and trial faced along the way. Hosea 14:9 implies that wise people learn from God, while others foolishly choose not to follow the God-revealed path of life: "Who is wise? Let them realize these things. Who is discerning? Let them understand. The ways of the LORD are right; the righteous walk in them, but the rebellious stumble in them."

It's important to note that the Old Testament portrayal of God as leader and guide is no less emphasized in the New Testament. One quick example in passing. Jesus (whom we understand to be fully God, Col. 2:9) portrays himself as the Good Shepherd who leads and guides his sheep, highlighting the intimate relationship between God and His people. In John 10:3-4, Jesus says, "The sheep hear his voice, and he calls his own sheep by name and leads them out. When he has brought out all his own, he goes before them, and the sheep follow him, for they know his voice."

Hodos and Early Christians

When Jesus called on his disciples to follow him, it was a unique form of followership. The invitation was first to believe in Jesus as the means to receive eternal life and then to live out that life by remaining spiritually attached to Jesus as their only Lord. Jesus called his followers to walk in his path, the path of the Lord as teacher, and thus to follow in his footsteps.

During the early days of Christianity, according to Acts 9:2, the followers of Jesus referred to themselves as "the way" (Greek: ἡ ὁδός, also see Acts 19:9, 23; 22:4; 24:14, 22).[7] This label was perhaps inspired by the text of Isaiah 40:3, which says, "Prepare the way of the Lord." Later, as stated in Acts 11:26, the term "Christian" (Greek: Χριστιανός), meaning "follower of Christ," was first used in the city of Antioch to refer to Jesus' disciples.

The term "the way" implies that the followers of Jesus were characterized by two things: (1) they followed a particular set of beliefs and Biblical teachings; and (2) they followed a way of life that was based on their spiritual relationship with the resurrected Christ as the Son of God. The loyalty of early Christians was exclusively to Jesus, whom they proclaimed as "the only way." They centered their faith on him and built their entire identity around the personal fellowship they claimed to have with him. That identity was rooted in their understanding of Jesus as the incarnate Son of God, as their Jewish Messiah, and as the Head of the newfound Church which he had instituted. His kind, loving, and sacrificial manner of life served as the model for their own conduct. Those first disciples of the early church formed a community based on love, forgiveness, and service to others, all of which flowed naturally out of their faith and devotion to God. Being a part of "the way" for those early followers also meant sharing the message of Jesus with others and inviting them to join in on this new way of life offered by their Lord.

The book of Acts, especially chapter 9, presents us with a graphic example of the Greek *hodos* exemplified in both its literal and metaphorical dimensions. The expression "the way" not only refers to the community of early Christians who worshiped Jesus ("The Way"), but also to the actual physical road upon which the Pharisee Saul was abruptly converted to Christianity while on "(his) way" (Acts 22:6) to the city of Damascus to persecute the Christians there.

According to Acts, chapter 9, Saul, who later became the apostle Paul, was a prominent religious figure violently opposed to the beliefs and practices of the early Christians ("the way"). On the journey to Damascus, however, he experienced a spiritually transformative encounter with the living Christ. That encounter would subsequently lead him not only to join the Christian community but also to become one of its more prominent leaders. As Darrell Bock so nicely summarizes that memorable journey: "Saul traveled on the way against the Way, yet he was stopped on the way to join the Way."[8]

The New Testament writers view Christian experience as a pilgrimage in a "new and living way" (Heb. 10:20), opened up by Jesus, who himself is the way. This way is spiritually transforming as believers cultivate a personal relationship with their Lord and take on the same way of life as that modeled by Jesus in the Scriptures. Christian spirituality, however, not only involves a relational aspect with Jesus but also entails ethical behavior. New commands, principles, and values become the new norms for conduct and behavior as stressed in such passages as I John 2:29, 3:9-10, 4:7, and 5:1-2.

Following Jesus involves a range of actions and attitudes, as seen in various passages in the Gospels. Showing love and kindness to others, being responsible with material possessions, serving others with humility, engaging in prayer, and sharing the message about Jesus, are but a few examples that highlight the new life in Christ. That these new behaviors are the expected rule of life for the Christian is further emphasized by the many warnings issued throughout the Scriptures against falling back into the old and godless patterns of life.

In Matthew 7:13-14, Jesus employs the metaphor of the "broad and narrow way" to describe two different paths that people can choose in life. He says that the broad way is easy to find and that many travel it, but it leads to destruction. In contrast, the narrow way is difficult to find and only a few ever travel it; but it leads to life. The broad way represents a life of indulgence, selfishness, and sin. It is the path of least resistance, but it leads to spiritual death!

The narrow way, on the other hand, represents a life of self-denial, sacrifice, and obedience to God. It is the path that Jesus himself took, and for his followers it leads to eternal life. This teaching of Jesus about the broad and narrow way is, in fact, a call of warning for us to choose the path of a God-honoring life, a spiritual, ethical and effective life – the one that makes tremendous leaders.

Love as the Most Excellent Hodos[9]

Leadership was a major issue in St. Paul's relationship with the Corinthian Christians. Most of Paul's converts in Corinth were part of a culture that prized self-importance, pride, and a competitive spirit. It's not surprising that in such an environment that the Corinthian believers fell far short in caring for one another and in pursuing a single-minded unity under the guidance of the Holy Spirit. Their factiousness is highlighted very early in Paul's first letter to them. In

1 Corinthians 1:10-17, Paul zeros in on the rivalries being played out in the Corinthian church—rivalries based on competing loyalties to Peter, Apollos, and Paul himself. He confronted the existing style of leadership based on power and a supposed wisdom being practiced within the church with the humble and vulnerable leadership of Christ, who in weakness yet in full submission to God and putting the good of lost humanity ahead of his own welfare, was obedient unto the death of the cross. (1Cor. 1:18-24).

In 1 Corinthians 13, Paul sets forth love. This is in contrast to the squabbling and infighting typified by the Corinthian believers of his day, as the ideal but practical way of life for every believer to follow. For him, a truly healthy church is molded and shaped by loving attitudes and actions shown by its members. Such attitudes and actions, in turn, reflect the love denoted by the Greek word *agapé*, a word whose meaning is perhaps best stated by Barrett as "an activity, the essential activity, of God himself; and when men love either him or their fellow-men, they are doing (however imperfectly) what God does."[10]

In his treatment of love in 1 Corinthians 13, Paul draws attention to three vital considerations: love's necessity (13:1-3), love's characteristics (13:4-8a), and love's superiority (13:8b-13). In verses 1-3, Paul deals with the necessity of love in the practice of spiritual gifts. For Paul, the possession and practice of gifts (tongues, prophesy, giving, etc.), however appealing it may seem, it's the practice of love in its truest Christian sense that is the most appealing. Exercising spiritual gifts merely as an end in themselves, says Paul, is devoid of any true value. Such a practice must be motivated by love. By extension, we might say that the more excellent way to be followed by the Christian in every area of life is to let love be the governing power in all that we think, say, or do.

In verses I Corinthians 4-8a, Paul describes love's characteristics, but not in the typical manner of drawing up a list of abstract attributes or properties. Instead, he rolls out a series of true-to-life verbs, thus showing that love manifests its true character in what it does and in what it does not do.

> *Love is patient, love is kind. It does not envy, it does not boast, it is not proud. It does not dishonor others, it is not self-seeking, it is not easily angered, it keeps no record of wrongs. Love does not delight in evil but rejoices with the truth. It always protects, always trusts, always hopes, always perseveres. Love never fails...*

In verses 8b-13 of the same text, Paul highlights love as indispensable and everlasting. Faith and hope, like all gifts, are important; but love, states Paul, is still the greatest and most influential. It's in love that all other virtues find their roots and value, thus establishing its status as the *summum bonum*[11] among the spiritual gifts and other moral qualities.

The practice of love in leadership is also the most excellent way to conduct oneself in an elevated position. The reasons behind such a claim are innumerable. Love is characterized by its resistance to all that is morally wrong and evil, and, conversely, by its embracing of integrity, patience, humility, kindness, diplomacy, cultural sensitivity, truth, concern for others, egalitarianism, and compassion. Love-motivated leadership unifies, welcomes, accommodates, and encourages all those falling within its sphere, ever developing among them a strong and growing sense of community. Love, as seen in a leader following "the way," isn't arrogant, nor is it ridden with an inflated sense of self-importance, ambitious, self-seeking, vindictive, jealous, or seeking prestige.

Tom Wright, a highly respected Pauline theologian, has suggested that Paul's model of love offers an alternative to Rene Descartes' (1637) famous axiom that "Cogito ergo sum," "I think, therefore I am." Paul's version: "Amore, ergo sum," "I am loved, therefore I am." [12] Penna has suggested: "I love, therefore we are,"[13] adding a further dimension to the relationship between love and what it means to be human.

Kendall, the author of *Just Love: The Most Excellent Way*, has said that love is not only the way to live, but for those in a leadership role, it is also the way to lead.[14]

4. HODOS TERMINOLOGY

Precise terminology is crucial for effectively disseminating knowledge, including the concept of *hodos leadership*, a concept which integrates spirituality and ethics with effective leadership practices. The terminology connected with *hodos leadership* is broad and encompasses a wide range of leadership practices and ideas. Following is a list of possible expressions that link the metaphors of "the way" and "showing the way" with leadership. Some of these leadership expressions are interpreted with a theological lens, while others are viewed from an organizational perspective or through the vantage point of personal leadership.

I AM THE WAY.
In the Christian faith, Jesus is often referred to as "the Way, the Truth, and the Life" (John 14:6). This phrase emphasizes the importance of following Jesus' example in all aspects of life, including leadership. By

knowing Jesus, following his teachings, and imitating his example, individuals can evolve into leaders who positively impact their churches, workplaces, and communities in general. Jesus is the ultimate example of selfless leadership, and by following his example, leaders cultivate the virtues of humility, compassion, and servant leadership.

BEING THE WAY.

"Being the way" in leadership refers to the idea of embodying and exemplifying the essential elements of leadership. It's leading by example. The phrase "being the way" can refer to the importance of authenticity, consistency, and integrity in leadership. It can also refer to the principle that leaders should align their actions with their words.

MODEL THE WAY.

This idea is a crucial aspect of effective leadership and leadership development. When leaders model the values and standards they expect from others, they equip and encourage those others to follow. Such modeling helps to establish trust and create a culture of integrity within a team or organization. Modeling the way is also an essential tool for any leader developing other potential leaders. People often learn more effectively from the examples set by others than from mere words or instructions.

FINDING THE WAY.

The expression "finding the way" refers to the process of forming a mindset that seeks direction, clarity, or solutions to problems. The phrase suggests that leadership is often associated with uncertainties or obstacles that require attentiveness and an alternate path or solution in order to move forward. Here, "finding the way" presupposes elasticity and a willingness to explore different options through active listening, creativity, and wisdom in problem solving or decision-making.

FOLLOW THE WAY.

The expression "following the way" implies adhering to a shared vision, mission, values, and strategies to achieve a common goal. It also suggests being committed to a leader's or organization's approach towards achieving the common goal trusting the leader's judgments and decision-making along the way. In essence, "following the way" emphasizes the importance of alignment between leaders and their followers where everyone works together towards a shared goal with a sense of unity and purpose.

SHOWING THE WAY.

This phrase should be understood within the context of relationships that exist among leaders, or those between leaders and their followers. In the dynamics at play in leadership and followership, different individuals could show the way – by pointing to what to do and how to do it. Showing the way can be executed in different styles or in the many different circumstances existing across the leadership spectrum. As Roger Gill says, showing the way can be demonstrated by helping or inducing others to follow. Showing the way presupposes, of course, knowing the way (honestly or not) and also taking responsibility for the outcome.[15]

LEAD THE WAY.

To "lead the way" in leadership refers to the act of guiding others toward a common goal. It implies setting an example for others to follow, being proactive to inspire them. "Lead the way" can also mean being the first to undertake a difficult task, paving the way for others to follow. The phrase is often used in military or team contexts, where leaders ensure that those under their authority are engaged in achieving what needs to be done.

STARTING POINT OF THE WAY.

This phrase refers to the initial point or step from which a journey or process begins. In the context of leadership, it can refer either to the starting point of a leader's development or to the start of a team's project. It can also refer to the foundational values and principles that guide leaders or teams as they embark on their journey. In essence, it's the point of departure, a crucial moment in any leadership venture, setting the tone and overall direction for all that follows.

END POINT OF THE WAY.

In a leadership context, this expression describes the desired outcome or destination towards which the journey or path is leading. This may include achieving a particular mission or vision, reaching a specific target, or progressing towards a set of objectives. Metaphorically, the phrase can also describe the arrival point of a development journey that individuals, teams, or organizations undergo as they follow a particular leadership philosophy. The saying "it's not how you start; it's how you finish" suggests that the end result or outcome is more important than either the initial starting point or the journey itself to get there. In any endeavor, it's important to keep the end goal in focus and to press towards it regardless of any setbacks or failures.

GOOD WAY.

This notion can refer to the spiritual, ethical and effective approaches in leading people and organizations. "Good ways" in leadership include building trust, communicating clearly, setting a positive example, providing guidance and support, recognizing and rewarding accomplishments, and fostering a collaborative and inclusive culture. These practices promote a sense of shared purpose, commitment, and accountability within a team or organization.

THE MOST EXCELLENT WAY.

This phrase is drawn directly from the Bible (1Cor. 12:31). It emphasizes the importance of love as the guiding principle, underpinning all spiritual gifts and actions. As it applies to leadership, this phrase means that leading with love, service, and empathy is the most effective way to inspire and motivate others. Jody Fry's model of spiritual leadership also highlights such aspects of altruistic love as patience, kindness, forgiveness, and trust - all virtues which lead to such positive outcomes as joy and peace.[16] By prioritizing love in leadership, leaders create a supportive and productive work environment, inspiring their teams to work towards common goals arising from shared visions.

BAD WAY.

The term "bad way" can describe an approach that's not ideal, but at the same time, not necessarily wrong either. For example, taking a "bad way" to a destination may cause delays, even if the destination is eventually reached. As to leadership, "bad way" refers to inadequate communication, neglected team needs, misguided strategies, and other similar issues. Such ways can hinder growth and productivity.

WRONG WAY.

In the context of leadership, the phrase "wrong way" implies a course of action that's not only inefficient but also unethical and potentially harmful to the team or organization. Leaders who take the "wrong way" are likely to disregard the values of honesty, integrity, and empathy, leading to a toxic culture in which trust among team members is greatly eroded. Furthermore, spiritual neglect, including little or no exercising of love, compassion, or service can lead to a narrow-minded approach to leadership, again resulting in decisions not in the team's or organization's best interests. Specific to Christianity itself, the "wrong way" refers to beliefs or actions that stand in direct opposition to the teachings of the Bible. Engaging in immoral or unethical behavior, neglecting one's relationship with God, or failing to follow the example of Christ in serving and loving others all aptly fit as examples of the "wrong way."

NEW WAYS.

In leadership terms, the expression "new ways" means adopting innovative and progressive ideas that depart from traditional ways, resulting in key shifts in determining end goals and on how to reach them. The "new ways" approach inspires individuals and organizations to embrace change in search of better solutions to problems.

OLD WAYS.

This phrase refers to established leadership practices that may be outdated or less effective in current circumstances. The phrase, however, can also suggest a sense of heritage and tradition. Depending on its context, then, "old ways" can be used either negatively or positively.

MY WAY.

"My way" leadership involves a strong sense of individualism, with decisions being made on the basis of personal biases and experiences. Leaders in this bracket are often resistant to change and feedback and are also prone to micromanaging their teams or organizations.

SIDEWAYS.

This term refers to a leadership approach that focuses on collaboration and working alongside team members rather than a hierarchical, top-down approach.

CIRCLE WAY.

In leadership theory, "circle way" refers to an inclusive decision-making process where participants sit in a circle and engage in dialogue, emphasizing relationships and consensus-building rather than hierarchical and power dynamics. This approach has been used in community-building, conflict resolution, and organizational development.

MULTIPLE WAYS.

The expression here suggests that there are several paths to achieving goals and objectives. "Multiple ways" acknowledges that there's no one-size-fits-all approach to leadership and that different situations may require different strategies. Leaders who understand multiple styles of leadership and the importance of multiple intelligences, can be more effective in addressing the diverse needs and challenges of their team members.

GIVING THE WAY.

The expression "giving the way" refers to a leader who makes room for others to lead and contribute ideas and skills. It can also refer to leaders who provide guidance and direction to their teams, allowing team members to make progress towards their goals. In addition, "giving the way" can involve preparing for succession by identifying and developing potential future leaders within an organization. A good leader not only prepares for his or her own future succession but also recognizes the importance of building a strong and capable team to handle unexpected situation along the way. This practice involves delegating responsibilities and providing opportunities for the team's growth and development to ensure a smooth transition and continued success.

ROADBLOCKING THE WAY.

This expression in leadership means creating obstacles that prevent change or impede others' efforts to function at peak performance within a team or organization. Such behavior is negative and counterproductive to effective leadership and team collaboration. Leaders who engage in roadblocking may need to address the underlying issues causing this behavior and work towards a wise and good solution.

WAY BACKWARD.
This expression can refer to regressing to old practices or strategies that are no longer effective, resulting in a lack of progress or growth. Leaders must avoid the shortcoming of "way backward" and instead focus on moving forward with change, innovation, and continuous improvement.

LEAVING THE WAY.
This phrase can refer to a leader who loses focus, disengages, or isn't sufficiently motivated to continue leading effectively. Such faults can lead to derailment where leaders fail to meet the expectations of their role, possibly causing serious harm to their teams or organizations. Derailment can manifest itself in various ways, such as a leader becoming arrogant, unethical, or incapable of handling stress. Leaders must regularly assess their performance, seek feedback, and address any personal or professional challenges that may negatively impact their leadership effectiveness.

The expressions listed above should not be considered exhaustive within the conceptual and practical realms of Hodos leadership. They underscore two key points: (1) leadership is inherently complex and requires nuanced and varied expression; and (2) the metaphors "the way" and "showing the way" are particularly useful because they provide powerful linguistic tools for conveying the intricate nature of leadership.

Endnotes

1. Gill, Roger. *Theory and Practice of Leadership*. 2nd ed. Sage, 2011, p. 8-9.
2. Ibid., p. 100.
3. King, Martin Luther Jr. *Strength to Love*. Beacon Press, 2019, p. 47.
4. Adiar, J.E. *Action-centered Leadership*. McGraw-Hill, 1973; see also his *The Leadership of Jesus and Its Legacy Today*. Pilgrim Press, 2002.
5. De Pree, M. *Leadership Jazz*. Currency Doubleday, 1992.
6. For Hebrew terms, consult standard dictionaries and lexicons such as: Botterweck, G. J., H. Ringgren, and H.-J. Fabry (eds.), *Theological Dictionary of the Old Testament*. Eerdmans, 1977–2021; and Koehler, L., W. Baumgartner et al. (eds.), *The Hebrew and Aramaic Lexicon of the Old Testament*. 3rd ed., 5 vols., Brill, 1994–2001 / study edition, 2 vols., Brill, 2001.
7. For Greek terms, consult standard dictionaries and lexicons such as: Bauer, Walter, Frederick W. Danker, William F. Arndt, and F. Wilbur Gingrich, eds. *A Greek-English Lexicon of the New Testament and Other Early Christian Literature*. 3rd ed., University of Chicago Press, 2000; Silva, Moisés, ed. *New International Dictionary of New Testament Theology and Exegesis*, 5 vols., 2nd ed., Zondervan, 2014; Louw, Johannes P. and Eugene A. Nida. *A Greek-English Lexicon of the New Testament Based on Semantic Domains*, 2 vols., UBS, 1988.
8. Bock, D. L. "A Theology of Luke and Acts: Biblical Theology of the New Testament," in *Biblical Theology of the New Testament*, ed. by A. J. Köstenberger. Zondervan, 2012, p. 307.
9. This section is based on a previously published article. See Gill Roger and Alexander Negrov. "Love as an Influence for Good in Leadership," *Theology of Leadership Journal*, 2021 4(1): 28-53.
10. Barrett, C.K. *The First Epistle to the Corinthians*. Harper & Row, 1968, p. 311.
11. A Latin term meaning "the highest good" or "the greatest good."
12. Wright, N.T. *Paul: In Fresh Perspective*. Fortress Press, 2005, p. 173
13. Penna, R. *Paul the Apostle: A Theological and Exegetical Study: Vol. 1: Jew and Greek Alike* (T. P. Wahl, trans.). Liturgical Press, 1996, p. 199
14. Kendall, R.T. *Just Love: The Most Excellent Way*. Christian Focus Publications, 1997, p. 18.
15. Gill, Roger. *Theory and Practice of Leadership*. 2nd ed. Sage, 2011, p. 9.
16. Fry, L. "Toward a Theory of Spiritual Leadership," *The Leadership Quarterly*, 14(6), 2003: 693-727.

Spiritual and practical wisdom shape our MINDSET. When moral values align with behavior, they create a MODEL for exemplary leadership. Shifting from doing to being fosters a MATURITY that deepens our connection to God, ourselves, and the world.

CHAPTER 3

THE 3M HODOS LEADERSHIP FRAMEWORK

1. MINDSET IN LEADERSHIP

Hodos Leadership is focused on promoting spiritual, ethical, and effective leadership. A key component of such leadership is cultivating a proper leadership mindset.

Recently, I was very delighted that one of my clients I was coaching indicated that he wanted to develop a better, more positive leadership mindset. In response, I asked him these questions:

1. What do you mean by a more positive leadership mindset?
2. Why is having a positive leadership mindset important to you?
3. What steps can you take to cultivate a positive leadership mindset?

As a Christian thinking about your leadership potential or development, have you ever thought about the importance of your *mindset*? Do you give attention to cultivating a leadership mindset?

What is a Leadership Mindset?

A leadership mindset is a mental framework that individuals adopt in approaching their roles as leaders and followers. It encompasses a set of beliefs, values, and assumptions that guide their decisions and actions. A *positive* leadership mindset is characterized by a focus on building strong relationships, fostering trust, and promoting collaboration. Such leaders are open to feedback, willing to learn from others, and committed to continuous growth and development. They are also adaptable and responsive to change, able to navigate challenges, and desiring to inspire others to achieve common goals.

Conversely, a *negative* leadership mindset is characterized by a lack of trust, rigidity, resistance to change, and a focus on self-interest. Leaders with this mindset create toxic work environments that hinder the growth and development of their teams. A positive leadership mindset is crucial for effective leadership and achieving organizational goals. Cultivating a positive mindset means embracing accountability, learning, and growth, and an openness to feedback, collaboration, innovation, creativity, and excellence.

Assessing and refining our mindset is crucial. It requires strong critical thinking skills, humility, and courage to understand our beliefs and assumptions, evaluate their validity, and replace unhelpful or invalid perspectives with better ones. In my leadership consulting practice, I have observed a significant transformation within a business where a new and relatively young CEO shifted the organizational culture from an authoritarian and toxic mindset of leadership to a democratic, servant leadership approach. (We have published a case study detailing this transformation.)[1] This transition allowed this company to embrace new values and implement the following key principles, such as:

1. **Purpose and Meaning:** Clarifying and determining the company's purpose is seen as a responsibility shared by all employees.
2. **Alignment of Goals:** Encouraging employees to align their personal purpose and objectives with the organization's mission.
3. **Profit and People:** Balancing profitability with a genuine care for people.
4. **Respectful Competition:** Fostering respect and encouraging ethical, virtuous competition.
5. **Work-Life Balance:** Maintaining equilibrium between professional success and personal and family well-being.
6. **Humility and Perseverance:** Cultivating both humility and perseverance—to achieve the highest levels of success and to be open to advice and criticism.

A genuine Christian mindset emphasizes a deep connection with God and an unwavering commitment to living out one's faith in every aspect of life – including in leadership. A Christian mindset is characterized by a set of beliefs and values that are aligned with the teachings of the Bible and Christianity in general. These beliefs and values, in turn, translate into exercising faith in God, practicing love and compassion towards others, striving for humility and selflessness, seeking wisdom and guidance through prayer and scripture, and embracing forgiveness and grace. It's vital to lead with a servant's heart and to empower others instead of seeking power and control for oneself. Being Christian means that such a mindset is naturally guided by the Christian principles of integrity, honesty, fairness, and decisions that align with God's will.

2. MODEL IN LEADERSHIP

During a recent research project, I asked participants what they considered to be the most effective leadership approach for Christian leaders in the public sector to follow. Most interviewees emphasized the importance of linking values to behavior. One Ohio-based CEO and founder of multiple companies stated, *"The best leadership model is when we live out what we say. If we talk about compassion, honesty, service and humility, the best leadership approach is simply connecting our spiritual and ethical principles to our actions."*[2] This CEO's response succinctly summarizes the consensus among participants of what an excellent leadership model.

Before I share with you my thoughts on what a leadership model entails, let me first ask you three questions:

1. How would you describe the leadership model practiced by the leaders in your team or organization?
2. How would you describe your own philosophy and style of leadership?
3. What kind of leadership do you think is needed for our time? For the future?

A Good Leadership Model

Leadership is a complex phenomenon that can be viewed as both a science and an art. Its complexity is often explained through empirical knowledge, figurative language, and conceptual frameworks. In these attempts to explain leadership, the phrases: "model of leadership" and "leadership model" are commonly used in various contexts to describe the different approaches, styles, or philosophies of leadership that exist. A particular model, philosophy, or leadership style provides a framework for depicting the nature and process of leadership. Many such leadership frameworks exist, each with its own labels, such as transactional, charismatic, situational, virtuous, authentic, task or relationship-oriented, toxic, etc.

But what is the best model of leadership? What is the most effective way to lead? To which leadership model should we pay the most attention?

In my opinion, to gain a deeper understanding of leadership and how to excel in its practices, it makes sense to learn from a variety of frameworks. While some of the following frameworks or methods are more well-known and better researched than others, here are a few examples of models that have been put forward in the effort to explain leadership:

- Situational leadership
- Connective leadership

- Transformational leadership
- Spiritual leadership
- Servant leadership
- Authentic leadership

By exploring various frameworks, we can develop a more comprehensive approach to leadership and discover new insights into what makes effective leaders.

Good leadership is a combination of spirituality, morality, and personal or organizational effectiveness. To ensure that all three of these components are realized, a meaningful model of leadership should therefore be comprehensive in nature and take into account the different elements and nuances offered by several leadership models. Better than adhering to just one model is to keep in mind the importance of investigating all possibilities.

If we wish to make a positive impact on our followers, teams, organizations, and society in general, what aspects of leadership do we need to keep in mind?

A comprehensive leadership model should prioritize the following elements:

- Vision, mission, values, strategies, empowerment, and engagement
- Spiritual and ethical awareness and competence
- Continuous development of leadership skills at both the personal and organizational levels
- A balance of good character and strong ability
- Fostering growth in both leaders and followers

A Great Leadership Model

The Bible contains numerous teachings and examples on what constitutes goodness and greatness. It emphasizes such principles as honesty, respect for authority, and treating others with fairness, respect, kindness, and compassion. In the New Testament, Jesus teaches that greatness is achieved through service and humility, rather than power and prestige. He tells his disciples that "whoever wants to become great among you must be your servant" (Matt. 20:26). Seeking personal greatness at the expense of others is roundly condemned by Jesus in that same passage.

In our day, many leadership concepts have been advanced to explain how leadership can be good or conversely, how it can be bad. What makes for good leadership has been detailed above; but what makes for bad leadership? Barbara Kellerman, a professor at Harvard University, offers one possible answer; she argues that "bad leadership" is a combination of immoral and ineffective leadership.[3] If, as I've argued here, good leadership represents a combination of spirituality, morality, and effectiveness, then when these components are missing, we arrive, not surprisingly, at what Kellerman calls "bad leadership."

Contemporary business philosophies emphasize that effective leadership models should consider the triple bottom line of profit, people, and planet. In my opinion, however, a truly exceptional leadership model applicable to all aspects of organizational life should prioritize economic sustainability, social responsibility, environmental stewardship (caring for God's creation) and, the spiritual well-being of all.

My approach to leadership, *hodos leadership*, prioritizes spiritual well-being and ethical practice over productivity and efficiency. It emphasizes the importance of aligning the behaviors of leaders and followers alike to key spiritual and ethical values. Cultivating spiritual and ethical practices serves as a guiding light that illuminates the hearts and minds of leaders. In the end, a leadership approach that values spirituality and ethical behavior creates a safe, supportive environment that is built on trust and mutual respect, resulting in teams and organizations marked by greater compassion, meaning, and peace.

3. MATURITY IN LEADERSHIP

Growth into maturity can be discussed in relation to various areas of life. As a desirable attribute, such growth may be applied to a wide range of personal realities such as our spiritual, emotional, cognitive, and physical maturation, not to mention our relational, social, and professional development. In our present context we'll focus on maturity as it relates to leadership.

Let me ask:

- What are some potential consequences when leadership maturity within a team or organization is lacking?
- Whom do you consider to be a good example of mature leadership in your church, team, or organization?
- What is an area in your leadership you'd like to improve to become a more mature and effective leader?
- What is an obstacle that might be hindering your development in leadership maturity?
- What is an action you can take today to begin cultivating greater leadership maturity?

The word *maturity* typically refers to an individual's physical and mental development from infancy to adulthood. Physical maturity pertains to bodily growth, while mental and emotional maturity involves the development of cognitive, emotional, and social traits. Maturity is, by any definition, a multifaceted process influenced by a variety of factors.

Leadership maturity is connected to psychological and spiritual development. It can be visualized as a progression along a scale from left to right; but the progression is complex, not always linear nor chronological. The end point of reaching and possessing maturity, however, is hugely important, and no more so than in leading or following in highly complex settings. Why? Navigating complexity entails dealing with multiple variables, uncertainties, and interdependencies. Sensemaking and decision-making in an environment characterized by *volatility, uncertainty, complexity, or ambiguity* (known as the managerial framework of VUCA) is a very difficult task. It's a task that calls upon leaders and followers alike to be at the one and same moment resilient, discerning, and adaptable; for complex and crisis situations by their very nature cannot be successfully managed except by those habitually attuned to ongoing learning, experimentation, and versatility, all hallmarks of a matured leadership.

Within Christianity, maturity is primarily associated with spiritual transformation, a process made possible by God's work in the human heart. This lifelong journey involves following Jesus and practicing His teachings along with other believers engaged in the same journey. When attained, spiritual maturity is characterized by wisdom, discernment, self-control, love, and a deeper understanding of how God guides. In this regard, New Testament writers encourage Christians not to remain as infants in their relationship to Christ (1Cor. 3:1-2), but to "become mature, attaining to the whole measure of the fullness of Christ" (Eph. 4:11-13). In theological terms, this means to live by the Spirit and thereby be transformed into Christ's image (2Cor. 3:18).

Contemporary scholars and practitioners discuss leadership maturity within a wide range of terms that include such concepts as self-awareness, self-reflection, emotional and spiritual intelligence, accountability, responsibility, courage, discernment, collaboration, integrity, and developing others. Certainly no one would argue with such a description of maturity, but as Christian leaders we should remember that such traits of character and leadership are only arrived at in a truly Christlike manner through the transformational growth process to which God's Holy Spirit subjects us.

Maturity and Leadership Development

Schools and organizations today offer various leadership development programs, each with its particular focus and objective. These programs have different names, such as leadership development programs, executive leadership programs, emerging leader programs, and high-potential programs. Their goal is to equip both emerging and experienced leaders with the necessary skills to effectively lead themselves and others. In this context, leadership development is usually understood within a pedagogical framework of aiding people to become better leaders and followers. Within this approach, development can either be defined in broad terms or be linked to more specific competencies.

Leadership development programs typically involve instruction in acquiring a range of techniques and skills, including brainstorming, exploration, solution search, strategizing, planning, experimentation, implementation, evaluation, and conflict resolution. Each of these skills is essential for effective decision-making. Although such skills are critical to any leader's all-around effectiveness, my colleague and leadership coach, Dick Daniels, asserts that leadership maturity necessitates the ongoing development of especially two key traits: character and competence. Character is demonstrated by a leader's ability to positively influence others, whereas competence pertains to a leader's capacity to devise strategies, execute actions, and achieve outcomes. Developing both character and competence enhances a leader's overall capacity to assume new opportunities and responsibilities at higher levels.[4]

According to Roger Gill, leadership development is the process of assisting leaders in "knowing what to do, how to do it, wanting to do it, and then actually applying it."[5] Leaders not only need to learn necessary knowledge and skills, but also need to develop intrinsic motivations and a sense of purpose that encompasses both the cognitive and spiritual domains. To be successful in their development on these fronts, leaders should conscientiously strive on an ongoing basis to integrate learned principles into their character and practice, while simultaneously being open and receptive to wise feedback.

To mature into a highly developed leader, it's important to focus on self-awareness, intentional learning, and resolute practice. Knowing both your strengths and areas that need growth is crucial. While consistent reading, training, and peer learning can provide knowledge and skills, true growth comes from taking risks and making mistakes, and then learning from those experiences. Leadership development through participating in team projects offers another practical approach to learning that can be more effective than traditional classroom methods. Such projects provide a dynamic way to learn and apply leadership skills in real-world situations, thus accelerating growth into maturity.

Maturity and Leadership Formation

Maturity attained through leadership education requires moving beyond the knowledge and skills typically focused on in the management sciences. We must, instead, adopt an integrated model of leadership that acknowledges and supports leaders on their spiritual journey toward maturity.

The late Andre L. Delbecq, a former professor at Santa Clara University and Senior Fellow of the Ignatian Center for Jesuit Education, offered through his lifelong work important understandings about leadership formation. I personally had the privilege of visiting him at his San Francisco home two years prior to his passing in October 2016. Largely as a result of that visit, his ideas have come to deeply influence my way of thinking about leadership maturity. Here is a summary of how my knowledge has evolved on this matter.

According to Delbecq, *leadership formation* is based on spiritual wisdom, while *leadership development* is rooted in the social and management sciences. He rejects the narrow emphasis often given to managerial and organizational skills in leadership development, but at the same time does not separate those social and organizational realities from the spiritual aspect of leadership. He calls, therefore, for an integrative approach to leadership that includes acquiring leadership skills, developing character, and attending to spiritual formation and well-being.

For Delbecq, leadership formation is a form of spiritual formation. He defines spirituality as the unique and personal inner search for and experience of the most complete personal development possible, an experience realized only through participating in the transcendent mystery of God. The test here for authentic spirituality is loving and compassionate service.[6]

In his attempt to define spiritual or leadership formation, Delbecq proposes the following themes as integral to its nature:

- The dignity of the individual person
- The nature of calling and spiritual gifts (*charismata*)
- The importance of community
- The virtues of patience, forgiveness, courage, hopefulness, etc. in support of community
- The sense of overarching mission

The focus of leadership formation is on fostering respect for the dignity and the honor of each and every individual, recognizing the value of their diverse talents and emphasizing the importance of spiritual discernment. Through this formation process, individuals are equipped to become productive members of communities that empower their members with freedom, a sense of worth, and the capacity to undertake activities for the greater good of the community.

With this understanding, Delbecq asserts that leadership formation from a Christian perspective is based on a two-sided theology – a theology of community on the one hand, and the theology of the individual on the other. He insists that leaders must recognize the presence of the divine in every human being and, consequently, treat all with respect and love. Leaders must acknowledge, moreover, that God grants to each person the talents to be employed for the greater benefit of the community, and that it's their responsibility to help their employees and volunteers mature through the discovery and application of their gifts, calling, and various ways of service.

Along with his focus on the individual, of course, is Delbecq's emphasis on community. He is a proponent of creating supportive and inclusive communities where participants strive for greater human effectiveness and virtuous character. In his overall philosophy of leadership formation is the importance on outcomes staying consistent with the mission of God. What is that mission? The mission of God is cosmic redemption!

Leaders, who want to promote their own spiritual growth need to be disciplined in Bible reading, prayer, and reflection. And it's through the ongoing practice of patience, deep listening, contemplative discernment, reexamining consciousness, and searching for the will of God that leaders experience true leadership formation.

Self-Transcendence and Beyond Dualistic Thinking

Professor Jody Fry, the founder of the International Institute of Spiritual Leadership, points out that leaders who are more spiritually developed are characterized by a number of notable qualities. Those qualities include a cultivation of spiritual awareness; the practice of various spiritual disciplines; a dedication to self-transcendence and interconnection, an altruistic love and service for the well-being of others, a capacity to reconcile apparent dualistic opposites, and unity with God, the one who transcends all things.[7]

Transcendence can manifest itself spiritually as individuals connect with God, the result being a sense of unity and purpose that goes beyond material concerns. Socially, transcendence occurs when individuals extend empathy and compassion to others. Self-transcendence, a concept rooted in Christian spirituality, shows itself when individuals rise above their own self-interests and limitations to connect with something larger and greater than themselves.

Such an experience transcends the ego and the result is a keen sense of unity with others, nature, and God. Manifestations of this self-transcendence include a sense of wholeness, altruism, and empathy – even towards those who may be "different" or adversarial. Associated with personal growth and a deeper understanding of the interconnectedness of all things, self-transcendence is a major contributor to a transformative journey leading to a higher form of fulfillment both in leadership and life in general. Besides transcending the self, leadership maturity reconciles within itself what we might refer to as "dualistic opposites." Entities or forces that appear, at least upon first sight, seem to be totally contrary to one another.

In everyday life, we often think in terms of opposites, such as hot and cold, big and small, or near and far. These contrasts help us navigate the world. However, it's crucial to avoid reckless oversimplifications when we deal with serious issues in life. It is dangerous. Extreme dualistic thinking divides everything into stark, black-and-white categories, insisting that life is strictly "either/or" and refusing to acknowledge its inherent paradoxes. Franciscan friar and ecumenical teacher, Fr. Richard Rohr, argues that such immature dualistic thinking is a hallmark of egocentric individuals. According to Rohr, their dualistic mindset fuels conflict and violence because it "it compares, it competes, it conflicts, it conspires, it condemns, it cancels out any contrary evidence, and then it crucifies with impunity".[8]

Immature dichotomous thinking thinks of leadership also solely in terms of counter opposites. For example, this kind of thinking believes that leadership is all about power and success, has little to do with suffering, is to praise for accomplishments, is engaged in a top-down-never-horizontal scenario, and so goes the thinking. People ensnared in this type of thinking are self-absorbed and stuck on "either-or" and "oversimplification" fallacies.

A dichotomous thinking involves over-simplifying complex situations into diametrically opposed, binary categories, such as, making an all-or-nothing claim or insisting on a solely right-or-wrong judgment. The binary categories involved in dichotomous reasoning are often totally contradictory or clashing in nature.

Let's cite a few examples:

- autocratic vs. democratic leadership
- task-oriented vs. people-oriented leadership
- centralized vs. decentralized leadership
- innovative vs. conservative leadership
- emotional vs. rational/logical leadership
- inclusive vs. exclusive leadership.

It's either one or the other, not both, nor is it anything in between. It's all important to note, however, that these dichotomies are not absolute. Mature leaders draw from what is potentially good and helpful on BOTH sides of the divide, and then successfully integrate them into their leadership. Such leaders are like tightrope walkers. Holding their arms straight out on both sides, each arm pointing in the opposite direction than the other. These amazing sky walkers are able to achieve a fine balance that enables them to successfully navigate their journey across the high wire. So it is with mature leaders. They find and achieve a fine balance between the dualistic options confronting their leadership and from there, they effectively continue on.

Shifting Focus from Doing to Being

Our society tends to prioritize busyness, productivity, and accomplishments over the cultivation of one's inner life. However, "doing more" or "doing better" does not necessarily equal personal growth and development.

In our fast-paced world, it's not difficult to see how easy it is to get caught up in the ever-constant rush of doing, achieving, and striving for more. But the question we need to ask ourselves in the midst of all this frantic activity is whether or not we really *should* expect ourselves to keep up all this busyness. Just *doing* things, and doing those same things right – does that make us successful *doers*? Or should we be looking for something more fundamental to our existence, and to which leadership should we turn?

Leadership maturity also presupposes a shift from inordinately valuing productivity and achievement over experiencing inner peace and contentment. If we continue to focus solely on doing and achieving, we risk compromising our inner spiritual lives and can develop a shallow understanding of God, ourselves, and others. To avoid these negative possibilities, we need to prioritize reflection and mindfulness. The shift "from doing to being" will then reap the benefits of more balanced and fulfilling leadership. The journey here is a personal one and will look different for each individual. However, by taking the time to cultivate a deeper sense of self-awareness and mindfulness, leaders will more consciously embrace the present moment, treasuring it as a gift of grace. The result? Finding greater peace and fulfillment in our lives!

That Christians are exhorted to focus on inner transformation rather than external conformity to the patterns and trends of the secular world is a major thrust in the teachings of the New Testament. In Romans 12:1-2, for example, the apostle Paul calls upon believers to "present your bodies as a living and holy sacrifice, acceptable to God, which is your spiritual service of worship. And do not be conformed to this world, but be transformed by the renewing of your mind, so that you may prove what the will of God is, that which is good and acceptable and perfect." Here we see that the shift from doing to being is closely related to the idea of surrendering oneself to God, discerning and accepting his will, and serving him in an attitude of worship.

In Christian terms, maturity in leadership is primarily associated with finding rest in God's love, acceptance, and grace. As to personal character, such maturity is reflected in the cultivating and acquisition of such inner spiritual qualities as love, joy, peace, forbearance, kindness, goodness, faithfulness, gentleness, and self-control, all traits listed in Galatians 5:22-23, and which the apostle Paul there calls the "fruit of the Spirit."

Secondly, leadership maturity is connected to the idea of living out our faith in Christ through our actions of service to others. This does not mean, however, that like the world around us, we make busyness a way of life as we live out that service. Busyness can be a serious hindrance to spiritual growth, distracting and disconnecting us from our spiritual purpose. The Bible warns against the dangers of busyness and encourages rest and Sabbath as essential for spiritual and physical health. Jesus himself modeled a life of rest and retreat, withdrawing periodically as he did to solitary places for prayer and reflection.

1. Find your identity and purpose in Christ.
2. Allow God to transform us from the inside out through faith and surrender to Jesus.
3. Focus on cultivating a deep inner relationship with God.

The pursuit of spiritual growth and maturity should never be neglected in the midst of the daily demands of life. Rather, it is crucial to maintain a balance between the things we need to do and the attention we need to give to our spiritual life. When we prioritize prayer and contemplation, we cultivate a deeper sense of awareness and connection with God. This deeper sense of purpose will bring meaning and purpose to all we think or do and help us approach our tasks with more focus, intention, and creativity. By nurturing our spiritual life, we can bring greater depth, wisdom, and maturity to all aspects of our existence, including leadership.

Endnotes

1. Gill, Roger & Alexander Negrov. "Perspectives on leadership development in post-Soviet Eurasia," *International Journal of Cross-Cultural Management*, 21(3), 2021, 409-429. https://doi.org/10.1177/14705958211051551
2. The face-to-face interview was conducted in May 2021.
3. Kellerman, B. *Bad Leadership: What It Is, How It Happens, Why It Matters.* Harvard Business School Press, 2004.
4. Daniels, Dick. *Leadership Briefs and Leadership Core.* Leadership Development Group, 2014. p. 26.
5. Gill, Roger. *Theory and Practice of Leadership.* 2nd ed. Sage, 2011, p. 365.
6. Delbecq, A.L. "Christian spirituality and contemporary business leadership," *Journal of Organizational Change Management*, (12/4) 1999: 345-354.
7. See these publications, for example, Fry, L. and Kriger, M. "Toward a theory of being-centered leadership: multiple levels of being as context for effective leadership," *Human Relations*, 62(11), 2009: 1667-1696; Fry, L. and Nisiewicz, M. *Maximizing the Triple Bottom Line Through Spiritual Leadership.* Stanford University Press, 2013; Allen, S. and Fry, L.W. "Spiritual development in executive coaching," *Journal of Management Development*, 38(10), 2019: 796-811.
8. Rohr, R. *A Spring Within Us: A Book of Dailly Mediations.* CAC Publishing, 2016, p. 97-98.

> Knowing and experiencing God is the key foundation in forming spiritual, ethical, and effective leadership.

CHAPTER 4

THE CONFLUENCE OF FAITH AND LEADERSHIP

In this chapter, the concept of "confluence" signifies the harmonious fusion of Christian faith with leadership. The seamless integration of personal convictions, values, and theological perspectives with leadership principles and practical application holds particular significance, particularly for Christians who find themselves navigating highly complex, secular environments. By leveraging this confluence, Christians have the potential to inspire and influence others in a more comprehensive and profound manner, leading by example and demonstrating their unwavering convictions.

1. THEOLOGICAL BEARINGS ON LEADERSHIP

It is difficult to pinpoint a single universal Christian theology that serves as the specific model for Christian leadership. Christianity encompasses a diverse range of theological perspectives after all. Throughout the history of the Church, various confessional theologies have emerged, reflecting the identities, viewpoints, and preferences of Catholic, Orthodox, and Protestant Christians. These theologies, in turn, have each been shaped by their own peculiar historical, political, social, economic, ecclesiastic, and cultural factors.

Instead of selecting one particular theological tradition over another as the authoritative source for discussion on leadership, it is more appropriate to consider a general biblical and Christian confessional heritage, along with a core of essential Christian convictions and character qualities, as the foundational elements of Christian leadership. Such an approach allows for a broad and inclusive understanding that acknowledges the rich diversity within the Christian faith and heritage overall.

In general, the main Christian theological traditions concur that God approves of a human leadership that embodies qualities reflecting God's character, such as obedience, trust, wisdom, courage, humility, loving authority, integrity, compassion, empathy, patience, the ability to handle criticism, selflessness, perseverance, operational excellence, and foresight. These virtues are seen as gifts bestowed by God, revealed through Jesus Christ, and mediated through the Bible's moral teachings, the empowerment of the Holy Spirit, and the presence of the Christian community. From a Christian theological perspective, ethical traits such as love, integrity, honesty, accountability, fairness, respect, empathy, and justice are seen as essential virtues that align with God's vision for leadership.

All Christian theological traditions further suggest that excellent personal and organizational leadership is possible because God provides leaders with the necessary skills and abilities to lead (and follow) within the historical and social contexts in which they find themselves. When leadership is so equipped by God, it serves divine purposes.

Biblical Theology and Leadership

When discussing leadership in relation to the Christian faith, it is more fruitful to approach it through the lens of Biblical theology rather than through the frameworks of systematic, historical, or comparative theologies. That's because biblical theology seeks to understand and interpret the teachings, themes, and overarching narrative of the Bible as a whole. It explores the unfolding plan of God throughout Scripture, tracing themes, motifs, and the development of key theological concepts from Genesis to Revelation. At the same time, biblical theology focuses on the theological structures and categories that arise from the individual books of the Old and New Testaments. Its goal is to explore the overarching mission of the Triune God (God the Father, God the Son, and the Holy Spirit) as depicted in such biblical themes as creation, the fall, redemption, and the new creation. It is in such a theological context that biblical leadership is most clearly seen.

According to Corné Bekker, the field of biblical theological studies tends to view leadership as being mimetic, power-conscious, follower-centered, and ultimately Christological.[1] This means that biblical theology recognizes that leadership in the Bible often involves imitating or modeling God's character and actions. It also acknowledges the practice of power dynamics within leadership roles. Furthermore, biblical leadership tends to be centered around the needs and well-being of followers. In short, theocentric (focused on God) and Christocentric (focused on Christ) concepts and ideas form the basis for understanding and approaching leadership within the framework of biblical theology.

Biblical writings often employ various concepts and metaphors to portray Christian leadership. Commonly used metaphors include shepherding, stewardship, and servanthood. These metaphors emphasize that being a steward, servant, or shepherd is not merely about skills or position, but it is about one's attitude towards God, people, and the tasks entrusted to the individual. Anacker and Shoup propose that at the core of the metaphor of Christian leadership lies transformational service that creates positive change or improvement in the lives of individuals or communities in a setting that is unfamiliar, foreign, or even hostile.[2]

Christians generally recognize that the Bible provides essential principles and guidance for leadership. By studying the Bible and incorporating its teachings into leadership practices, individuals gain valuable insights and guidance for their roles as leaders. Developing good leadership skills involves more than simply studying the Bible or other relevant Christian and secular texts; it also requires experiential learning, reflection, and continuous personal growth.

2. WHY THEOLOGICAL INQUIRY?

In a secular setting, leadership excellence relies solely on personal strength, wisdom, knowledge, and skills—an approach that centers on human capabilities. In a Christian community, leadership distinguishes itself by acknowledging that individuals must exert their personal efforts, yet ultimate success rests upon God and his will. This notion of leadership neither implies passivity, relying solely on God without any concurrent cooperation in carrying out his will, nor does it suggest autonomous action apart from God.

Christian leadership embraces:

- collaborating *with* God,
- recognizing his presence in one's life,
- experiencing his work within and through the individual person,
- valuing the community of believers,
- understanding the significance of God's kingdom,
- and acknowledging his role in human history.

Without theological inquiry, it is difficult to gain Christian insights into leadership concepts and practices. Such inquiry involves exploring and studying religious beliefs, practices, and texts to gain a deeper understanding of God, faith, and the human experience. It is a dynamic and ongoing process that encourages individuals to delve into deep intellectual and spiritual exploration while seeking to make meaningful connections between theology, personal faith, and the broader human experience.

A few years ago, I had the opportunity to participate in the *Coaching Mastery Certificate Program* led by Dr. Keith Webb. This program provided a solid theoretical foundation along with the introduction to numerous coaching practices. During one of the coaching sessions, I was paired with an experienced Anglican priest from Canada as my coach. At the beginning of our session, he asked me what I wanted to discuss during our thirty-minute time together. I expressed my struggle with a short essay (titled "The Mission of God and the Leadership of God") I was working on at the time. Although I was interested in the topic, I was having difficulty making progress. My coach responded with a series of insightful, thought-provoking questions:

- What do you mean by the Mission of God and the Leadership of God?
- Why are these subjects important to you? How are they connected?
- How do you plan to develop your theme?
- What have you learned about yourself in relation to your interest in the topic of your essay?

My coach's guidance here encouraged me to think at a much deeper level about the topic I had been struggling with, and as a result, I arrived at the following understandings:

1. A theocentric focus on leadership helps to negate an interest in pursuing leadership for the wrong reasons. It neutralizes egocentrism, narcissism, and a toxic passion for power. In contrast to these self-centered evils, a theocentric focus inspires us to establish a relationship with God – the one who will provide us with the needed faith, hope, and love to execute excellent leadership. Accordingly, then, we need to think less about our personal and leadership accomplishments and focus more on contemplating the Mission of God and the Leadership of God.

2. Leadership development, as we know, is about developing leaders with excellent leadership characteristics and skills. But if we approach framing leadership development around the Leadership of God, then we will ask:

- What does God desire to accomplish within, without, and around us you?
- What is God accomplishing through you without you even being aware of it?
- Where - and how - is God taking you to carry out his work in this world?

3. If a leader's mindset is rooted in the Mission of God and the Leadership of God, then the leadership becomes a case of spiritual followership rather than merely human leadership.

4. Christian theological inquiry can contribute to enriching leadership if it addresses key fundamental questions surrounding leadership development and practice:

- What is the Mission of God and how does it relate to the Leadership of God?
- How do Christians relate to the Mission and Leadership of God? What is their role?
- What are the Whys and Ways of being godly leaders and followers in participating in God's mission?
- How can Christian leaders balance the tension between following Jesus and leading others with authority and humility?
- What is the relationship between leadership and followership in Christian thought, and how can leaders foster a sense of unity and collaboration?
- How can Christian leaders engage with secular leadership theories and practices while remaining faithful to their Christian beliefs?
- In what ways does God entrust his people with the task of nurturing unity, encouraging inclusivity, and establishing environments for worship, fellowship, and service?

From a Christian point of view, leadership is both a theological and spiritual phenomenon. The study of theological realities involves exploring the nature of God, religious practices, spiritual experiences, the nature of faith, and the interpretation of sacred texts. It also encompasses developing theological concepts and themes. The theological consideration of leadership aims to uncover the meaning, purpose, and significance of leadership within Christian traditions and the broader human experience.

3. THEOCENTRIC APPROACH

Henri Nouwen (1932–1996) was a Dutch Catholic priest and theologian who taught for many years at the Universities of Notre Dame, Yale, and Harvard. Later in his life, Nouwen worked in Canada with people who had cognitive or developmental impairments. In his book, *In the Name of Jesus: Reflections on Christian Leadership*, Nouwen states that very few contemporary Christian leaders think theologically.

He says:

> Most Christian leaders today raise psychological or sociological questions even though they frame them in scriptural terms....The task of future Christian leaders is .... to identify and announce the ways in which Jesus is leading God's people out of slavery, through the desert to a new land of freedom. Christian leaders have the arduous task of responding to personal struggles, family conflicts, national calamities, and international tensions with an articulate faith in God's real presence....The Christian leaders of the

> future have to be theologians, persons who know the heart of God and are trained – through prayer, study, and careful analysis – to manifest the divine event of God's saving work in the midst of the many seemingly random events of their time.[3]

Over the course of my leadership research, I have conducted interviews with hundreds of Christians, including seminary-trained pastors and theologians. Among other inquiries, I have posed open-ended questions like: "How do you understand leadership?" and "What does leadership mean to you personally?" Through these interviews I, like Nouwen, have discovered that the majority of respondents perceive leadership as a social phenomenon. They acknowledge the presence of leaders, followers, and the dynamics of leadership in various contexts ranging from sports and politics to business and religion. Occasionally, they even reference group dynamics in the animal kingdom. However, I have also observed that mature Christians with professional experience often describe leadership solely within social or organizational contexts, rather than from a theological standpoint. They rarely establish a direct connection between the notion of leadership and ultimately, the leadership of God. This observation highlights the importance of revitalizing theological knowledge when discussing leadership.

The Theocentric Approach of Hodos Leadership

For Christians, the foundation of understanding leadership lies in recognizing God as leadership's primary person, source, and dimension. It is essential for every Christian to shape an understanding of leadership in the nature of God and in the "Leadership of God."

When it comes to the concept of the "Leadership of God" there are numerous avenues that can be explored. Christian teachings rooted in diverse texts, accounts, and narratives offer a wealth of information that contributes to the understanding of leadership. They provide a rich tapestry of data, including:

- God's nature, attributes, and character.
- God's mission, vision, and values.
- God's plans and how he decides upon them, along with the strategies he employs to implement them.
- God's ways of calling, appointing, and empowering his people.
- God's will for his creation, including humans.
- God's loving care for the world.
- Etc.

Based on revelation given in the Bible, what can be known about God's person or character? What is revealed about him as Leader?

Here are a few essentials:

1. **God is revealed as the Supreme Being.** As such, God is endowed with the highest authority and power.
2. **God reveals himself as Father, Son, and Holy Spirit.** The Bible depicts the united work of the Triune God as the Father acting in the Son through the power of the Spirit. Working in such unity, the Trinity serves as the real content and conceptual framework of God's leadership.
3. **God makes himself known as Lord** in various ways, especially through his Son Jesus Christ.

4. **God is regarded as the Creator, Author, and First Cause of the universe.** He initiates when needed and implements what he initiates with effectiveness.
5. **God acts according to his understanding** of what and when something is needed. And when he acts, his actions are always worthy, just, and complete.
6. **God sovereignly rules over the universe, the world, and the affairs of men.** As the Leader, he governs, and his government is eternal.
7. **God is the Supreme Judge.** He sets the moral standards and laws for all his created beings and holds them accountable to follow his will.
8. **God is Father. God is love.** He tenderly cares for his creation and for his children.
9. **As the Leader, God is a powerful communicator.** Throughout the Biblical narrative, we see him employ various ways to communicate his will, whether it be by the written word, angels, Old Testament prophets, New Testament apostles, or even by his Son, the Lord Jesus Christ.
10. **God tempers his justice with mercy.**
11. **God is always at work fulfilling his purposes**, even in the most adverse circumstances, including those in which he is either ignored or outrightly rebelled against. God acts out of his own will, but often does so through chosen agents, whether they be individuals or nations. God establishes teamsmanship in which he leads and others are invited to follow. This following of sorts represents a select community in which all have the privilege and responsibility of being God's sub-creators, co-workers, and servants.
12. **God's Holy Spirit is the divine presence** who leads and directs individuals in their spiritual journey and decision-making. He brings spiritual transformation and

growth and fosters fellowship with a sense of unity despite any diversity that might exist among Christ's followers. He empowers, equips, and enables God's people to fulfill their calling and to carry out their responsibilities. And it is the Holy Spirit who empowers individuals with specific gifts and talents for service in the Church and society in general.

For your reflection:

- What principles about God's leadership do we find in Scripture?
- How is God guiding and leading us, and in what ways do we actively follow him?
- What areas of our life do we need to improve upon to reflect God's way of leadership more truthfully?

4. PLAN FOR A THEOLOGICAL JOURNEY

Imagine yourself on a car journey with multiple stops, guided by a tentative plan that provides a basic sense of direction. Throughout your trek, a real-time digital navigation system assists you with valuable information such as landmarks, points of interest, alternative routes, and live traffic updates. Your trip represents a process of progression and exploration, with each stop holding significance as a point of interest or a milestone on the drive to the next destination.

Similarly, thinking about leadership theologically is akin to a journey with multiple stops. This theological expedition can benefit from a tentative map, a guide providing a rough outline of the route to be followed. Like a traveler embarking on a journey, individuals on this theological expedition encounter different stops, each serving a distinct purpose. These stops encompass studying foundational beliefs, engaging with biblical texts, exploring historical perspectives, grappling with contemporary issues, and engaging in personal reflection. The presence of a foundational map or framework for the theology of leadership enriches the transformative journey of growth, exploration, and discovery in the domain of leadership practice.

The construction of this map entails addressing pivotal questions, including:

- What theological truths are crucial for understanding the leadership phenomenon?
- What core themes and practices of leadership are presented in biblical texts?
- Which theological insights should guide God's people in their leadership and followership?

Knowing and experiencing God is the key foundation in forming spiritual, ethical, and effective leadership. From a Christian point of view, godly leadership is based on *faith in God*, which presupposes a leader's readiness to follow Jesus and lead people in accordance with God's plans. This kind of godly leadership is attainable, in turn, if a person is willing to learn from God (Gal. 1:11-12), recognizing that the ways and means by which God perfects his followers and teaches them effective leadership are diverse. This being the case, reflecting on the theology of leadership becomes crucial.

Seven Waypoints on the Theological Map

Christian theology speaks to the character and actions of God, especially to the exercising of his will towards a wayward humanity.

A Christian theological map outlining the route to leadership must include numerous theological destinations (i.e. understandings), each needing to be carefully explored.

Among the key ones, the following should be noted:

1. God the Creator. There is a God who created the universe and humanity, and he loves both. Through his self-revelation, God communicates to humanity his divine plan for its existence (John 1:1-18; 14:23; Rom. 1:19-20; 1 Cor. 12:4-6; Heb. 1:1-3). The Triune God (as understood by orthodox Christian teaching) is the Creator of all that exists, the First Cause of everything. For members of the human race, standing in a personal relationship with the Creator and understanding and obeying him are the most important steps in reflecting his image in their lives.

Understanding leadership as an existential phenomenon is contingent upon this knowledge of God and His role in human history – a role in which God is the main actor (creating, directing, allowing, influencing, etc.). The Triune God represents a perfect basic model for understanding leadership and management. From this perspective, it can be said that Christian leadership is based on a theocentric, Trinitarian theology. In God the Father, the inherent ability to create and foresee is revealed to us. In God the Son, it is service and redemption, and in God the Holy Spirit, it is the multiplication of potential and transformation. God reveals to all of humanity, not only himself, such pursuits and activities as planning, plan implementation, evaluation, interaction; as balancing such tensions as community and individual freedom, unity and diversity, and individual fulfillment and collective responsibility, practicing justice, honesty, love, and other such related personal and social virtues.

2. Purpose of Human Beings. Human beings have been created by God for a definite purpose (see Gen. 1:26-27; 9:6). At creation, he placed them in the world, perhaps the most significant locale in God's overall creation. This natural world is characterized by an interconnectedness and interdependence among all living and nonliving entities and has been particularly entrusted to us by the Creator. Over this world and its inhabitants, God exercises the highest authority and power, executing his own mission, vision, and strategies, etc. Created in his image, humans are capable of communication with God. It's because he has invited humans to become his co-workers in fulfilling his divine will on Earth. Man has been created for the glory of God (Is. 43:7, 1 Cor. 10:31).

God is the source of all that might be called *good*. He created the world, which had a definite beginning, and which one day will also be brought to an end as we currently know it.God is the Source, Architect, and Creator of anything and everything constructive, effective in accomplishing its purposes, and sufficient to meet the requirements and needs of the human creatures whom he has created. God initially destines all for his glory, a glory which is realized in creative and constructive service to God and fellow human beings (Rom. 11:36). Within this framework, then, it can be said that knowledge of God, imitation of his person and character (1 Peter 1:13-16), and the understanding of his divine will are the basis of godly and effective leadership (Mark 12:30).

3. Reality of Evil. There is an ancient enemy of God and humanity: Satan (the devil). (Gen. 3:1-6, Matt. 4:1-11, John 8:44, 2 Cor. 4:4, Gal. 4:4). Evil is a concrete reality in our world. It's a presence which seeks to destroy God's plans and his people. Evil manifests itself through its agents, with the main agent being Satan himself. Dominant as it is, however, evil is not an equal rival to God. Make no mistake, God is infinitely more powerful than Satan! He will ultimately prove victorious over evil on a universe scale. Due to the Fall (Gen. 3), which witnessed humanity's fall from a perfect state into one of vulnerability, weakness, and sinfulness, the entire human race was left under the power of the devil. Stripped of its God mandated authority and dominion over the earth by sin and Satanic deception, the race now experienced a major leadership crisis. God's plan that his newly created earth be ruled over by what may be referred to as a "theocratic administrator" was seriously disrupted.

To not leave human beings in their fallen state, and thus under his judgment, God provided redemption for them. This redemption, which includes all divine actions (through God the Father, Jesus Christ the Son, and the Holy Spirit), made it possible for humans to be spiritually reborn and reinstated to eternal communion with God, and become once again co-workers with him. Redemption, by its very definition, implies a human's escape from his or her most fundamental spiritual crisis – alienation from God. When redeemed, we acquire new and positive character traits. In relation to leadership, redemption can be most succinctly defined as redeemed humans regain the potential for godly leadership.

4. Spiritual Redemption. The Savior delivering us from evil and sin is the God-Man Jesus Christ who became for humans "wisdom from God, righteousness and sanctification and redemption" (1 Cor. 1:30, 1:18). The role of Christ is important in both the Revelation of God (Heb. 1:1-2) and in the redemption of the world. According to John the Evangelist, Jesus Christ, through his own self-sacrifice (Rev. 1:5), created the conditions necessary for the forgiveness of sins and the eternal salvation of humankind. It only remains for each individual to appropriate the benefits of this sacrifice of Christ through faith (Rom. 3:21-30; 5:1).

The life and death of Jesus Christ serve as an example of true godly leadership. Figuratively speaking, the cross of Christ clearly defines what it means to live a godly life (as a follower of Christ), namely: "Whoever wants to be my disciple must deny himself and take up his cross and follow me" (Mark 8:34). Thanks to the cross of Jesus Christ, believers possess a renewed life (Rom. 6:3-4; Gal. 2:19-20), a crucified sinful nature (Gal. 5:24-25), a oneness with Christ and with each other (1 Cor. 12:12-13), a realization that their fellow brother or sister is also one for whom Christ died (Rom. 14:13-15; 1 Cor. 8:9-11), a ministry endowed with spiritual power (2 Cor. 13:1-4), and relationships with spouses, children, bosses and subordinates characterized by the way of the cross (for the benefit of others – Eph. 4:31-6:2). From a biblical point of view, leaders and followers should serve each other for mutual benefit (John 13:1-17), forgiving one another since others' sins too have already been cleansed by the death of Christ (John 3:16).

As just mentioned, this redemption that is the totality of divine actions (through God the Father, Jesus Christ, and the Holy Spirit) on fallen humanity's behalf, makes it possible for humans to return to eternal communion with God. Redemption implies a way out of crisis, one in which the race is totally helpless to extricate itself (Col. 2:13-15, Rom. 6:6). What changes, then, does a redeemed person undergo upon entering into this new redeemed life? The individual departs from a self-centered, sinful way of life, and in its place takes on new character traits defined by love for others, becomes an active participant in society, and becomes a co-worker with God (1 Cor. 3:9a) in carrying out his redemptive mandate (Matt. 28:18-20) for the world. In regard to leadership, redemption provides for the believer the distinct possibility of a leadership now empowered to do God's work in God's way.

5. The Word of God. The Bible is the authoritative Word of God, a source of wisdom from God himself (Ps. 119:105-112). In this revealed wisdom is to be found the secret of exercising a living and beneficial influence upon the lives of one's fellow human beings. The superior path of leadership is in harmony with the nature, character, and way of God's own actions. That's why one of the key factors in the development of a leader is a coming into an understanding of the Holy Scripture–the Word of God–not only at the level of familiarity with its content, but also through actualizing (embodying) that content into attitude and practice.

It is in the pages of Scripture that we find the principles that lay the spiritual foundation for a truly God-ordained existence. The Bible testifies about how the lives of historical figures were shaped and formed, how they interacted and influenced each other, and how they related to God. As for leadership examples, innumerable accounts of both effective and ineffective leaders abound in the Bible. There are those whom God chose and molded into successes, and there are those who by their own flawed and sinful choices were failures. It is these real-life stories and accompanying instructions that believers throughout history have repeatedly turned to for understanding of true biblical leadership.

6. The Body of Christ. The church is a great example of how a community of people can harmoniously interact to achieve a common goal. Despite having many members (individual believers), the church remains one body – the body of Christ: "For as the body is one and has many members, but all the members of that one body, being many, are one body" (1Cor. 12:12). The body of Christ exists because all believers have been placed in it by the Holy Spirit (1Cor. 12:13). God, in the three persons of the Trinity, is the source of spiritual gifts (abilities and actions) that members of the Church receive by grace for serving God and each other in building up the body of Christ.

7. Two Horizons: Biblical-Theological and Secular Understandings of Leadership. In my view, the understanding of spiritual, ethical, and effective leadership requires an understanding of both religious and secular perspectives. A theological understanding of leadership emphasizes the importance of spiritual wisdom and divine guidance, while secular models of leadership recognize the importance of personal development, setting clear goals, motivation, communication, skills development, and so on. Secular leadership can (and does to a measurable extent) uphold ethical values and prioritize the welfare of the community, but at the same time, it is not only incomplete, but also inadequate due to its disregard for God. For a proper understanding of leadership, a multidisciplinary approach is certainly required, but Christian leaders must first and foremost in their approach engage in theological reflection on leadership theories and practices. Joint exploration of theology and leadership can and does influence mindsets, develop models, and foster the maturity required for true leadership.

5. LEADERSHIP IN THE BIBLE

The books of the Bible introduce us to the foundational aspects of faith and life. As such, they also unveil the spiritual, ethical, and impactful nature of leadership. Throughout the Bible, God is portrayed as the Mighty Creator, offering humanity the potential to exercise an authority and creativity that mirrors his own character. More specifically, the biblical concept of leadership is deeply rooted in Christology, that is, in the person and work of Christ, the second person of the Trinity. This portrait of leadership directs individuals toward a distinct way of life – one centered on Christ who exemplified discipline, humility, unconditional love, and genuine concern for the well-being of others. He was, after all, the leader *par excellence*.

More generally, the Bible serves as a valuable resource for instruction, admonishment, correction, and guidance in righteousness, empowering individuals who seek to follow God's path to be whole and fully equipped for virtuous endeavors (2Tim. 3:16-17). Its teachings encourage making choices that embrace abstinence over permissiveness, order over disorder, and love and humility over arrogance and injustice. Upon these understandings, the biblical approach to leadership further promotes a sincere and unconditional love for God and a selfless dedication to serving others. As a manual for godly leadership, then, the Bible is complete in its sufficiency.

According to Norwegian theologian, Karl Inge Tangen, the Bible appropriately portrays exemplary leadership as both doxological, accomplished for the glory of God, and serving, directed towards God and one's neighbors (Matt. 6:9-33; 22:37-39). Conversely, when individuals exhibit leadership driven by self-aggrandizement, characterized by self-indulgence, psychological manipulation, and a single-minded pursuit of power, wealth, and status, the Bible categorizes such leadership as idolatrous and detrimental.[4]

How to Study the Bible and Learn About Leadership

The Bible helps people build relationships with God and creation, enabling spiritual, ethical, and effective leadership. Learning leadership from the Bible involves interpreting biblical texts and formulating practical lessons for application in personal or organizational life. It is about actualizing biblical teachings in real-world leadership scenarios.

To study the Bible and what it has to say about leadership, you can follow this systematic process involving six steps:

1. **Selection of the Text:** Choose a specific book or passage from the Bible that focuses on leadership or contains relevant narratives, teachings, or examples.

2. **Collection of Additional Material:** Gather supplementary resources, such as commentaries, historical background, linguistic tools, and relevant scholarly works to support a proper understanding and analysis of the chosen text.

3. **Detailed Study and Interpretation:** Engage in a thorough examination and interpretation of the selected text through a process called exegesis. This involves scrutinizing the original language, historical context, cultural background, literary style, and theological themes to extract a comprehensive understanding of the text's intended meaning. (The depth of biblical study will vary based on one's level of preparedness and background, yet the key objective remains to engage with the text as thoroughly as possible, applying all available resources and methods—whether linguistic, historical, or theological—according to one's ability. The goal is to pursue the fullest understanding possible, given one's knowledge and tools, striving for excellence in interpretation.)

4. **Systematization of Observations:** Organize and categorize the insights, observations, and themes derived from the study of the text. Identify patterns, recurring motifs,

and key principles related to leadership that emerge from the analysis.

5. **Formulation of Leadership Insights and Recommendations:** Based on the systematic study and analysis, distill the observations into practical leadership insights and recommendations. Identify the principles, values, and practices that can inform and guide contemporary leadership contexts.

6. **Contextualization:** Reflect on the connection between the meaning of the biblical text and its relevance to modern personal and organizational life. Consider how the insights and recommendations derived from the study can be applied and adapted to address current leadership challenges, values, and cultural contexts.

By following this six-step process, you can delve into the study of leadership in the Bible and derive valuable insights and guidance for personal and organizational leadership for the present day.

One can also read the Bible and study leadership in a purposeful way by following a thematic approach. First, choose a biblical story or passage that depicts the harmonious or conflicting activities of biblical characters. Second, make observations that will help you see a broader and more multifaceted picture of the leaders and followers presented in the text.

Here are some questions to help guide you in this process:

- Who are the characters involved in this story?
- What role does God play in their thinking and actions?

- Where are they, who are they with, and what are the circumstances in which they find themselves?
- What skills and competencies do they possess? How are those skills reflected in the decisions and actions they take?
- How do they manage their tasks, especially as carried out in conjunction with others?
- What vision do they adhere to, and how do they strive to achieve that vision?
- What strategies, approaches, methods, and resources do they follow in pursuing their goals?
- What are their values and motives? What drives them?
- What do they understand clearly, and how do they effectively communicate that to others?
- How do they serve, impact, and contribute to the development of others?

I also propose incorporating Roger Gill's leadership theory of six themes and practices into the study of biblical texts.[5] When reading the Bible from this angle, one should consider the following six questions:

1. What does the Bible teach about vision? Explore the significance of vision and the ways for developing and effectively communicating it.
2. What does the Bible say about mission/purpose? Examine the understanding and communication of the purpose behind specific behaviors.
3. What does the Bible say about the formulation, communication, promotion, and preservation of spiritual, moral, personal, and communal values?

4. What does the Bible say about strategic thinking and planning? Explore aspects such as planning, implementation, and the ability to adapt initial plans to changing circumstances.
5. What does the Bible say about empowerment? Focus on resourcing and creating the necessary conditions to empower others to fulfill their tasks.
6. What does the Bible teach about engagement? Consider the creation of spiritual and emotional conditions that inspire active participation and actions that surpass basic expectations.

6. CHRISTIAN WORLDVIEW AND LEADERSHIP

Understanding the impact of your worldview is crucial to cultivating spiritual, ethical, and effective leadership practices.

What is meant by one's worldview? Simply put, a worldview refers to an individual's entire orientation towards life and the world, encompassing that individual's fundamental beliefs, values, assumptions, and interpretations of reality, all of which, in turn, influences his or her understanding of themselves, others, and the nature of leadership itself. In fact, worldview plays a vital role in shaping leadership perspectives and practices, acting as it does as a lens through which leaders perceive and evaluate their world, make decisions, and choose their actions.

A leader's worldview influences not only how he or she perceives and interacts with more immediate and like-minded followers, but also with a diverse array of individuals, groups, and communities who may not necessarily share the same worldview. Effective leaders, however, are very self-aware of their worldview. They acknowledge its power and influence over them, while still remain open to engaging in dialogue with people from other worldviews.

What these leaders understand is that interacting with different worldviews leads to diverse leadership approaches, priorities, and outcomes. For instance, a leader with a humanistic worldview may prioritize empathy, collaboration, and social justice, while a leader guided by a Christian worldview might, without in any way minimizing these values, emphasize spiritual transformation and fulfillment of God's will as the first priority in life and leadership. Recognizing this distinction, the Christian leader will make the necessary accommodations that will enhance his or her status as an effective leader without compromising the Christian stance they represent.

Anacker and Shoup[6] provide the following comprehensive list of eleven foundational elements for a Christian leadership model derived from the Christian worldview:

1. Following Jesus Christ
2. Being filled with the Spirit of God
3. Discerning and pursuing a vocational calling from God
4. Understanding vocation as an ambassador of Christ and a citizen of heaven
5. Stewarding God's gifts and talents for the advancement of God's Kingdom
6. Experiencing Christian fellowship
7. Knowing and applying the Word of God in daily life
8. Engaging in unceasing prayer
9. Participating in the ministry of the Church and finding belonging within it

10. Integrating general truths from general revelation with special revelation to guide practices
11. Trusting in the Lord rather than relying solely on self-understanding

These elements form the foundation of a Christian leadership model that aligns with the Christian worldview.

What is Christian Leadership?

The term "Christian leadership" is widely used in today's world, but its ambiguity leads me to prefer avoiding its use. Generally, it refers to leadership practiced by Christians from various traditions and denominations, characterized by adherence to Christian faith, principles, and values. More specifically, when Christians pursue Christian leadership, they aim to highlight the fundamental distinctions that exist between a secular and a Christian understanding of leadership. The primary contrast lies in the fact that in a secular mindset, leadership is viewed on the whole as humanly based.

The theological approach inherent within the Christian faith, however, suggests that Christian leadership should be conceptualized in relation to God and his redemptive mission in the world, particularly as realized through the Church. Within this context, leadership presupposes the guidance and wisdom of the Holy Spirit, while simultaneously incorporating insights from both special revelation (such as Scripture) and general revelation (such as the natural world and human experience).

The Christian understanding of leadership is deeply rooted in the Bible. Although Scriptures provide valuable insights and principles, truly effective leadership also requires thoughtful interpretation and application of those principles to contemporary contexts. A holistic approach that integrates biblical teachings with general knowledge gained through research, reflection, and practical experience is a must for those who aspire to true Christian leadership.

How, then, might "Christian leadership" be best summarized? To begin with, leadership (and, of course, followership as well) requires the active involvement and participation in the redemptive mission to which God has called all believers. How does leadership in such a context play out? Martin Hanna highlights several essential elements that factor into its successful execution. He states that Christian leaders, through the guidance of the Holy Spirit, are called to collaborate in the divine-human synergies of conviction-confession, conversion-repentance, consecration-obedience, and confirmation-perseverance. They are tasked with fostering dissatisfaction with the status quo, encouraging shifts in perspective, empowering others, providing long-term motivation, and developing flexible short-term action plans. In doing so, Christian leaders also promote synergy among fellow leaders and followers. Ultimately, Christian leaders exemplify a follower's heart in their approach to leadership.[7]

Leading from a Christian perspective ultimately involves following Jesus Christ as a fellow co-worker of God, fulfilling God's will for all of Creation. This entails adhering to Jesus' teachings, and in so doing, reflecting his values and behaviors. Jesus exemplified oneness with the Father in demonstrating sacrificial love in service to a lost humanity. Following Jesus entails cultivating a spiritual relationship with God, being obedient to God's will, and serving others with Christ-like love. Among other aspects of Christian living, this encompasses serving the local church, caring for one's fellow human beings, and giving oversight to the environment. In my understanding, Christian leadership can be said to be partnering with God and other individuals to achieve goals that are ideally driven by God's purposes. As such, Christian leadership serves as a channel for expressing godly love, faith, and hope on earth.

Endnotes

1. Bekker, C. "Towards a Theoretical Model of Christian Leadership," *Journal of Biblical Perspectives in Leadership*, 2(2), 2009: 142-152.
2. Anacker, G. J. and Shoup, J. R. "Leadership in the Context of Christian Worldview," in Burns, Jack, Shoup, John R, and Simmons Jr., Donald C. (eds). *Organizational Leadership*. InterVarsity Press, 2014, p. 35-64.
3. Nouwen, Henri J. M. *In the Name of Jesus: Reflections on Christian Leadership*. Crossroad, 1989, pp. 86-88
4. Tangen, K. I. "Leadership as Idolatry. The case of Stalinism and beyond," *Scandinavian Journal of Leadership and Theology*. 5(1) (2018), doi.org/10.53311/sjlt.v4.24; Tangen, K. I. "Leadership as Participation in the Hospitality of God. A Reading of Luke-Acts," *Journal of Pentecostal Theology*. 27(2), 2018: 284-306.
5. Gill, R. *Theory and Practice of Leadership*. 2nd ed. Sage. 2011.
6. Anacker, G. J. and Shoup, J. R. "Leadership in the Context of Christian Worldview," in Burns, Jack, Shoup, John R, and Simmons Jr., Donald C. (eds). *Organizational Leadership*. InterVarsity Press, 2014, p. 61.
7. Hanna, M. "What Is 'Christian' About Christian Leadership?" *The Journal of Applied Christian Leadership*, 1(2), 2006: 21-31.

Spiritual leaders are truly effective only to the extent that they connect themselves to Christ: seeking him, cultivating their personal relationship with him, submitting to his headship over them.

CHAPTER 5
SPIRITUALITY AND LEADERSHIP

1. SPIRITUALITY AND RELIGION

The terms "spirituality" and "religion" are often used to encompass personal beliefs, practices, and the institutional frameworks within which those beliefs and practices are enshrined and exercised. We normally categorize these concepts differently, such as representing religion as objective and spirituality as subjective, or representing religion as public and spirituality as private. Relative to these two concepts, it is important to acknowledge that individuals worldwide identify themselves in different ways. Some claim to be religious but not spiritual, others claim to be spiritual but not religious, and some do not align themselves with being either religious or spiritual. And, of course, there are those who claim to be both.

As might be expected, differing viewpoints on what constitutes the relationship between religion and spirituality have advanced:

- Some see the two as distinct and mutually exclusive of each other.
- Others consider them as synonymous, with no real distinction between them.
- Some acknowledge their differences but believe that they can be successfully integrated into one general notion.

It is widely accepted that spirituality can exist independently of organized religion, allowing individuals to cultivate their own personal sense and practice of spirituality outside of traditional religious boundaries. However, it is also widely accepted that religious traditions provide nurturing environments for spiritual exploration and growth. In this respect, Christianity serves as an excellent example, offering established frameworks and practices that support Christians in their spiritual journeys.

Non-Religious Spirituality

Non-religious spirituality refers to a form of spirituality that lies outside religious doctrines and organized religious institutions. As such, it encompasses a broad range of beliefs, practices, and experiences independent of the teachings of such traditional religious structures as local churches, synagogues, or mosques. Instead, such spirituality focuses on individual quests for meaning, purpose, and transcendence, guided by personal values, introspection, and connections to nature, humanity, or the universe at large. Deeply personal and individual, this form of spirituality seeks to explore and connect with something greater than oneself.

In leadership literature, particularly from non-religious authors, spirituality is commonly defined as:

- informal, unstructured, and lacking any affiliation with a religious institution
- pursuing and experiencing connections to oneself, others, nature, and the transcendent
- inclusive, embracing diversity
- universal and timeless in nature
- shaping the meaning and purpose of human lives
- encompassing inner peace, a state of heart and mind devoid of angst
- instilling hope and optimism
- inspiring courage in pursuing justice, compassion, and service.

People who embrace spirituality outside of religion often engage in such practices as meditation, mindfulness, yoga, and other activities that promote inner peace, harmony, and self-awareness. They may find inspiration in philosophical teachings, ancient wisdom traditions, or from various spiritual and mystical sources.

People who embrace spirituality outside of formal religion indicate that their non-religious concepts and practices of spirituality are governed by a flexible and personalized approach toward self-discovery, as well as a sense of social and environmental responsibility. In their opinion established religion is not needed to forge a unique path that resonates deeply with their understanding of the world.

Religious Spirituality

The concept of "religious spirituality" is something more objective than "non-religious spirituality," and as such is more "public" than "private." Although experienced subjectively, as is also the case with non-religious spirituality, this objective and more public dimension of religious spirituality is attributable to its beliefs and practices being grounded in a highly developed and sophisticated religious system.

Religious spirituality is linked to such established and highly organized religions as Judaism, Christianity, and Islam, and to religious traditions that incorporate philosophical inquiries into their body of beliefs and practices, such as Hinduism, Buddhism, and Confucianism.

Spirituality growing out of a defined religious context may be characterized by the following traits:

- A connection to the Divine; an experiencing of the transcendent or sacred.
- The practice of prayer, meditation, and contemplation.
- A reliance on sacred texts or teachings.
- A concern for personal spiritual transformation.
- The promotion of ethical behavior.
- A search for the meaning of life from a religious perspective.
- Serving others; practicing compassion.
- Mastering self-control; striving toward ethical and social self-transcendence.
- A concern for the holistic well-being of people.

Key Differences Between Religious and Non-Religious Spiritualities

Key differences between religious and non-religious spiritualities encompass worldviews, beliefs, practices, and social structures. In religious spirituality, transcendence involves connecting with God or some sublime spiritual dimension guided by specific doctrines and practices as defined within the parameters of a definite religious institution. Self-transcendence is marked by inner transformation, surrendering personal desires to the will of God and serving others, and to live with an eternal perspective.

Non-religious spirituality, on the other hand, focuses on self-transcendence through empathy, compassion, and interconnectedness with others. It lacks specific doctrines, is more individualistic, and emphasizes personal autonomy. Non-religious spirituality is flexible and adaptable to individual preferences and does not rely on any external spiritual authority. While religious spirituality emphasizes communal gatherings and worship within the context of a religious community, non-religious spirituality is more individually focused but with less emphasis on prescribed communal practices.

In discussing differences between religious and non-religious spirituality, it is also worth noting that some individuals find they incorporate elements from both frameworks as they experience an evolving spirituality over time.

2. CHRISTIAN SPIRITUALITY FRAMEWORK

Christianity is a monotheistic religion centered on the life, teachings, death, and resurrection of Jesus Christ. Its central emphasis is salvation and eternal life through faith in Jesus. The spirituality that grows out of this salvation experience is comprised of various important theological truths and practices, and at its core, includes the following features:

- Understanding personal salvation and God's forgiveness as possible through Christ's redemptive work and as a result of this understanding.

- Believing in Jesus as divine Savior and as the way to eternal life.
- Recognizing life's temporary nature, and thus seeking ultimate fulfillment in God's presence.
- Developing a personal relationship with God through Bible study, prayer, and worship.
- Seeking a sense of God's presence and guidance as well as spiritual nourishment through prayer, Bible study and contemplation.
- Recognizing and trusting in the Holy Spirit as the one who brings inner renewal and who shapes the believer into Christlikeness.
- Following Christ's teachings and reflecting his values in daily life.
- Engaging in a supportive community of believers.
- Serving others, empowered by the Holy Spirit's gifts.

A Christian framework for spirituality lays the foundation for truly authentic leadership. Here are several important elements that formulate that foundation:

- The path to spiritual leadership begins with an obedient following after Jesus Christ.
- Spiritual leaders are truly effective only to the extent that they connect themselves to Christ: seeking him, cultivating their personal relationship with him, submitting to his headship over them.
- The essence of spiritual leadership lies in embodying the life of Christ.
- The measure of a believer's spirituality can be recognized as the measure to which that individual's character and lifestyle reflect the person of the indwelling Christ.

- The Spirit of God is the key to discernment and engagement in fruitful work with others.
- Christian leaders draw upon spiritual strength that springs directly from the Lord God.
- Spiritual leadership means serving one another in providing necessary authority, knowledge, skills, resources, and freedom.
- Some key practical indicators of a leader's spirituality are the biblical values of love, service, reciprocity, humility, wisdom, contentment, and integrity.

Christ as the Center of Christian Spirituality

While religious individuals align themselves with the beliefs and rituals of a particular religious tradition, it is crucial to recognize that spirituality extends beyond formal religious practices. Not all religious individuals possess a strong inclination towards spirituality. Merely identifying as a Christian and engaging in superficial observance of rituals, for example, does not necessarily reflect the essence of Christian spirituality. Genuine Christian spirituality entails a profound reverence for God, being filled with the Holy Spirit, actively seeking personal growth through the Word of God, embodying love, mercy, humility, self-sacrifice, and other fundamental qualities that exemplify spiritual vitality.

In my first year of undergraduate theological training, I encountered the statement, "Jesus Christ is the end of religion." I was an insight which left a profound impact on me. This theological statement suggests that Jesus, through his role in the salvation and spiritual transformation of the believer, makes observance of a traditional religious system in and of itself unnecessary or inadequate as a means to come to and know God. It highlights the idea that a personal relationship with Jesus and the transformative power of his message are more significant than strict adherence to religious rules and practices. Jesus' life, death, and resurrection bring fulfillment and completion to humanity's religious strivings and aspirations.

Indeed, in his teachings, Jesus emphasized that true transformation begins with the heart. He highlighted the significance of cultivating a heart filled with love, forgiveness, humility, and righteousness. He expressed this idea innumerable times during his earthly ministry, and in such memorable words as the following:

- "Blessed are the pure in heart, for they will see God" (Matt. 5:8).

- "What comes out of a person is what defiles them. For it is from within, out of a person's heart, that evil thoughts come—sexual immorality, theft, murder, adultery, greed, malice, deceit, lewdness, envy, slander, arrogance and folly. All these evils come from inside and defile a person" (Mark 7:20-23).

- "Woe to you, teachers of the law and Pharisees, you hypocrites! You clean the outside of the cup and dish, but inside they are full of greed and self-indulgence. Blind Pharisee! First clean the inside of the cup and dish, and then the outside also will be clean" (Matt. 23:25-26).

Christian spirituality promotes the notion of establishing a direct and personal connection with Jesus rather than solely relying on Church teachings or legalistic interpretations of faith. This emphasis on a personal relationship underscores the belief that Jesus is the ultimate fulfillment of religious longing, and that his teachings guide individuals towards an ever-deepening spiritual experience.

As mentioned above, a truly Christian message emphasizes that Jesus Christ fulfills and surpasses the requirements and regulations of religious practices. He offers rest, freedom from the burden of the law, and a new way to approach God based on faith in him. In Christ, the focus shifts from external religious spirituality to an inner personal relationship with Jesus where true spiritual transformation and righteousness are found. Again, these basic truths are highlighted in such Scripture passages as:

- Romans 10:4: "For Christ is the culmination of the law for righteousness to everyone who believes."

- Matthew 11:28-30: "Come to me, all you who are weary and burdened, and I will give you rest. Take my yoke upon you and learn from me, for I am gentle and humble in heart, and you will find rest for your souls. For my yoke is easy and my burden is light."

3. TRINITARIAN GUIDANCE

Kees Waaijman (1942-2023), one of the leading European academic voices on the history and systematics of spirituality, stated: "Relationality is a basic category in spirituality."[1] Spirituality is like a river, a dynamic and ever-flowing entity that both shapes and observes the myriad interconnections within its realm. The river interacts with its surroundings—nourishing lands, shaping landscapes, and joining with other bodies of water; it embodies connections and relationships. Spirituality is about interactions within the spiritual and social worlds and the phenomenon of being connected and transformed.

In this context, the Trinity serves as a profound model of relational dynamics within the nature of God, illustrating how the Father, Son, and Holy Spirit exist in a unique and eternal communion. The Trinity not only reveals the inherent relationality within God's nature but also invites and guides humans into a transformative relationship with God which is characterized by love, communion, and co-participation in the divine life and mission.

Guidance from the Father

In Christian tradition, God the Father serves as the perfect guide for individuals embarked upon a spiritual journey. As the Creator of all things, God's wisdom and guidance are unparalleled. Christian spirituality, however, recognizes God not only as a Creator of infinite wisdom and sovereign control, but also embraces him as a good, loving, and caring leader. The Bible highlights the role of God the Father as that of a shepherd, guide, and leader, providing direction, protection, and wisdom to those who trust in him.

> **Two Examples**
>
> Psalm 23:1-3 - "The Lord is my shepherd; I shall not want. He makes me lie down in green pastures. He leads me beside still waters. He restores my soul. He leads me in paths of righteousness for his name's sake."
>
> Isaiah 58:11 - "And the Lord will guide you continually and satisfy your desire in scorched places and make your bones strong; and you shall be like a watered garden, like a spring of water, whose waters do not fail."

In creating human beings in his own image, God embedded in them a yearning for personal development, self-expression, and connection with others within community settings. He also blessed them with a desire to serve and help others, and to value and demonstrate love, justice, friendship, artistic inspiration and creativity, as well as with an intellectual and professional tendency.

Christian teachings recognize that spirituality permeates every dimension of our existence and involves a transformative relationship between God and humanity, guided by God's wisdom, goodness, and caring nature. God the Father guides those who trust him in discovering their true identity, the meaning of life, and their personal calling, along with giving them that sense of belonging so necessary for a healthy, wholesome spirituality. Truly God's goodness and care are everywhere, evident in his interactions with humanity, as most notably exemplified and proven in the life and teachings of Jesus Christ.

Guidance from Jesus

Remember the metaphor of "showing the way" and how it is connected to spirituality and leadership? From a Christian perspective, this metaphor also reminds us of the role that Jesus Christ plays as the ultimate guide, leading his followers on a spiritual journey toward God and with God. From a follower's perspective, the metaphor of Jesus as guide also emphasizes the responsibility of aligning one's life with the path Jesus shows.

For Christians, Jesus is the ultimate spiritual teacher who (even now) offers rest, humility, and guidance for living a blessed and fulfilling life. His emphasis is the importance of love, both for God and for others. Jesus is the way to a deep relationship with the Father.

- Matthew 22:37-40: Jesus says: "'Love the Lord your God with all your heart and with all your soul and with all your mind.' This is the first and greatest commandment. And the second is like it: 'Love your neighbor as yourself.' All the Law and the Prophets hang on these two commandments."
- John 14:6: "I am the way, and the truth, and the life. No one comes to the Father except through me."

Following the teachings of the Bible and leaning on God's Holy Spirit, Christians can and should demonstrate their Christ-like spirituality before the society in which they live – abstaining from, instead of indulging in all things selfish, worldly, and ungodly. This creates order in the world, rather than creating disorder. It exhibits love instead of pride, arrogance, injustice, and other such evils. The Bible leads Christians toward a distinctive way of life–a life with Christ who set an example of discipline, unconditional love, humility, caring for the well-being of others, and a host of other God honoring virtues.

Guidance from the Holy Spirit

Jesus assured his followers, "But the Advocate, the Holy Spirit, whom the Father will send in my name, will teach you all things and will remind you of everything I have said to you" (John 14:26). In the pursuit of a life aligned with God's will, guidance from the Holy Spirit is crucial. As the Apostle Paul instructs in his letter to the Galatians, "So I say, walk by the Spirit, and you will not gratify the desires of the flesh" (Gal. 5:16). Acts 13:2-4 illustrates how discernment and guidance for Christian leaders involve a combination of spiritual practices, direct revelation from the Holy Spirit, communal affirmation, and purposeful commissioning for service. The passage describes a group of Christians in Antioch who "were worshiping the

Lord and fasting." During this time, the Holy Spirit said, "Set apart for me Barnabas and Saul for the work to which I have called them." Following further fasting and prayer, the leaders placed their hands on Barnabas and Saul, sending them off. Thus, the two were "sent on their way by the Holy Spirit" and proceeded to Seleucia and Cyprus to fulfill their mission.

In 1 Corinthians 2:6-3:4, the Apostle Paul reflects on the relationship a believer possesses with the Holy Spirit. Through the Spirit, a person communicates with God. The Spirit reveals to that person God's will and truth. Without the help of the Spirit, an individual merely possesses knowledge of the world but lacks discernment, true wisdom, and genuine spiritual power. (This "soulfulness" is anthropocentric, while spirituality is theocentric, placing God's revelation and the action of the Holy Spirit at the forefront.) Moreover, the Holy Spirit guides followers of Christ along a dynamic and personal journey that involves love, faith, trust, worship, obedience, and ongoing growth in knowledge and understanding.

Within the Christian perspective, true spirituality emerges from the inner depths of the human heart, soul, and mind, stirred by the self-revelation of God through the Holy Spirit. As such, it is not something obtained solely by personal efforts and actions, but an actuality resulting from the encounter with the transcendent nature of God. This supernatural reality is a gift and comes from experiencing God's self-disclosure through the Scriptures as well as the interaction of the believer with the Holy Spirit.

Within the journey of relationships with God, the Holy Spirit facilitates awareness of a profound connection between believers and their inner selves, between them and their fellow human beings, and between them and a transcendent, immaterial God whose power surpasses anything within their limited human existence. To the submitted heart the Holy Spirit generates a profound sense of completeness, unity, and contentment. Through the guidance of the Holy Spirit, God encourages his people to desire and practice compassion, diligence, compassion, honesty, righteousness, justice, empathy, reverence, accountability, and faithfulness.

4. SPIRITUAL DIRECTION AND COMPANIONSHIP

In 1997 and 1998, I accepted two invitations from Vladimir's Orthodox Theological Seminary in Crestwood, New York, to conduct short-term research as a visiting fellow. During my tenure at the seminary, I had numerous profoundly insightful dialogues with the well-regarded Dean, Father Thomas Hopko (1939-2015). He helped deepen my understanding of Orthodox spirituality and shared several foundational principles of spiritual formation: go to church, say your prayers, be attentive to God, and practice spiritual friendship with other Jesus followers. I agree! A healthy spiritual journey cannot be accomplished without the Trinity, the church, and the presence of someone in your life who can serve you as a spiritual mentor, coach, guide, or friend.

Christian leadership is about following Jesus and practicing the way of Jesus within God's Kingdom. Christian spirituality helps conceive leadership as the expression of relationship with the Trinity, neighbor, and self. Christian spirituality presupposes that a reverent following of Jesus Christ will help overcome the temptation of an egocentric life.

Our metaphor of "showing the way" can also be applied to the spiritual journey of an individual or a team. Every journey implies there is a presence of travelers, a purpose, a plan, and a process. When a team of people embarks on a journey, each member may (and should) have different roles.

Consider the serene setting of a monastery where an elderly and well-respected priest asks the monks, "If we follow Jesus Christ by taking him as our Shepherd who spiritually tends, herds, feeds, and guards us, who do you think we are to each other?

> The first monk says, "Well, I think one role could be as supporters. We should encourage and help each other, especially in tough times, just like Jesus supports us. We are companions, right? We should treat each other with love and kindness, just as Jesus did."
>
> The second brother says, "We could be accountability friends. If someone is struggling or getting off track, we gently remind them of Jesus' teachings and help them get back on course."
>
> The third monk adds, "I also think being mentors, spiritual guides to each other, is important. Sharing our understanding and experience of God's, helping to be aware of God's presence could help us grow spiritually."
>
> The Priest says, "Excellent insights! By embodying these roles in humility, we can foster a community that truly reflects Jesus' mind and heart."

This hypothetical dialogue reveals facets of spiritual direction or spiritual companionships. There are many good books on these topics and practices.[2] The essence of spiritual direction and spiritual companionships lies in continuous discernment, ongoing development, and a desire for a deeper connection with God and adherence to divine guidance.

Spiritual direction implies there is some differentiation in terms of spiritual life's experience and maturity. A spiritual director is someone who possesses more experience and maturity in the spiritual life, offering guidance based on their extensive knowledge and experience. In contrast, a seeker is an individual who voluntarily searches for spiritual guidance and support, seeking to deepen their own spiritual understanding and practice.

Spiritual direction focuses on the journey of an individual's inner life and their relationship with the Trinity. The dialogues aim to discern and understand the influence of the Holy Spirit in the seeker's life. Through thoughtful questioning and reflective responses, the director assists in uncovering and interpreting the seeker's faith journey, encouraging deeper understanding and informed decision-making based on the nuanced realities of their faith. This process is enriched by the Scriptures, the wealth of spiritual wisdom, and traditional practices.

Spiritual friendship (spiritual companionship) implies more horizontal, peer-to-peer relationships. In both cases, the relationship between Christians is based on trust, confidentiality, and mutual respect. In this spiritual journey, both Christians share their spiritual experiences, insights, and struggles in a trusted space. There must be a willingness to be open and vulnerable and to foster a deeper connection with God through prayer, contemplation, and Scripture reading. Companions may offer insights and ask deep, thought-provoking questions to help one another live fully and authentically as followers of Jesus Christ. Spiritual companionship offers an opportunity to support one another by focusing primarily on God's presence and guidance amidst everyday life.

The Trinity and Spiritual Direction/Companionship

Spiritual friendship and companionship presuppose that God is the primary spiritual Director and Friend. It entails listening and being attentive to the voice of God. Spiritual friends or companions are co-listeners for that voice.

Christian teaching about God is foundational to the concept of spiritual relationships. Each Person of the Trinity—Father, Son, and Holy Spirit—as revealed in Scripture, is inherently relational. This is not a purely theological concept. "The doctrine of the Trinity is an eminent practical teaching, expressing not only who and how we understand God to be, but what we think human persons are called to be and become: created to glorify God by living in communion with God and one another through Christ in the Spirit."[3]

Spiritual friendship and companionship play an auxiliary, not a leading, role. It suggests that God shows the way to his children, and spiritual Christian's friends assist one another in discerning God's guiding voice. Spiritual transformation cannot be done without God's Spirit and Jesus promises the indwelling gift of the Holy Spirit to his followers. In the Gospel of John, Jesus refers to the Holy Spirit as the Paraclete (John 14:16, 14:26, 15:26, 16:7) from a Greek word, "parakletos" that can be understood as "advocate," "helper," "counselor," or "comforter." Jesus promised his disciples the comforting, guiding, and sustaining presence of the Holy Spirit which guides the believers to be transformed into his image by ever-increasing glory (2Cor. 3:18).

Exploring the depths of Christian spirituality, David Banner provides a compelling perspective on the intricate path towards a deeper connection with God. He says, "Christian spirituality is a journey toward union with God. First and foremost, therefore it is a relationship.... Union is not fusion. In union with God, human personality is neither lost nor converted into divine personality."[4] The journey toward union with God is a transformative process toward Christlikeness. Banner adds strongly, "No one get far on the path of Christian spirituality without two things – space for contemplative reflection and engagements with other who share the journey."[5]

Spiritual direction and/or companionship, through their relational character, allows the followers of Christ to partake in a divine symphony where each note resonates with the harmonious melody of God's eternal love and purpose.

> Reflect on your spiritual journey. How do you perceive your relationship with God, and in what areas do you seek growth or change? How can other Christians (mentors, spiritual directors) contribute to your spiritual journey?

5. SPIRITUAL INTELLIGENCE IN LEADERSHIP

Throughout the centuries, the term "intellect" has been used to emphasize a specific human attribute that distinguishes humans from other living organisms. The term, along with its companion word "intelligence," is often used when referring to the human capacities to think abstractly, reason, learn, understand, interpret, solve problems, retain, plan, and communicate.

Human cognitive abilities are largely influenced by genetic factors, but also can be shaped and developed through various other factors such as learning, practice, and intellectual stimulation. As mental phenomena, cognitive abilities are measurable through an instrument developed by psychologists known as the Intelligence Quotient (IQ) test. This test provides valuable information about an individual's intellectual strengths, weaknesses, and potential academic or cognitive performance in given areas.

In more recent times, it has been commonly accepted that humans are blessed with numerous intelligences, not just with cognitive ability (IQ). In his book, *Frames of Mind: The Theory of Multiple Intelligences*, Harvard University professor Howard Gardner defined intelligence as "the ability to solve problems or to create products that are valued within one or more cultural settings."[6] With this definition in mind, Gardner proposed several distinct intelligences, each with its own specific set of abilities that can be observed and measured. He categorized them as visual/spatial, verbal/linguistic, mathematical/logical, bodily/kinesthetic, musical/rhythmic, intrapersonal and interpersonal.

Turning to leadership, contemporary research indicates that effective leadership is also connected to different forms of intelligence: cognitive, emotional, social, cultural, moral, spiritual and behavioral.[7] In this vein of thought, then, it is the view arising from the concept of *hodos leadership* that high quality leadership requires the development of these intelligences. Spiritual, ethical, and effective leadership can be demonstrated by people with high cognitive abilities (IQ), but also with developed emotional intelligence (EQ), cultural intelligence (CQ), spiritual intelligence (SQ), moral intelligence (MQ), etc. A balanced development of these different intelligences can support wise, resilient, sustainable, and effective leadership.

Developing Spiritual Intelligence

Spiritual intelligence is particularly and crucially fundamental. What is spiritual intelligence and how does it relate to leadership? SQ is the intelligence with which people ask the most essential questions one might ask about life and human existence, and the intelligence with which they explore the answers to those questions. To speak of spiritual intelligence means to focus on several interrelated queries:

- The existence of a transcendent God.
- The interior life of the human being.
- The purpose and meaning of human life. Exploring the meaning inherent in such questions as "Who am I?" "Why am I here?" and "What ultimately matters?"
- The distinguishing of reality between illusion, truth, and falsehood.
- The capacity to see the sum totality of things as an interconnected reality.
- The capacity to bridle egocentrism.
- The capacity to love, believe, and hope.

Further, within the Christian worldview, spiritual intelligence is linked to a God-centered (transcendental) spirituality, a "Christian Spiritual Intelligence" comprised of a set of capacities God grants to those who believe in him. These capacities would encompass the following:

- The capacity to connect with and learn from God.
- The capacity to experience a spiritually transformed consciousness.
- The capacity to connect life with all its ventures and happenings to God's presence and the exercising of his will in this world.
- The capacity to apply spiritual insights and giftings for the common good.
- The capacity to make proper choices in life, and thus to exhibit such virtuous behaviors as being thankful, forgiving, humble, and caring.

How is spiritual intelligence developed? Spiritual intelligence can be developed through the disciplines involved in cognitive learning, in practicing spiritual exercises, and in understanding the spiritual significance of daily life experience. Breaking down this development process into further details, its path might follow any one or more of the following:

- The work of the Holy Spirit in the heart and mind of the believer (God's Spirit is the key agent that is active in all spiritual development.)
- The work of the Spirit coinciding with a conscious search for and pursuit after God
- Engaging in meaningful and trustful conversations with spiritual directors, pastors, and other believers. The local church is, of course, the hallmark community where spiritual growth is first pursued and nurtured.
- Practicing vital spiritual disciplines,
- Committing to consistent and systematic learning and feedback. Partnering with other spiritually mature people such as church leaders, mentors, coaches, friends, family

members, and professional Christian counselors serves this purpose well.
- Monitoring one's life in general and reflecting on how God is working there, equipping for leadership and service.

Overall, then, it may be said that the development of spiritual intelligence operates on four levels:

- A developing of one's own worldview and sense of self-awareness.
- A coming into and enlarging of a perception of the interconnectedness of all of life.
- A deepening of submission to God and in seeking guidance from the Holy Spirit.
- An ongoing growth of a compassionate, anxious-free, healing, and spiritually positive presence in the world in all spheres of life, be they the home, workplace, church, or larger society.

If an individual embraces the concept of multiple intelligences but lacks access to a spiritual mentor or coach, he or she must do some self-determining learning. A good place to start would be to find some time to process the thoughts and feelings relative to this matter. These thoughts, along with any ensuing inquiries and potential solutions, will influence the individual's emotions. The incorporation of these thoughts and emotions will then act as a driving force for the subsequent actions taken to achieve a meaningful spiritual intelligence. Of course, it is important to note that a fundamental principle in entering and following this journey is a prayerful dependence upon God's Holy Spirit, which perpetually serves as the catalyst for growth and transformation in a Christian's spiritual journey.

Continuing the path to attain spiritual intelligence, it is advisable to allocate time for contemplation of the following questions:

- Who am I? Why am I here? What ultimately matters in life and human existence?
- How well am I connected to God and to what I am learning from him?
- How well am I connecting my life and ventures to a sense of God's presence and actions in the world at large and in my life in particular?
- What do I want to learn in this pursuit of spiritual intelligence? Upon what would I like to improve? Why?
- What basic spiritual knowledge and principles help me to navigate in life generally?
- How well do I understand spirituality in myself and others?
- How do I act in different social settings such as family, church, or workplace?
- How discerning am I in differentiating right from wrong, the spiritual from the non-spiritual?
- To what extent am I aware of the difference between what I desire to be and what I *ought* to be?

Today it is somewhat customary for churches and Christian organizations to focus on Christian leadership formation. As they engage in this task it would be good that they pay attention to the following indicators of spiritual intelligence as principles applicable to all Christians generally, even as they focus on their relevance to Christian professionals in particular:

- A connection with and peaceful surrender to God, remembering that this requires believing that God exists and that human life is part of the divine will for time and eternity.
- A self-awareness as to the personal beliefs, convictions, values, and motives one holds.
- A dealing with the fundamental questions pertaining to life: What is the meaning of life? What does it mean to sacrifice for others? Where does suffering fit into the grand scheme of things? And all such like questions upon which humans have always pondered.
- An acting out of biblical teaching and the deep beliefs it gives rise to.
- A searching for and realization of one's calling and vocation.
- A mastery over the egocentric self.
- A gracious compassion that engenders love and empathy for others.
- A discerning of the larger patterns, relationships, and connections that make up life, and possessing a sense of belonging to that larger network.
- A seeking after truth, motivated by a lively curiosity.
- A caring attitude for the welfare of God's creation.
- An acceptance and celebration of the interconnectedness and diversity existing within Christian communities.
- An inner freedom to act honestly and responsibly.
- A wisdom and willingness to learn and grow from mistakes.

6. SPIRITUALITY AND PERSONAL LEADERSHIP

Personal leadership can be explained as taking charge of oneself and effectively influencing one's thoughts, emotions, and behaviors to achieve personal and professional goals. It involves self-direction, self-motivation, and self-management. Personal leadership relates to self-awareness, personal convictions, and intrinsic motivations essential for individual advancement and excellence.

Embedded within the metaphor of "showing the way" is the concept that leading others begins with leading oneself. By assuming the responsibility to lead oneself through the challenges and growth opportunities life presents, a leader acquires the skills, confidence, and experience necessary to guide and inspire others in their journeys.

A true notion of leading oneself, however, also implies a personal spirituality existing within the heart and character. This spirituality involves a journey of self-reflection and seeking guidance and inner strength from God. During life's difficult moments, it is this reliance upon God that can provide a sense of peace, joy, and hope.

From a Christian perspective, as personal leadership and personal spirituality merge into one, they often express themselves in seeking a greater purpose or meaning in life beyond material pursuits and, instead, find fulfillment through a connection with God and service to others.

Key Elements of Personal Leadership

In their book, *Maximizing Triple Bottom Line Through Spiritual Leadership*, Jody Fry and Melissa Nisiewicz define personal leadership as the self-confident ability to define life's direction, commit to it, and take determined action to achieve ultimate goals. It involves developing a positive self-image, making conscious choices to satisfy needs, persevering, and taking responsibility for outcomes.[8] Personal spiritual leadership, on the other hand, augments personal leadership (as just defined) with a vision of serving others through altruistic love. Such a vision springs from a rich inner life rooted in spiritual attentiveness, an attentiveness that nourishes and shapes the individual into being more mindful, self-aware, and focused on others.

Fry and Nisiewicz argue that it is important in personal leadership to possess clarity about personal calling, purpose, values, and vision. A personal vision, in particular, defines an individual's aspirations, purpose, and direction. It serves as a compass, outlining one's personal journey and why it is being followed. One might say that vision reveals the tension between what currently exists in a person's life, and what ought to be. While Christian spirituality, comparatively speaking, does not explicitly address goal setting as a specific practice, it does provide such principles as seeking God's guidance, pursuing spiritual goals, embracing a vision, and living with purpose in a godly manner.

I wholeheartedly agree that the practice of developing a personal vision for life is very important. Not everyone can muster the courage to develop such a vision and the personal goals to complete them all. Not all have the needed diligence and discipline to think through what they want to achieve in life. Of course, while creating a list of goals is undoubtedly easier than actually achieving them, the exercise still remains a crucial step towards personal growth and fulfillment. By gaining clarity on our priorities and aspirations through such a step, we equip ourselves with the strength to navigate challenges, learn from setbacks, and persevere in the face of hardships. And, of course, it must forever be remembered that wherever we are going, and whatever our long-term goals are, that we were never meant to strive towards meeting those goals by our own ingenuity and efforts. We need to remember the ever-poignant words of Jesus, "I am the vine; you are the branches. If you remain in me and I in you, you will bear much fruit; apart from me you can do nothing" (John 15:5).

Personal Leadership as Service and Stewardship

Several decades ago, the renowned Swiss psychiatrist and psychoanalyst, Carl Jung (1875–1961), articulated what has since become a well-known quote: "If you are a gifted person, it doesn't mean that you gained something. It means you have something to give back."[9] This quote aligns well with Christian principles of stewardship, selflessness, love, and humility. It emphasizes the idea that one's gifts and talents are meant to be used for the betterment of others and to serve a higher purpose beyond personal gain. The quote echoes Jesus's parable of the talents in Matthew 25:14-30. In that parable, a master entrusts different amounts of money (talents) to his servants before going on a journey. The servants who invest and multiply their talents are praised, while the one who buries his talent out of fear and fails to use it is reprimanded. The parable thus teaches the importance of using one's gifts and abilities to serve others and God faithfully.

According to the Christian faith, human life is a precious gift from God. As such, human beings possess inherent dignity and worth. They also, however, have been given the responsibility of being good stewards. Stewardship translates into living within God's appointed purposes, and therefore with an integrity that goes beyond mere self-interest to working for the common good and caring for God's entire creation. In short, stewardship simply means to demonstrate social and environmental responsibility.

Stewardship aligns perfectly with the whole concept of personal leadership (understood more accurately perhaps as personal spiritual leadership) as that idea is discussed above. Biblically, this association between stewardship and personal leadership is expressed in such passages as I Peter 4:10, "As each has received a gift, use it to serve one another, as good stewards of God's varied grace," all underscoring that as talents are developed, better stewards of what has been received from God are created.

The exercise of personal leadership in service and stewardship can become a guiding light, paving the way for others to follow and thrive. In Matthew 5:14-16, Jesus states, "You are the light of the world. A city set on a hill cannot be hidden. Nor do people light a lamp and put it under a basket, but on a stand, and it gives light to all in the house. In the same way, let your light shine before others, so that they may see your good works and give glory to your Father who is in heaven." Jesus's words here suggest that when the initiative is taken to lead oneself, that individual becomes a shining light, guiding others towards what is good and meaningful. Just as a lamp illuminates a dark room, personal leadership illuminates the paths of others, showing them the way to God's truth and love.

7. SPIRITUALITY AND MARKETPLACE LEADERSHIP

In his book, *Good to Great*, Jim Collins introduces a leadership principle he refers to as "First Who, Then What." This principle prioritizes the importance of finding the right individuals before embarking upon a planned course of action. Exceptional leaders, he says, ensure that they have the right people on board before deciding on how to reach a desired destination.[10] This principle is not only relevant to a strictly business context but also applies to Christian spiritual leadership.

For Christian leaders, the first and foremost focus in life should be on developing an intimate connection with Christ and faithfully following him. This deep connection serves as the foundation for all subsequent motivations and endeavors. Before engaging in various organizationally related projects, be they social or otherwise, it is crucial for Christians in leadership to be nurturing a deeply personal relationship with God. Whether within family life, community involvement, church service, or workplace engagements, knowing God must come before serving God.

Marketplace Leadership

Spirituality is not confined to just religious settings; it encompasses every aspect of life, including the workplace. While writing this book, I have been reflecting deeply on the challenges and opportunities Christian professionals face. It is my conviction that to successfully meet those challenges, it is crucial for today's young Christian professionals to first embrace the abundant blessings that fill their lives and to recognize the ever-present love and care of God showering those blessings upon them. Undeniably, these young professionals, in whatever fields of endeavor they may find themselves, are being afforded a grand opportunity by God to cultivate a spiritual worldview and a depth of meaning to their careers and life journeys.

An unprecedented freedom is seemingly theirs to engage unhindered in cultivating spiritual disciplines and to cherish communities of like-minded individuals who support their growth. I am convinced that seizing this opportunity, along with the responsibilities that accompany it, is what will produce this generation's truly, and so badly needed, "personal leaders."

Spiritually healthy leaders sense the presence and purpose of God's mercies and interventions in the workplace throughout their working hours. Aligning their person with God's intentions, these leaders experience a profound sense of fulfillment. Why? Because their lives have taken on a purposeful and meaningful trajectory, bringing glory to God in all spheres of work and life. Spiritually healthy professionals not only love God but also demonstrate care for others. They strive to contribute to a workplace culture that stresses essential core values, the observance of which promotes the well-being of all. These values may include:

- Excellence
- Compassion and empathy
- Interrelationships
- Integrity and honesty
- Responsibility and reliability
- Justice and fair play
- Mutuality and understanding
- Openness and receptivity
- Respect for self and others
- Trust and authenticity

As Christian spirituality is lived out, regardless of whatever segment of society in which it is practiced, it always fosters creativity and collaboration. And in the workplace – in whatever form it may take – Christian spirituality transforms how individuals respond to job-related circumstances:

- In place of restlessness, *calmness*
- In place of intransigence and stubbornness, *flexibility and adaptability*
- In place of indifference, *care*
- In place of suspiciousness and cynicism, *trust*
- In place of ignorance, *awareness (mindfulness)*
- In place of egocentrism and narcissism, *altruistic love*
- In place of autonomous behavior, *accountability*
- In place of resistance to change, *adaptability*
- In place of passivity, *initiative*
- In place of sluggishness and laziness, *motivation and punctuality*
- In place of dishonesty, *integrity*
- In place of individualism, *teamwork*
- In place of a complaining attitude, *a problem-solving mindset*

8. TOXIC RELIGIOUS LEADERSHIP

Leadership in accordance with Christian spirituality is validated whenever the embodiment of Christ-like qualities is witnessed within leaders. Leadership at this level reflects genuine faith and a deep relationship with God. Conversely, unhealthy religious leadership can be detected by the absence of these Christ-like attributes and by a lack of authenticity in personal faith and connection with God.

One type of leadership fosters dignity, fairness, integrity, trust, collaboration, prudence, stability, and constructive goal achievement, benefiting all. However, a contrary type (negative or toxic) leads to deceit, suspicion, self-interest, chaos, and disorganization.

The Bible cautions against – in fact, openly condemns – wicked practices within leadership, commanding that righteousness be observed instead. The Bible teaches that by seeking God's guidance and resisting evil, leaders can align their leadership with God's character and righteous ways. This open denunciation of ungodliness among leaders, along with a call to uprightness is clearly seen, for example, in the Gospels. There, Jesus is frequently seen criticizing religious leaders for their hypocrisy, using their positions for personal gain and lacking compassion for outcasts. In distinct contrast to these behaviors, Jesus emphasized inner transformation, love, and genuine faith as the defining traits that would characterize his followers.

As a researcher, I have conducted interviews with many Christian leaders both in the USA and abroad, aiming to gain a comprehensive understanding of leadership dynamics within Christian communities. Throughout these insightful conversations, a recurring and thought-provoking theme has emerged: the sobering realization that identifying as a Christian does not automatically exempt one from exhibiting ineffective, unethical, and unhealthy spiritual leadership. Christians of different traditions grapple with the challenge of truly embodying Christ-like attributes – a grappling that often results, unfortunately, in expressions of an unhealthy spirituality rather than the desired display of positive and transformative leadership. Surprisingly (and sadly), even those in such revered positions as priests and pastors who are tasked with guiding others on their spiritual journeys often face personal struggles and challenges that seriously handicap them in fulfilling their callings.

Some common themes and practices that have arisen from my research include a tendency towards authoritative and controlling behavior, a lack of genuine care and compassion for others, and a failure to acknowledge one's own imperfections. Additionally, my interviews revealed that it is not uncommon for some leaders to prioritize ritualism and legalism over fostering authentic spiritual growth, a regrettable practice leading to an environment where superficial displays of faith prevail.

The Toxic Ways of Religious Leadership

Different facets of negative religious leadership can manifest themselves in various ways, depending on individual circumstances and contexts. Traits such as egocentrism, inflated self-esteem, arrogance, and a focus solely on personal ambitions act like destructive bacteria that can infiltrate the hearts of believers. These negative qualities lead to contagious diseases that spread like infections, adversely impacting not only the individuals themselves but also their surroundings, including the teams and larger communities in which they (supposedly) serve.

Based on my observations and research, below are the key characteristics that define negative religious leadership, ordered from more religious-specific to more universal.

- **Neglecting the Gospel:** Toxic religious leadership fails to uphold this essential biblical truth and the values of love and grace accompanying it, prioritizing, instead, external ceremonials over genuine spiritual transformation.

- **Dogmatism, Intolerance, and Exclusion:** Toxic religious leadership promotes strict adherence to non-essential doctrinal nuances, fostering intolerance towards different viewpoints or observers. They exclude non-loyalists from their religious communities.

- **Closed-mindedness:** Toxic religious leadership discourages intellectual exploration, dialogue, and questioning, clinging rigidly to religious fundamentalism.

- **Hypocrisy:** Toxic religious leadership may demonstrate hypocritical behavior, imposing strict expectations on others while exempting themselves, creating false public images for personal gain.

- **Approval of War:** The toxicity of religious leadership becomes starkly apparent when those who profess values of love, peace, and compassion simultaneously discount or covertly support aggressive international warfare. When religious leaders fail to speak out against or remain passive in the face of their government's initiation of conflicts, they do more than merely observe—they become complicit in the resulting violence and war crimes. Such leaders undermine their own moral authority, betraying the very principles they claim to uphold. Their silence or tacit approval reveals a dangerous disconnect between their proclaimed values and their actions, illustrating how their leadership becomes toxic. This hypocrisy not only compromises their integrity but also perpetuates a culture of violence and injustice, fundamentally contradicting the core tenets of their faith.

- **Prioritizing the Spreading of Belief Over Genuine Service:** Toxic religious leadership prioritizes spreading religious beliefs over genuinely serving and caring for people.

- **Manipulative Propagation:** Toxic religious leadership involves manipulative propagation of conspiracy theories to control and manipulate followers. It exploits these theories to foster an environment of unhealthy suspicion.

- **Authoritarianism, Cult-like Atmosphere:** Toxic religious leadership adopts a dictatorial style. It suppresses dissenting voices and imposes its will on others, reinforcing its control over followers and discouraging critical thinking and independent judgment.

- **Inflated Self-esteem:** Toxic religious leadership displays an exaggerated sense of self-importance and superiority, disconnecting from the reality of personal limitations.

- **Arrogance:** Toxic religious leadership often possesses a sense of superiority, leading to an overbearing and condescending attitude towards others.

- **Egocentrism:** Toxic religious leadership prioritizes personal interests and ambitions, neglecting the welfare of followers and the broader community.

- **Disinterest in Collaboration:** Toxic religious leadership lacks interest in partnerships and collaboration with others, acting, instead, out of suspicion and cynicism and therefore, missing valuable opportunities for learning and problem solving.

- **Devious Behavior:** Toxic religious leadership uses deceitful tactics to control and influence its followers, rather than empowering them.

- **Lack of Empathy:** Toxic religious leadership lacks genuine understanding and concern for the struggles and needs of those being led.

- **Materialistic Motivation:** Toxic religious leadership prioritizes personal financial gain, indulging in lavish lifestyles and misappropriation of funds.

- **Lack of Accountability:** Toxic religious leadership evades responsibility for its actions and refuses to be held accountable for its mistakes.

- **Division and Conflict:** Toxic religious leadership fosters division and conflict among its followers and communities.

- **Animosity and a Judging Spirit:** Toxic religious leadership fosters a culture of passing judgment, emphasizing punishment and shame over grace and forgiveness, leading to intolerance and abuse in the name of religion.

- **Control and Abuse of Power:** Toxic religious leadership concentrates decision-making power without meaningful checks and balances, suppressing individual autonomy and discouraging diversity of thought.

Endnotes

1. Waaijman, K. "Spirituality – a Multifaceted Phenomenon," *Studies in Spirituality*, (17) 2007, p. 112.
2. See, for example: Benner, David. *Sacred Companions: The Gift of Spiritual Friendship and Direction*. InterVarsity, 2004. Smith, Gordon. *Spiritual Direction: A Guide to Giving and Receiving Direction*. InterVarsity Press, 2014; Nouwen, Henri. *Spiritual Direction: Wisdom for the Long Walk of Faith*. Harper San Francisco. 2006; Barry, William. *Spiritual Direction and the Encounter with God: A Theological Inquiry*. 2nd rev. ed. Paulist, 2004.
3. Mowney, M. 'Trinity and spirituality,' in: Philip Sheldrake, P. (ed), *The New SCM Dictionary of Christian Spirituality*. SCM Press, 2005, p. 624.
4. Benner, David. *Surrender to Love: Discovering the Heart of Christian Spirituality*. InterVarsity Press, 2015, p. 100.
5. Ibid., 105.
6. Gardner, Howard. *Frames of Mind: The Theory of Multiple Intelligences*. Basic Books, 1985, p. x.
7. Gill, Roger. *Theory and Practice of Leadership*. 2nd ed. Sage, 2011, p. 287-320.
8. Fry, L. W., and Melissa Sadler Nisiewicz. *Maximizing the Triple Bottom Line through Spiritual Leadership*. Stanford University Press, 2013.
9. This quote is assigned to Carl Jung, but the exact source is not known.
10. Collins, James C. *Good to Great: Why Some Companies Make the Leap ... and Others Don't*. Harper Business, 2001.

From a theological perspective, every valuable and God-glorifying work done by people is made holy by God through Christ and strengthened by the Holy Spirit.

CHAPTER 6

HODOS LEADERSHIP AT WORK

1. MISSIONAL LEADERSHIP

From a theological standpoint, *hodos leadership* is not a philosophy of leadership limited to professional missionaries or Church leaders, but also - and primarily - applicable to those who have been termed by practical theologians and missiologists as "missional professionals."[1] *Hodos leadership* holds a particular significance for "missionary professionals," identified as individuals who ardently seek to create a positive impact and exemplify Christ-like virtues within their workplace. These professionals perceive their careers as avenues to serve both God and others, embracing a profound purpose in life that transcends mere financial gain or personal success. They live out their faith without resorting to aggressive or coercive methods of sharing their Christian beliefs.

The realm of faith, mission, leadership, and work holds within it a captivating intersection with the world around it, an intersection where the lives of Christians can potentially take on new and exciting dimensions. For Christian working adults, day-to-day jobs and professional activities carry with them tremendous challenges and potential that are intricately woven into the very fabric of their identity as Christ followers. Their Christian identity beckons to a life of following Christ in purposeful ways in different spheres of life; nevertheless, few Christians contemplate how they might embody Christian leadership in their day-to-day existence, including within work and marketplaces.

I want to underscore that *hodos leadership* is a missional leadership because it is rooted first and foremost in a higher purpose or mission, one that is grounded in faith and values. It is a leadership involving a dedicated commitment to positive transformation and impact, the outcome of which is the consideration and care for the well-being of individuals and communities alike. From the Christian perspective especially, missional leadership entails integrating day-to-day activities into the larger mission of God.

In this chapter, I invite you to engage with a series of thought-provoking questions - questions which serve as a pathway to self-discovery and a deeper understanding of faith and work and their relationship to each other. I hope this chapter will catalyze transformation on your journey of unearthing the significance of marketplace leadership and embracing the transformative presence of God in the workplace.

Let me begin with a few observations from my research practice.

Research Insights

From 2016 to 2018, I had the privilege of leading two international research projects that delved into the crucial issues of Christian leadership, faith, and work. Alongside a dedicated team, I meticulously gathered and analyzed research interviews and several questionnaire surveys from Christians residing in Ukraine and several Eurasian countries. The study encompassed a vast participant base of over 500 individuals, including young professionals from various employment sectors.

Below, there are nine questions we asked in our research:

1. How do you personally understand the notion of "calling?"
2. How do you perceive your unique and personal calling as a reality that currently impacts your life?
3. How do you view your main sphere of work or professional activity? What significance does it hold in your personal and career journey?
4. How do your goals and aspirations in your work/professional realm align with your faith and calling?
5. What does Christian service truly mean to you? How do you envision living it out in your daily life?
6. How do you actively practice your Christian service?
7. What is your understanding of Christian mission? What does it encompass?
8. Where do you practice Christian mission in your immediate life and in the broader world around you?
9. How does your local church play a role in supporting you in your professional life and fostering you in your leadership development?

Here are six key observations stemming from our research:

1. Most Christians understand "calling" as a vocation from God, an understanding that God-given interests and talents predispose a person to certain kinds of work. However, only 25% see "calling" as related to their work and professional activities.
2. Most Christians regard work primarily as a means to earn money, and only to a lesser degree as a service to God.
3. Most Christian young adults indicate that their practice of leadership and mission is largely confined to the local church. They do not associate Christian leadership, calling, and mission with their day-to-day work or career. A pastor of a large church raised his concern about this lack of connecting calling and mission to the everyday workplace, saying: "We must explain to young believers that the choice is not between doing a mission or leading 'in church' or 'outside church,' but rather how to lead and serve not only in the local church."
4. Church pastors generally think that leadership is needed in all spheres of life (church, work, family, etc.). They focus Christian leadership development programs mainly on how leadership relates to life as experienced within the church, with very little attention being paid to associating it with professional work.
5. For many church pastors, the main question in dealing with young professionals is not how to minister to them, but rather how to utilize them for the benefit of the local church.
6. Many Christians reduce Christian mission to evangelism through verbal witness and short-term missionary trips. Only a few participants in our study expressed the

conviction that Christian mission is connected to all spheres of life, including the workplace.

Although our research was conducted outside the USA and other Western countries, it is quite evident that the challenges surrounding the integration of faith and work are strikingly similar around the world. The prevailing misconceptions about Christian service and mission within the context of faith and work transcend geographical boundaries and point towards a universal challenge that demands further thought and consideration.

2. REVAMPING A WORK MINDSET

It is rather disheartening to observe that for many Christian young adults, the fusion of faith, work, leadership, and mission remains only as a conceptual ideal rather than a lived reality.

From the research I have conducted, I can say that when today's Christian young adults are asked about what motivations drive their jobs and careers, their responses typically encompass:

- earning a livelihood
- providing for their families
- utilizing their skills and education
- generating passive income for retirement
- contributing to society
- being in the company of others
- engaging in something meaningful
- avoiding boredom at home
- and other such answers.

Some see their work somewhat in the following vein: an obstacle to spiritual growth, "the vanity of earthly life," a distraction from "true Church life," and even as "a secular temptation." For these individuals work is never viewed as a sacred service to God and others, but something like a curse to be endured.

The shared perspectives cited above are often rooted in how young people are raised in their families and educated in their local churches. Quite often, parents, youth leaders, and pastors teach young people that Christian faith is only about saving the soul. However, it is not just that. It is also about creatively living life daily, maturing spiritually, and co-working with God to bring positive changes to one's surrounding circumstances.

This connection with God isn't restricted to specific places or moments—it is a partnership that influences every aspect of our lives where God's plan is unfolding. Believing in God is tied to the presence of God's plan throughout our entire lives—at home, school, work, and beyond. Faith unifies everything. When someone believes, they undergo an internal transformation. God's influence touches every facet of their existence in countless ways. This influence is not confined to church-related activities; it extends to our families and the jobs we undertake.

In respect to the issue being discussed here, I would encourage every Christian working adult to carefully think through the following questions:

- What role does God play in my work?
- How does God's mission relate to my work?
- What do I perceive as God's influence in my workplace?
- What aspects of my work can I align with God's mission?
- How do I exemplify Christian leadership at work?

In one of the research interviews I conducted in Kyiv, Ukraine, a local pastor provided the following insightful recommendations that I found to be very valuable:

> "Embrace a broader perspective by exploring the profound interconnection between your faith and daily activities. Recognize that your everyday work and professional tasks hold the potential to serve God and embody his purposes in your life. Extend your spirituality into your workdays, allowing your actions to mirror your beliefs. Exercise discernment and challenge the inconsistency between the emphasis on short missionary trips and the neglect of everyday spiritual experiences at the workplace. Engage critically with the existing literature on the theology of work, evaluating its resonance with your own work experiences. If needed, seek out local congregations or support groups that genuinely prioritize the integration of faith and work, encouraging Christian professionals to infuse their careers with spiritual significance."

Theological Reflections on Work

In the consumer society that surrounds us today, we observe that the value of human work is often reduced not to the practical significance and utility of the final product, but to the pleasure and self-expression experienced by the person creating that product. We see the idealization of creative self-realization together with its consequential narrow focus on individual pleasure. This approach to work (and to life in general) can does lead to a shallow and short-sighted view of life's purpose and meaning. Work is primarily perceived as a context for prioritizing individual expressions and experiences of self-fulfillment, a preoccupation that negates the more ethical view of work as a contribution to the greater good of society.

Various secular perspectives exist on the conduct and meaning of work. Some of them, admittedly, are quite constructive. The so-called work-life balance approach emphasizes the importance of maintaining a healthy balance between one's professional and one's personal life. Other trends highlight finding purpose and meaning in one's work, engaging in environmentally sustainable and socially responsible work, and pursuing flexible and independent work arrangements. These and other philosophies coexist and often overlap, with individuals resonating with different aspects of this or that philosophy based on their own personal values and circumstances.

A Christian Theology of Work

A theology of work is typically conceptualized in three dimensions:

1. instrumental (work satisfies one's own and others' needs),
2. social (collective work and/or work products form a community of people), and
3. ontological (people by nature are workers, created in the image of God the Worker).

Throughout Church history and across geographical divides, Christians have occasionally disconnected everyday life from their individual spiritual journeys, confining active engagement with God to church spaces and services. Work, professional activities, and community involvement are perceived within this mindset as lacking spiritual significance, while attending church gatherings is seen as true service to God.

Christians often perceived work as merely secular or non-spiritual, a task with its own peculiar set of rules, goals, and reasons. Here, "at work," spiritual values and principles do not apply. As a result, this separation between church and the workplace as places to practice one's Christianity causes inner conflict. The dichotomy also leads to a shallow spiritual experience, one in which the hope of experiencing the faithful presence of God is reserved only for Sundays or other moments of rest set aside from day-to-day work.

In recent decades, there has been a growing global interest among Christians in exploring the interplay between faith and work, embracing Christian leadership within the workplace, and emphasizing Christian missions through one's profession. Many contemporary authors rightly argue that God's presence and mission transcend local church events (see John Hughes, Timothy Keller, Dorothy Sayers, Miroslav Volf, Darrell Cosden, and many others). In this vein, Fr. Dumitru Stăniloae, one of the greatest Eastern Orthodox theologians of the twentieth century, in his book "The Experience of God," addresses the sanctification of daily life, including work, and advances the notion that the professional journey is a path where encountering God also happens.[2] He points out that Christian prayer, the gift of being present with God, is not limited to solitary practice but should also be viewed and practiced as a communal activity. In the same way, God honoring work should not be confined to monastic life, but be embraced as part of the ordinary day-to-day routines of life.

Christian theology places human labor within the context of a journey from the present creation to new creation. Against this backdrop the selfless and public-spirited efforts of redeemed individuals, wherever and whatever they may be, can and should be regarded as contributions to an emerging new creation. In this light, of course, the resurrection of Jesus Christ serves as the pre-eminent model for this transformative process. His bodily resurrection exemplifies the seamless connection between the present 'fallen' state of creation and the glorified state that lies ahead.

From a theological perspective, every valuable and God-honoring task or work has been sanctified by God through Christ and strengthened by the Holy Spirit. Christianity raises an individual's perception of work to a high and noble level, viewing it both as an honored service for God and as a responsibility for the collective benefit. Hence, the terms "work" or "calling" are linked not to the pursuit of personal gratification, self-fulfillment, or individual gain, but rather to a form of spiritual asceticism. In this context, the individual engaged in professional work is predominantly focused on the welfare of others.

A Christian theology of work is connected to several themes:

1. God himself is the Worker. God created and ordered the entire universe (Gen. 1-3). God continues to work even now. The psalmist states that God "does not slumber or sleep…" (Ps. 122:4). And Jesus said, "My Father is working until now, and I am working" (John 5:17). Because God is the prototypical worker, human work is also invested with value and meaning.

2. God, being God the Worker, created humans in His own image. Work is thus an integral expression of human nature (see Gen. 1:26-27).

3. God has commanded man to work with him for his purposes, a command known as the Mandate of Creation (or the Great Command). In Gen. 1:28 God commands Adam and Eve to "be fruitful and multiply and fill the earth and subdue it." The words "fill" and "subdue" imply active labor. Gen. 2:15 expands on the meaning of 1:28, saying, "And the Lord God took the man, and put him into the garden of Eden, to dress (cultivate) it and keep it." The Hebrew word here for "cultivate" is avadh, meaning "to work or serve," and "keep" means "to make an effort." Man, thus, became God's sub-creator, or sub-worker: God planted a garden (Gen. 2:8), and man cultivated it (Gen. 2:15). In addition to gardening with the physical labor such activity called for, God also accorded man intellectual labor by assigning him the task of categorizing and naming all members of the animal kingdom (Gen. 2:19). The fourth commandment also recognizes work as part of man's nature; he must work six days of the week (Ex. 20:9) and rest on the seventh. The book of Proverbs is full of appeals to diligent work along with warnings against laziness (e.g. Prov. 6:6). And several New Testament passages further reveal work as a moral duty, an attitude towards work that should be characteristic of all Christians: Col. 3:22-4:1; Eph. 6:5-9; 1Tim. 6:1; Tit. 2:9; 1Pet. 2:18-25.

4. Work did not come about due to the Fall, and therefore is in no way a curse. However, because of the Fall, the effort now needed to be put forward in work became much greater (see Gen. 3:17-19). What had previously been enjoyable was now relegated to toil.

5. God through Christ redeems and transforms all creation (see Rom. 8:18-23, Eph. 1:9-12, Col. 1:15-20, 3:18-25, 4:1). Man becomes God's co-worker in this work of redemptive salvation. Thanks to the redemption received through Christ, every work that reflects the work of God has importance, purpose, and meaning.

6. Human labor can be filled with eternal meaning if motivated and executed with an eternal perspective in view. God keeps the work of every person in memory and will reward everyone for work well done (Col. 3:23-24).

7. The current creation awaits the fulfillment of Christ's redemption – the transformation into a new creation (see Rom. 8:22, Col. 1:20). The value of work depends on our understanding of the concept of a new heaven and a new earth. Scripture is clear that there will be "new heavens and a new earth" (Rev. 21:1; 2Pet. 3:13; Is. 65:17, 66:22), but there are two theories about how they will come: (1) the present earth and heaven will be destroyed and replaced by a new heaven and new earth through a cataclysmic "act of new creation" rather than renewal; (2) the new heaven and new earth will be the result of a transformation of the present heaven and earth. If God destroys the old earth (by fire, for example), then the understanding of work in this age as an investment in the new creation becomes meaningless. If, however, the new creation is a transfiguration of the present order, and God credits human work towards that new earth into eternity, then each man's work does possess eternal value and meaning in the eyes of God.

8. Christians find a sense of purpose and meaning in work when they perceive their work as a reflection of God's work on earth. If Christians serve the real needs of others - spiritual or physical, they reflect God's work to meet the needs of the larger society. Ideally, the Christian should be able to say in all honesty, "My work is God's work!"

3. NAVIGATING WORKPLACE REALITIES

What do individuals who are either self or otherwise employed face in their day-to-day work commitments? And what, in particular, are the challenges and opportunities for the practice of leadership within that context?

First, it should be noted that some general opportunities and challenges can vary depending on the industry, organizational setting, or the work dynamics specific to a particular workplace. For example, workers or professionals in settings like hospitals, car manufacturing factories, or restaurants might be afforded opportunities for learning and skill development, steady employment, and social workplace relationships, while at the same time, facing demeaning challenges such as monotonous tasks, limited advancement, unsatisfactory wages, unpredictable hours, and heavy physical demands.

Second, relative to the opportunities and challenges facing leadership within the workplace, keep in mind that effective leadership and followership must be adaptable and skillful in addressing those opportunities and challenges. According to Roger Gill, individuals holding leadership roles in teams and organizations commonly find themselves involved in six core themes and practices inextricably tied to leadership: vision, mission, values, strategy, empowerment, and engagement.[3]

In my view, these six elements present both opportunities and challenges for leadership.

1. The opportunity to develop an inspiring **vision** is challenging because it necessitates balancing the vision with the reality of what is attainable.
2. The opportunity to create a unifying **mission** or purpose for the organization is challenging because the mission needs to resonate with the various stakeholders.
3. The opportunity to establish the strong **values that are** foundational for decision-making within any organization is challenging to implement.

4. The opportunity to think strategically and to develop a sound **strategy** is challenged by constant, unpredictable changes and instabilities, both internal and external factors.
5. The opportunity to **empower** and provide resources and conditions for organizational success, is challenged by how hard it is to strike a delicate balance between equipping and empowering while also inviting accountability.
6. The opportunity to cultivate employee **engagement** through effective communication, recognition, creating growth avenues, and fostering a positive work environment is challenged by inconsistent motivation levels over time. It becomes necessary to address diverse employee needs, ensuring effective communication and manageable workloads.

Christians at Workplaces

Working Christian adults encounter various realities associated with their work environments. These encompass addressing the complexities associated with diverse personalities, inhouse competition, the pursuit of fairness, the drive for excellence, the quest for equilibrium, the embracing of diversity, the acceptance of limitations, and the pursuit of a holistic and meaningful concept of success. There are several trademarks that shape the collective experience of Christians in the marketplace.

Professional Development

Seeking growth in professional skills and knowledge is very important. However, embarking upon a journey of professional development should be intertwined with spiritual transformation. This involves discernment in the selection of training and other career development experiences that foster both professional growth and spiritual well-being. It is this integration of professional development and spiritual transformation that exemplifies the core tenets of Christian values.

Ethical Dilemmas
Christian professionals often encounter situations where workplace practices conflict with their beliefs and personal values. This necessitates keen discernment. Christian professionals facing conflicts between workplace practices and faith values can navigate this challenge by seeking advice from mentors or fellow believers. Reflecting and praying can offer clarity, and understanding organizational policies and compromising with supervisors can help find a balance. Open dialogue with colleagues about faith convictions and personal ethical values can also foster understanding and resolution.

Workplace Evangelism
For Christian professionals, sharing their faith in the workplace is both a privilege and a responsibility, demanding a thoughtful approach. While direct conversations about faith may be suitable in certain contexts, they might not be appropriate in others. It is vital to keep that distinction in mind. It is also important to recognize that excellent work performance can be a potent form of evangelism. Demonstrating outstanding work with integrity, ethical behavior, and compassion can mirror the values of one's faith without explicitly attesting to it verbally. Colleagues observing consistent dedication, honesty, and kindness often find their curiosity piqued, potentially leading, in turn, to deeper conversations about God and one's Christian faith.

Diverse Personalities

Interactions in the workplace involve individuals with varying personality types and distinct perspectives on work related issues. Effective, ethical and spiritual leadership, however, involves respect for others and genuinely serving regardless of differing viewpoints or beliefs.

Competition

Competitiveness, when channeled constructively, stimulates innovation and creativity. Within the professional world, the inclination to compare oneself with peers often arises, necessitating the resolve to focus on personal growth and progress rather than the rivalry. We must foster collaboration over competition.

Fairness Concerns

Professional circumstances may give rise to issues related to injustice, unethical behavior, and negative interpersonal dynamics. Good leadership encompasses safeguarding those treated unfairly and holding everyone involved to high ethical standards.

Performance Standards

In team and organizational settings, others' mistakes or lack of quality performance are often all too easy to see. However, as Christian professionals, it is essential to focus the spotlight, not on others, but on self when considering how well the work is being carried out. This orientation toward one's own personal level of performance does not mean ignoring the mistakes or poor performances of others, but rather, it emphasizes the individual's first priority as being that of self-assessment and improvement.

Juggling Priorities
Frequently, a professional career can hinder personal health and the well-being of the family. It is not uncommon to feel pulled in too many different directions between work, personal life, and commitments to the local church. Finding a balance between work demands and personal responsibilities is really important.

Embracing Diversity
Professional settings feature individuals with distinct methodologies, styles, and leadership models. Countering the potential problems such a reality poses, effective leadership acknowledges the absence of a single, correct approach to motivating, managing, and coordinating people. Success emerges as individuals adapt, bridge differences, resolve conflicts, and collaborate towards shared objectives.

Recognizing Limitations
Demonstrating effective, ethical, and spiritual leadership involves acknowledging that not everything is under one's control. Understanding that not every factor bearing upon a work environment or employee assignment is subject to being personally managed reinforces the need to persist despite challenges and to learn from mistakes, while maintaining a sense of humility and hope.

Pursuit of Success
Workplaces often prioritize a strong emphasis upon accomplishment, thoughtlessly linking it to financial gain and career progression. Christian professional success, however, represents something different. It denotes a combination of godly character, competence, and favorable individual and organizational results. Within this context, true success is measured by the positive impact exercised upon one's organization and the general community. An attitude of

honoring God for a lifetime keeps the emphasis on serving both God and others through one's talents and actions.

Stress and Burnout

The pressures of fulfilling work commitments, managing family responsibilities, and maintaining spiritual well-being can lead to stress and burnout. Developing coping strategies and seeking support are essential for sustaining well-being.

God's Presence During Working Hours and at the Workplace

For many, this reality is often declared but not fully experienced. Cultivating an awareness of God's loving presence requires intentional effort. This belief is rooted in the understanding that God is actively involved in every aspect of a Christian's life, including professional context. It acknowledges that God's presence does not pause during work but continues, enriching, transforming, and influencing how one behaves. God's presence helps us make decisions and interact with others.

Brother Lawrence (c. 1614–1691), a lay brother in a Carmelite monastery in Paris, is best known for his spiritual teachings, which were compiled posthumously in a small book titled *The Practice of the Presence of God*. He believed in maintaining a continuous awareness of God's presence, not just during prayer or religious worship hours, but also in the ordinary tasks of daily life. Brother Lawrence famously said that he could experience God as much in the kitchen while performing mundane tasks as he could in formal prayer. Indeed, it is a wonderful blessing to have a constant sense of divine connection, regardless of the circumstances.

Endnotes

1. On the concept of "missional professionals" see Sharp, Larry. *Missions Disrupted: From Professional Missionaries to Missional Professionals*. Tyndale House Publishers, 2022.
2. See Stăniloae, Dumitru. *The Experience of God, Vol. 4: The Church: Communion in the Holy Spirit*. Holy Cross Press, 2012; *Ibid., The Experience of God, Vol. 5: The Sanctifying Mysteries*. Holy Cross Press, 2012.
3. Gill, Roger. *Theory and Practice of Leadership*. 2nd ed. Sage, 2011.

Ethical leadership is attentive to the moral framework established in the Bible and encompasses a balanced concern for both personal and collective interests.

CHAPTER 7
ETHICAL LEADERSHIP

1. WHAT DEFINES ETHICAL LEADERSHIP?

In the end, good leadership is based on ethical values. Negative, toxic leadership traits and processes, for example, are invariably linked to ethical failure. Conversely, what we would deem good leadership is intricately connected to the display of ethical and principled behaviors.

To understand what properly constitutes ethical leadership, we must first turn to the notion of "personal morality." The practice of one's morality extends across various domains: personal relationships, work habits, and community involvement. In short, practically every area of life is included because they play a significant role in shaping a leader's character and ethical conduct. What is personal morality? It may be defined as the system of beliefs and standards by which an individual makes judgements about what is ethically right or wrong, good or bad. Since leaders for their part, like everyone else, arise naturally out of the cultural and community milieus in which they have been reared, it is not surprising that they will reflect those communities' moral codes in their own personal beliefs and behaviors.

Although shaped by family, cultural, societal, and religious norms, moral and ethical behaviors are still invested with highly subjective components. Choices, for example, characteristically reflect the moral philosophies and convictions that inform them, but nonetheless, they are still ultimately subjective in nature. A choice is made from within by an act of the will, either in accordance with one's moral beliefs or in violation of them. It is this subjective element within a person's moral outlook that often accounts for the variance in ethical behavior from person to person, often among even those who share a common worldview.

If choices are made, or not made, in accordance with personal moral convictions, they possess a subjective dimension to them. No less subjective is the sense (or lack thereof) of duty and responsibility than the sense (or, again, lack thereof) of exercising integrity and accountability in all interactions with others. The point to be made here, however, is that no matter how real and in what direction these subjective elements of morality may be exercised, what always lies behind and informing them are a person's moral precepts. And subsequently, then, what may be defined as ethical behavior is simply in one way or another subjectively adhering to those moral expectations or, looking at it in reverse, subjectively refraining from what one considers to be unethical.

Ethical concerns are to true leadership as important as any economic, political, or social factors that might also bear upon its success. In fact, in both leadership and followership, hardly anything falls outside the realm of ethical considerations. Why? Because leadership decisions and the actions that follow from them directly or indirectly impact the lives and well-being of others. Often, many others. Within teams and the organizations in which they operate, ethical or unethical leadership will, respectively, positively or negatively impact internal dynamics such as job/ministry satisfaction, sense of safety, level of engagement, team or organizational attractiveness, trust among team members, recruitment and retention, productivity, and performance levels.

Unethical leaders are characterized by a lack of honesty, integrity, fairness, and credibility. Their effect upon the individuals and organizations they lead is patently negative. On the other hand, studies indicate that organizational executives perceived to be ethical exhibit such traits as trustworthiness, integrity, honesty, humility, and compassion. Furthermore, they are viewed as ethical leaders when they demonstrate personal morality, a concern for people beyond just short-term interests, and a refraining from "using" individuals for personal or organizational gain.

Ethical leadership should not be regarded in mere simplistic terms, but rather, it should be understood as an extensively nuanced and comprehensive undertaking. In this respect, I concur with Bernice

Ledbetter and his colleagues that ethical leadership is characterized by four dimensions:

1. **Ethical Awareness:** Ethical leadership involves more than just recognizing what is right or wrong; it requires a heightened awareness of the ethical challenges confronting it.
2. **Ethical Commitment:** The willingness to act ethically is a pivotal aspect of ethical leadership. While some leaders may align themselves with ethical ideals in principle, their commitment may at times waver in practice, leading to inconsistent ethical behavior.
3. **Ethical Competence:** The ability to discern and act ethically is another critical component of ethical leadership. Ethical competence implies the possession of ethical intelligence, adeptness in discerning ethical issues, and skill in applying ethical principles effectively in various situations.
4. **Ethical Development:** Ethical leaders and followers exert mutual influence on each other; thus, the cultivation of ethical leadership grounds itself to a large degree in social learning.[1]

Researchers (M. Brown, L. Treviño and D. Harrison) argue that employees perceive their supervisors to be ethical when those leaders exhibit a host of distinctive behaviors that include:

- conducting their personal lives in an ethical manner,
- defining success not only by results but also by the way those results are obtained,
- listening to what employees have to say,
- disciplining employees who violate ethical standards,

- making fair and balanced decisions,
- inviting trust,
- discussing business ethics and values with employees,
- setting an example on how to do things ethically,
- having the best interests of employees in mind, and
- asking, "When making decisions, what is the right thing to do?"[2]

And, again, highlighting the nuanced and complex nature of ethical leadership, Peter Northouse suggests that its foundation lies in five important themes: respect, service, justice, honesty, and community.[3] According to Northouse, ethical leadership means to:

1. **Respect Others:** Treat others as worthy of your attention and time. Such treatment involves taking pains to listen, demonstrate empathy, and nurture the well-being of others.
2. **Serve Others:** Prioritize the interests of others, acting in a way that benefits them and refrains from advancing your self-interest at their expense.
3. **Act Justly:** Provide fair and equal opportunities to one and all as based on individual needs, rights, efforts, performance, contributions, and ethical behavior.
4. **Act Honestly:** Strengthen relationships and trust within a team or organization by being open and truthful.
5. **Build Community:** Aim to achieve shared goals for the common good through fostering a sense of community.

2. THE WAY OF ETHICAL LEADERSHIP

Ethical leadership is connected to the perennial hope that as spiritual and moral beings, people can work together toward the betterment and well-being of themselves and others. It aims to serve people both individually and collectively to the end that they might flourish physically, mentally, materially, morally, and spiritually. Unethical leadership, on the other hand, is a negative because it violates the principles of fairness, integrity, and responsibility that are so essential for fostering a healthy and productive environment in which to work for the common good.

Most people have a fairly good grasp on what constitutes good or bad leadership, especially if they have had experience working with others in teams. Accordingly, during my seminars and workshops, I frequently pose a crucial question to the participants: "What characterizes an exemplary leader, or put more abstractly, what constitutes exemplary leadership?" Such a question is intricately linked to the call for a brand of leadership that is not only effective but also morally and spiritually grounded. In contemporary leadership circles, however, a pronounced tendency exists to applaud leaders solely on the basis of their effectiveness, independent of any moral or personal virtues they may practice. This trend is particularly observable in political and professional arenas where, given the desire to achieve or maintain positions of influence, leaders often place less than ideal emphasis upon balancing success with ethical considerations.

Coming up with a concrete list of moral values and ethical practices applicable to all leaders everywhere has proven to be a rather elusive endeavor! Moral perspectives, themselves varied and often subject to possible change, differ—sometimes dramatically—across many divergent cultures and communities. Despite this reality, there do exist certain moral principles that are recognized universally and provide a foundation for ethical leadership that will transcend borders and cultures.

One such principle towering above the array of ethical beliefs and serving as an enduring compass is the Golden Rule: "Treat others as you would like to be treated."

This virtually universal principle is an ethical understanding that rises above cultural disparities and fosters a collective commitment to a moral responsibility rooted in compassion, empathy, reciprocity, and respect for others. Approached from the angle of the Golden Rule, ethical leadership becomes synonymous with a value-based leadership to be observed and practiced on a grand scale.

Beyond the Golden Rule, there are fundamental virtues that from time immemorial have been posited as central to living what has often been called "the good life." The same virtues could be put forward as pivotal in practicing "ethical leadership." These virtues, often associated with servant leadership, transformational leadership, and virtuous or spiritual leadership draw inspiration from the writings of such influential historical figures as Plato, Socrates, Aristotle, Aquinas, and Christian spirituality in general. This set of virtues comprises prudence, temperance, justice, courage, faith, hope, and love, which together form a comprehensive framework for guiding ethical and meaningful living.

Genuine ethical leadership also necessitates the presence and cultivation of moral intelligence, the ability to discern right from wrong coupled with a given set of essential values crucial to moral practices. Following is a concise compilation of key virtues that form a path to ethical leadership for teams and the organizations where they exist:

- **Prudence.** Ethical leadership wisely contemplates the long-term implications of possible courses of actions.

- **Temperance.** Ethical leadership avoids recklessness, exercising in its place discipline and balance.
- **Justice.** Ethical leadership strives for decision-making that expresses fairness for all.
- **Courage.** Ethical leadership upholds what is right, even in the face of potentially negative consequences, courageously protesting and initiating change in the presence of injustice.
- **Faith.** Ethical leadership expresses faith in others.
- **Hope.** Ethical leadership focuses on a positive and compelling vision for the future, actively supporting and uplifting others.
- **Love.** Ethical leadership demonstrates concern for how actions impact others, thus displaying compassion toward fellow colleagues in the workplace.
- **Empathy.** Ethical leadership identifies with and genuinely feels the concerns of others.
- **Conscience.** Ethical leadership not only recognizes the right and decent way to act, but consistently chooses to do so.
- **Self-control.** Ethical leadership regulates one's thoughts and actions so as to resist both internal and external pressures.
- **Respect.** Ethical leadership aims to value others by treating them courteously and considerately.
- **Kindness.** Ethical leadership exhibits genuine concern for the welfare and feelings of others.
- **Tolerance.** Ethical leadership acknowledges the dignity and rights of everyone, even those with differing beliefs.

The Apostle Paul, in Philippians 4:8, provides a Christian perspective that resonates with the virtues essential for ethical leadership.

He emphasizes the importance of focusing on positive and virtuous thoughts in all aspects of life and leadership. He says: "Brothers and sisters, whatever is true, whatever is noble, whatever is right, whatever is pure, whatever is lovely, whatever is admirable – if anything is excellent or praiseworthy – think about such things."

3. ETHICAL VS. UNETHICAL LEADERSHIP IN TEAMS

Good or bad (negative) leadership determines the success of a working team, influencing not only the long-term sustainability of the team but also the more immediate personal welfare of its members. If you have had any present or past experience working within a team, give some careful thought to each of the following questions:

- What would you consider to be ethical behaviors that should be exemplified within a team?
- Can you think of an example of a leader or team member who has demonstrated exemplary ethical behavior? What impact did that behavior have on you and your team?
- Have you ever experienced a team related situation in which unethical leadership was involved? How did that impact you and your team members?
- Reflect on a time when you had to confront unethical behavior within your team. What actions did you take to address the issue?

Unmasking Unethical Behaviors in Team Dynamics

Together with my Ukrainian colleagues, I study team leadership practices. In our research inquiries spanning 2022-2023 in Ukraine, 257 adult participants shared their insights on negative leadership from the contexts of their own teamwork. Of these participants, 82% were between the ages of 18 and 40, a group comprised of 142 males and 115 females. These individuals brought to the study a wide range of teamwork experiences from business, non-profits, and government sectors. Our research highlighted five prevalent unethical behaviors that were identified by respondents as characteristic of negative team leaders:

- Prioritizing personal interests over the team's interests (80% - the percentage represents the proportion of participants who mentioned this behavior)
- Distrustful (63%)
- Arrogance (62%)
- Dishonesty (60%)
- Injustice (60%)

Between 2020 and 2022, I conducted several leadership seminars at various churches in the USA. These seminars were attended by middle-aged working professionals and church leaders. Before the seminars, participants completed a questionnaire answering the prompt: "In your opinion, what are the most characteristic signs of negative leadership within a team environment? (Choose any number of responses)." Listed below is a compilation of the results of those questionnaires. Ranked on a percentage basis from the greatest number to the least, the listings show what characteristics of negative leadership (within a team context) the study participants prioritized:

- Pursuing personal interests at the expense of team interests (70% of participants chose this answer)
- Dishonesty, injustice (59%)
- Distrustful (57%)

- Inability to resolve conflicts (57%)
- Inability to define a common goal and strategy for the team (56%)
- Arrogance (55%)
- Unwillingness to support others (44%)
- Lack of understanding about the place and function of roles within the team (38%)

A comparison between the two studies (the one conducted in Ukraine, the other in the USA) on perceptions of negative leadership displayed within team contexts reveals some interesting insights. First, certain negative leadership behaviors appear to be consistently identified by participants in both studies. Prioritizing personal interests over team interests, dishonesty, injustice, lack of trust, and arrogance are recognized as prevalent negative behaviors in both contexts. Second, the findings from these studies collectively suggest that certain negative leadership behaviors are widely recognized regardless of cultural or organizational differences. The consistency in identifying these behaviors across different settings emphasizes the universality of the concerns related to unethical team leadership.

Where, then, is the objectionable element in each of the negative leadership behaviors identified above? The following points offer the explanations:

- An egocentric approach that neglects the well-being and goals of the team is unethical because it contradicts the fundamental values of cooperation, mutual support, and shared accomplishments, all crucial for a thriving team environment.

- Distrust within a team can undermine collaboration, fostering a toxic environment. Establishing and nurturing trust is vital for ethical relationships and effective teamwork.

- Arrogance often entails an inflated sense of self-importance, leading to disrespectful behavior and a lack of consideration for others. This behavior contributes to an unhealthy and unethical work environment.

- Dishonesty and injustice constitute clear violations of ethical standards, eroding trust, damaging relationships, and generally inflicting negative consequences upon individual members as well as the team as a whole.

4. DEEPENING ETHICAL LEADERSHIP

The path to ethical leadership has several starting points. We need, however, to do more than consider the starting points; we must go beyond them. The journey along the path on which ethical leadership travels is somewhat analogous to peeling away the layers of something like an apple or orange, for example. Delving below the mere surface uncovers richer facets of understanding and practice.

Beyond learning

Recognizing the importance of ethical leadership is just the beginning. It is essential to understand what ethical leadership entails and how to put ethical principles into practice. Ethical leaders move beyond a theoretical understanding of ethics (secular and/or theological) to the effective implementation of ethical leadership in real-world scenarios. From the standpoint of Christian spirituality, ethical learning involves - above all - seeking and embracing God's guidance and practicing love for others.

Beyond deciding

For many, the initial step in ethical leadership involves making a conscious decision to be ethical. This initial intention to lead ethically is all important! However, like deciding to change to such positive habits as healthy eating or regular physical exercising, this decision is merely a starting point. It should be remembered that the decision to act ethically should not resemble a New Year's resolution, made today but broken tomorrow. Just as deciding to adopt healthier habits involves discipline and consistent effort, ethical leadership also requires sustained dedication. The issue here is not merely about being convinced on the necessity of ethical leadership or about actually making the decision to be ethical; it is about the embodying of ethical principles on a regular basis and in every facet of leadership.

Beyond meeting societal expectations

In Christian spirituality, ethics goes beyond simply conforming to social standards or widely accepted moral norms. Instead, it emphasizes a deeper, transformative, and transcendent approach to ethical living that surpasses conventional human expectations. The focus is on seeking a more profound and spiritually grounded way of life with God. This emphasis, in turn, implies that ethics involves a commitment to values and principles that are rooted in God and as such transcend what is commonly accepted in mainstream society.

I am convinced that while aligning with human expectations often serves as a foundation for ethical behavior, it is not the full picture and certainly, from the viewpoint of Christian spirituality, not the final end-point of ethical leadership. What do we know about the ethical standards promoted in contemporary societies? In our present day, being a 'good person' means (at least in most of the Western world) believing in the inherent dignity and worth of every individual; promoting the general welfare of all; refraining from the discrimination against others based on race, gender, or belief; advocating for fair treatment for the marginalized and downtrodden; and standing for equal rights and opportunities. Western societies emphasize that compassion, empathy, social justice, personal responsibility, recognition of the interconnectedness of human experiences, and the promotion of collaboration are guiding principles in ethical decision-making. Workers in modern organizations are expected to act with integrity; to be generous and act beyond their own interests; and to demonstrate environmental responsibility, cultural sensitivity, and open inclusivity. Ethical leadership as practiced in the best organizations promotes the ideas of altruistic love, humility, and forgiveness - traits that are foundational for producing harmony on both the individual and societal levels. All these principles are noble and honorable. Yet, as a final and absolute system of ethics, they are only partial and not sustainable.

Why then would these moral standards just enunciated, commendable as they might be, still be judged from a Christian vantagepoint as insufficient as a true and enduring ethical system? The answer is quite simple. They fail to take God into account. Human-centred, they are subject to all the moral foibles and weaknesses of what Christians often refer to as 'fallen' human nature. In contrast, Christian spirituality, believing that God is the ultimate moral authority, provides in biblical teachings a compass to guide Christian leaders in distinguishing good from evil in decision-making and acting ethically. Furthermore, the truly Christian leader, having experienced spiritual regeneration from the Spirit of God, now finds him or herself equipped and empowered to live a moral and ethical life with a stability and consistency that adheres to God's will, even when faced with opposition and disapproval from others.

Beyond Being Complacent

Ethical leadership recognizes that success calls for continuous growth and improvement. Sitting back on one's laurels, regardless of how splendid they might be, can lead to a self-congratulatory spirit that sees no need for growth. In contrast to such an attitude of self-satisfaction, true ethical leadership operates out of a sense of humility, recognizing the maxim that what is considered right and moral in a specific situation today may not be sufficient or true in how the principle is applied tomorrow or the next day. Yes, we can, to some degree, admit that there are timeless, unchangeable ethical principles. It is unwise, however, to become overly pleased in past or current achievements. The temptation will be to fall into complacently thinking that now they can be rigidly applied to all future contingencies. Such complacency is but a form of self-assuredness not too different from moral smugness.

The Bible cautions against such self-righteousness, emphasizing humility and the recognition of one's dependence on God's grace. It states that "Pride goes before destruction" (Prov. 16:18). King David, the greatest among the ancient Israelite kings, prayed: "Search me, O God, and know my heart; Try me, and know my anxious thoughts; And see if there be any hurtful way in me; And lead me in the everlasting way" (Ps. 139:23-24).

Ethical leadership, like the psalmist's prayer, involves recognizing the need for continuous improvement, an ever-evolving betterment that is realized in a spirit of humility rather than pride. Just as the psalmist sought guidance to overcome potential shortcomings, ethical leaders should remain vigilant in guarding themselves against a self-applauding attitude. Ongoing self-reflection, seeking feedback, and attending to God are the true signs of a commitment to improvement in both spiritual and leadership contexts.

Beyond Personal Performing

The choice to be ethical in our own lives is the starting point to ethical living. As the common saying goes, "All positive initiatives begin with oneself." To effect change in the world around us becomes challenging if we do not first effect change within ourselves. However, restricting ethical living only to oneself may not be sufficient for positively impacting the well-being of a family, team, community, or organization. True ethical leadership necessitates that individuals not only cultivate living ethically out of personal interests but also out of concern for promoting and improving collective commitments.

5. PROFESSIONAL ETHICS

Because they contribute specialized knowledge and expertise, working professionals play a crucial role in modern communities. They enhance overall economic and technological development as well as strengthen social cohesion. The knowledge and skills of working professionals helps ensure that communities stay innovative, adaptive, and resilient. Professionals also serve as positive role models. They can, for example, inspire and encourage others to pursue education and service, thereby contributing to the continuous advancement of society. Or, conversely, in the case of unethical and/or incompetent performance, they might serve as negative role models, both within their respective fields and within society in general.

Addressing fundamental ethical principles is crucial for the development of today's professionals. A few years ago, when I visited a country in Central Asia, I chatted with a Christian business consultant from Canada who travels frequently to Asia to conduct business training for young professionals. We discussed how we each assisted today's young generation of business leaders. I said that the Hodos Institute focuses on advancing spiritual, ethical, and effective leadership, and then he responded by highlighting the importance of ethics, emphasizing that we cannot solely focus on the mechanics of how to make businesses thrive from a pure economic perspective. He mentioned that it is crucial to address not only the basics, such as emotional intelligence, communication, and strategic business planning, but also the fundamental aspects of doing business ethically. The participants in his workshops worldwide, he said, often grapple with basic ethical dilemmas in their daily lives, making it essential to integrate ethical considerations into the broader spectrum of leadership training for business entrepreneurs.

Harvard professor, Barbara Kellerman, in her book *Professionalizing Leadership*,[4] argues that professional education must aim to develop individuals who are not only effective in their chosen occupations but also ethical in how they execute their responsibilities within those occupations. Her distinct push is that leadership must be practiced more ethically **and** more effectively.[5] Why? It's for one simple reason. Communities and those within them should not have to suffer from professionals who are ineffective and unethical. Kellerman posits that if professionals are not properly trained and held accountable, they eventually transition from ethical to unethical and from effective to ineffective.[6] In her book, *Leadership from Bad to Worse*, Kellerman also stresses that unethical and inefficient leadership and followership only get worse unless somehow, by someone or something, they are slowed or stopped.[7]

Ethical Codes in Professional Fields

It is obvious that ineffective and unethical conduct among professionals (doctors, lawyers, pastors, journalists, and engineers, just to mention a few) can have serious consequences for individuals, society at large, and the professions themselves. Therefore, to ensure ethical conduct among specialists, professional organizations worldwide establish codes of ethics for their practitioners to abide by. These codes define the fundamental values and ethical commitments essential for guiding professional behavior and decision-making particular to given professional fields. Typically, these documents and the policies they contain encompass such areas as integrity, confidentiality, professional competence, and the welfare of clients and responsibility to the public. In short, these codes set the ethical framework for practitioners. The expectation is that professionals affiliated with these associations will possess a thorough understanding of and a strict adherence to the code of ethics directly applicable to their respective practices.

Depending on the particular profession the foundational principles of an ethical code may include:

- **Autonomy:** Fostering the right of clients to control the direction of their own lives.
- **Nonmaleficence:** Avoiding actions that might cause harm.
- **Beneficence:** Advocating for the well-being of both the individual and society in general by promoting mental health and overall welfare.
- **Justice:** Treating individuals equally and fairly.
- **Fidelity:** Honoring commitments, keeping promises, and fulfilling responsibilities of trust in professional relationships.

- **Veracity:** Dealing truthfully with those with whom contact exists within one's professional capacity.

I once participated in the training program of Creative Results Management, a Christian coaching training company. During that training, I was introduced to The International Coaching Federation (ICF, www.coachingfederation.org). The ICF accredits programs that provide coaching education, develop cutting-edge core competencies, and lay out a code of ethics for coaching practitioners. The ICF's own Code of Ethics serves as an excellent example of what such a code entails.[8] It lists twenty-eight ethical standards, grouping them into four categories:

1. **Responsibility to Clients.** Responsibility in this category includes confidentiality, clarity and accuracy in financial arrangements, respecting a party's right to terminate the coaching relationship.

2. **Responsibility to Practice and Performance.** Responsibility in this category specifies the importance of ongoing personal, professional, and ethical development; the willingness to resolve conflicts in a proper manner; and respecting the privacy of ICF members and their contact information.

3. **Responsibility to Professionalism.** Responsibility in this category includes accurately representing coaching qualifications, making truthful statements about coaching offerings and the coaching profession in general, setting appropriate and culturally sensitive boundaries, and avoiding romantic engagement with clients.

4. **Responsibility to Society.** Responsibility in this category means refusing to engage in discrimination, upholding fairness and equality, recognizing the contributions of others, and respecting other people's intellectual property.

6. ETHICAL LEADERSHIP AND WORKPLACE SPIRITUALITY

From the perspective of Christian spirituality, working professionals face several challenging tasks: (1) discerning and realizing their calling, (2) striving for personal development (such development is essential for cultivating their talents and abilities), (3) fostering self-awareness, and (4) seeking their place in serving God, their neighbors, and God's creation at large.

Biblical teachings and Christian spirituality in general encourage working persons of all stripes to approach their work and leadership with a sense of purpose and commitment, recognizing that their efforts contribute to the well-being of themselves and others. While the Bible does not explicitly use the term "professionals" or otherwise refer to them as they are understood in the modern sense, it does provide guidance and principles relevant to various aspects of work, ethical behavior, and community contributions that are directly applicable to today's professional world. Colossians 3:23-24, for example, states: "Whatever you do, work at it with all your heart, as working for the Lord, not for human masters, since you know that you will receive an inheritance from the Lord as a reward. It is the Lord Christ you are serving."

The notion of working "for the Lord" elevates our work to acts of worship and service in God's kingdom. Inherent within these acts of worship and service is the assumption of a high level of excellence in their execution and a high standard of morality behind how and why they are performed.

Within the workplace that is the complex landscape of one's professional life, people are consistently confronted with multifaceted challenges related to fairness, work ethics, and interpersonal dynamics. Authentic Christian leadership, in its truest form, necessitates not only navigating these intricate issues but also taking a principled stand in advocating for individuals who may have encountered various forms of injustice, trauma, or lack of work-related opportunities.

A profound commitment to ethical standards and an unwavering dedication to promoting moral values within the organizational framework is what is demanded in such cases. As for its part, on the other hand, "negative, unethical leadership," as assessed from a Christian perspective, is to be judged as nothing more than a thirst for control, a pursuit primarily to satisfy one's own interests, and a conspicuous display of arrogance, greed, deceit, and dictatorial behavior.

Good leadership goes beyond mere adherence to established ethical norms. It also involves setting a personal example by voluntarily subjecting oneself to even more stringent moral behaviors than those expected of others. Christians in leadership roles should be the beacons of integrity and moral fortitude, inspiring their teams to embrace a culture of fairness, service, accountability, and social and environmental responsibility. By consistently upholding a higher ethical bar for themselves, Christian leaders can create an environment where integrity, humility, and compassion become the guiding principles, fostering trust and social cohesion among team members.

For the Christian professional, it is important to foster a workplace culture characterized by a distinctive standard, an ethical bar that includes a genuine concern for the general welfare of every individual within the organization. Here, effective Christian leadership is expressed in establishing the necessary conditions for people to achieve goals in line with God's will. Such leadership is also evident whenever a spiritual and emotional environment is created where workers are inspired to do more than what their job descriptions require of them. All of which is to say that in the end, the essence of Christian leadership is nothing more or less than effective love for God and people. Such love is produced by the Spirit of God in the heart of the believer and is based on God's perfect love revealed to the world in Jesus Christ.

Here is a list of some key theological and ethical principles that, when observed, can potentially result in ethical leadership being practiced as the norm in the professional workplace:

1. Recognizing and submitting to the authority of God. The acknowledgment of God as Creator and Lord should lead believers to prioritize him in their lives.

2. Accepting the reality of God's sovereign presence within the workplace. Such an acceptance should motivate Christians to be diligent in the workplace as faithful stewards. Christian leadership means to be God's co-worker there, a distinction that is both honorable and responsible.

3. Appropriating God's wisdom. In carrying out one's work responsibilities, this means to rely on his guidance, rather than relying solely on one's own or another's human ideas or resources.

4. Living a balanced life. A wise professional will juggle career and work obligations with personal and family responsibilities in such a manner that the latter are not compromised in any way.

5. Taking time to rest from work. The mental, emotional, spiritual, and even physical benefits from observing this principle are incalculable.

6. Embodying great qualities. These leadership traits promote a high ethical value: honesty, approachability, accountability, authenticity, sincerity, fairness, respectfulness, and patience. These are the traits of leadership ethicality.

7. Appreciating simplicity, beauty, and good taste. This fine attribute stems from a foundation of love and a commitment to serving God and the best interests of others.

8. Being faithful to the marriage bond. This commitment precludes any sexual impropriety.

9. Embracing God's moral standards. Such an embrace entails a commitment to safeguarding the sanctity of human life, cherishing and nurturing God's creation, demonstrating a deep respect for the property and possessions of others, and steering clear of such destructive tendencies as jealousy and gossip.

7. ETHICAL LEADERSHIP CHECKLISTS

Ethicality refers simply to identifying an individual or action as ethical. True ethical and moral behavior extends across diverse realms of life reaching into such areas as personal behavior, professional engagements, and public interactions. In various occupational fields such as business, healthcare, law, education, etc., ethicality is a crucial aspect that governs the conduct of professionals and the organizations in which they work. Carole Jurkiewicz and Robert Giacalone propose a valuable list of factors that can be confidently regarded as indicators of ethical leadership.[9] Organizational leaders and the teams they lead can assess their ethical standing by focusing on these themes and engaging in thoughtful self-reflection relative to each one.

- **Transparency:** Would we feel embarrassed if our decisions and actions were made public?
- **Universalizability:** Are we willing to be treated as we treat others?
- **Justice:** Do we ensure the dignity and freedom of others?
- **Rights:** Do we prioritize the well-being of minorities and otherwise socially marginalized individuals, or only those with privilege but without accompanying merit?
- **Egoism:** Do we pursue self-centered interests and personal gain at the expense of others?
- **Training:** Do we address both potential and actual ethical dilemmas in meetings and training sessions?
- **Communication:** Do we communicate in a straightforward and transparent manner with all stakeholders, minimizing gossip and rumors?
- **Utility:** Do we strive to act in accordance with my/our espoused ethical principles? Are we careful not to violate the spirit of our organizational policies and standards?
- **Social Benefit:** Are we committed to achieving the greatest good for the greatest number, or we committed to ensuring the least harm for the fewest?
- **Response:** Do we respond to claims of wrongdoing in a timely and unbiased manner?

Spirituality and Leadership Ethicality

From a Christian viewpoint, the ethical decisions made in everyday life are closely intertwined with one's theological beliefs and spiritual understandings. The foundation and backdrop for ethical leadership find their roots in biblical and theological teachings.

Ethics that can be recognized as distinctly Christian center around an apprehension of God's nature, his character, his interactions with humankind, and his sovereign rule over the universe and the unfolding of human history. This belief system, however, extends beyond its intellectual tenets to embrace the conduct of individuals who exercise faith in God, worship him, obey his commands, and follow his guidance. Such individuals stand in marked contrast to those who disregard God, those who adhere to their own or the socially induced moral standards that arise from and are shared generally by the larger community around them.

Christian ethical leadership is not, by the very nature of the Christian faith, a rigid checklist of rules and prohibitions. It encompasses a range of ethical principles anchored in the biblical commandments to "love God with all our heart, soul, and mind' and 'to love our neighbor as ourselves" (Matt. 22:37-40). Christian spirituality emphasizes the importance of the Old Testament's ten commandments. However, in its practice, this spirituality goes beyond a mere external observance of the moral law (Matt. 5:21-22, 27-28) to embrace the very spirit of love upon which it is founded (1Cor. 13:4-8).

In navigating the principles of ethical leadership through a Christian lens, it is natural for leaders grounded in biblical teaching to prioritize ethical precepts that align with Christian tradition. They do this by assessing their ethical path and priorities in the light of Scripture, thereby engaging themselves in self-reflection. In this respect, the

Bible presents a richness of ethical material for such self-evaluation and reflection. Below are listed several important biblical principles that, united to spiritual formation as they are, naturally lend themselves to an ethical way of life.

Seeking God's Guidance

Proverbs 3:6 instructs, "In all your ways submit to God, and He will make your paths straight." Acknowledging and submitting to God's voice in our daily lives empowers us to make decisions that are firmly grounded in his moral principles.

A thoughtful reflection relative to Proverbs 3:6 might involve asking, "In what ways have I sensed God speaking into my life lately?"

Relationship with God

The Bible says, "Come near to God and he will come near to you" (Jam. 4:8a). A close and intimate relationship with God forms the foundation of ethical leadership. The influence of such a relationship with God will be reflected in the practices and habits of believers right down to the ethical choices related to everyday life.

An appropriate question to reflect upon here might be: "Do I regularly draw near to God so that I might sense the ongoing nearness of His presence in every aspect of my career, occupation, and life in general?"

Responsiveness to the Spirit of God

On the relationship of the Holy Spirit to the believer successfully living the Christian life, the apostle Paul instructs, "Since we live by the Spirit, let us keep in step with the Spirit" (Gal. 5:25).

Every Christian would do well to frequently ask, "Am I open and responsive to God's Spirit? If not, why? If so, how can I fine tune my responsiveness yet further?"

Serving and "Building Up" the Community

The early Christian community was devoted to teaching, fellowship, breaking bread, and prayer. It was characterized by a shared purpose among the believers (see Acts 2:42-47). The apostle Paul compares the members of this community to a body, each member entrusted with a different function, but all working together for the general well-being of the body as a whole (Rom. 12:4-5; 1Cor. 12:12-27). In his letter to the Colossians, Paul calls upon believers to carry out this joint venture by clothing themselves with compassion, kindness, humility, gentleness, and patience, thus promoting harmonious relationships within the community (Col. 3:12-15).

Self-assessment questions related to building community per biblical teachings might include:

- Am I actively involved in various aspects of community life?
- How am I using my individual gifts and talents to contribute to the overall well-being of the community?
- How do I contribute to creating a supportive and encouraging atmosphere within the community?

Love and Compassion

Jesus's words: "Love your neighbor as yourself" (Matt. 22:39).

A self-assessment question in respect to this verse: Am I actively cultivating love and compassion in my leadership? (Am I consistently striving to treat others with the same care and consideration that I desire for myself?)

Respect for Others

The essence of ethical leadership lies in promoting an other-centered, empathetic, and collaborative approach in working toward achieving mutually agreed upon goals. Ethical leadership involves a balanced concern for both personal and collective interests. By looking out for the interests of others, leaders contribute to the robustness and overall long-term success of their teams and organizations. Such an approach is only possible, however, as leadership both exemplifies and promotes common respect for one another. In Philippians 2:4 (ESV), the apostle Paul writes: "Let each of you look not only to his own interests but also to the interests of others."

A self-assessment for ethicality in this regard would be to think through the following question: Am I faithfully considering the interests of others in my leadership, showing genuine respect for their well-being and viewpoints on matters of joint concern?

Integrity and Honesty

Moral integrity and honesty are at the core of ethical leadership. In Proverbs 11:3, it is said that "The integrity of the upright guides them, but the unfaithful are destroyed by their duplicity."

A fitting question to prompt serious self-assessment in this area would be: Am I exercising the kind of integrity that would serve me well as a guiding principle, thus avoiding the pitfalls of duplicity that could lead to destruction?

Justice and Fairness

Micah 6:8 says, "He has shown you, O mortal, what is good. And what does the Lord require of you? To act justly and to love mercy and to walk humbly with your God." This and other biblical passages reveal that goodness is exemplified through the practice of justice, mercy, and humility. Ethical leaders, recognizing God's requirements of them, integrate these values into their leadership style, fostering an environment of fairness, compassion, and humility. Two apt questions to stimulate meaningful introspection concerning this topic would be:

1. In what ways do I actively practice justice in my leadership role, and how can I further strengthen my commitment to fairness?
2. What steps can I take to foster a work environment that reflects the values of fairness, compassion, and humility, aligning with God's requirements as outlined in Micah 6:8 and other biblical passages?

Humility

The classic Scriptural exhortation for the practice of this virtue is found in Philippians 2:3-4, "Do nothing out of selfish ambition or vain conceit. Rather, in humility value others above yourselves, not looking to your own interests but each of you to the interests of the others." An excellent self-assessment to follow here is to ask: Am I unwaveringly practicing humility in my leadership, valuing others above myself and prioritizing their interests over my own?

Forgiveness

In the Christian tradition, believers are reminded of the imperative to "Bear with each other and forgive one another if any of you has a grievance against someone. Forgive as the Lord forgave you" (Col. 3:1). This biblical injunction underscores the significance of forgiveness in interpersonal relationships, drawing a parallel between divine forgiveness and the call for human forgiveness. Understanding forgiveness in leadership extends beyond the mere act of pardoning wrongdoings is critical. It also involves actively cultivating a mindset that transcends criticisms, seeks reconciliation, and embraces the transformative power of grace.

A pertinent question that emerges from Colossians 3:1: "Am I cultivating a spirit of forgiveness in my leadership and extending grace to others in the same way as the Lord has graciously forgiven me?" Reflecting upon this question should help engender a willingness to imitate the Lord's forgiveness in the restoring of fractured relationships.

Faithfulness
Faithfulness in leadership encompasses consistency, commitment to shared values and plans, trust-building, support for others, integrity, and leading by example. Faithfulness does not mean blind loyalty to something or somebody, but rather a steadfast dedication to principles and a genuine commitment to the welfare and success of the team or organization.

Faithfulness for Christian professionals means a holistic and integrated approach to work, interweaving professional endeavors with a commitment to Christian values, service, and a purpose-driven life. It involves a conscientious effort to live out personal faith authentically in the workplace, positively influencing the lives of those around them. The Bible teaches, "Let love and faithfulness never leave you; bind them around your neck, write them on the tablet of your heart. Then you will win favor and a good name in the sight of God and man" (Prov. 3:3-4).

To assess one's standing on this important trait of ethical leadership, give some careful consideration to questions such as the following:

- In what ways am I setting a positive example for others to follow in terms of commitment and a strong and consistent work ethic?
- How am I internalizing and expressing faithfulness in my actions and interactions, both professionally and personally?
- Do my actions and decisions consistently reflect my Christian beliefs, serving as a positive witness to others?

Endnotes

1. Ledbetter, B. M., Banks, R., & Greenhalgh, D. *Reviewing Leadership: A Christian Evaluation of Current Approaches*. 2nd ed. Baker Academic, 2016, p. 48-49.
2. See Brown, M. E., Treviño, L. K., & Harrison, D. A. "Ethical Leadership: A Social Learning Perspective for Construct Development and Testing," *Organizational Behavior and Human Decision Processes*, 97(2) 2005: 117-134.
3. Northouse, P.G. *Leadership: Theory and Practice*. 9th ed., Sage, 2022, p. 433-439.
4. Kellerman, Barbara. *Professionalizing Leadership*. Oxford University Press, 2018.
5. Ibid., 162.
6. Ibid, 137.
7. Kellerman, Barbara. *Leadership from Bad to Worse: What Happens When Bad Festers*. Oxford University Press, 2024.
8. See https://coachingfederation.org/app/uploads/2021/01/ICF-Code-of-Ethics-1.pdf. Accessed 3 Sept. 2024.
9. Jurkiewicz, C. L., & Giacalone, R. A. You Can Lead a Man to Oughta, But You Can't Make Him Think. In *Radical Thoughts on Ethical Leadership*. Information Age Publishing, 2017, p. 12.

A reputation built patiently, founded on effectiveness, integrity, and a deep connection to God, represents leadership that transcends any positional power or job title.

CHAPTER 8
EFFECTIVE LEADERSHIP

1. DEFINING EFFECTIVE LEADERSHIP

Recognizing it as a topic of great significance, this chapter delves into the vast and pivotal realm of leadership effectiveness.

In accordance with the logic followed overall in this book, the chapter on spiritual and ethical leadership was intentionally placed before this chapter in which effective leadership is the focus. In my observation, contemporary discussions on leadership sadly lack a due emphasis on spiritual or ethical dimensions. While most specialists in leadership discourse prioritize effectiveness, the more vital aspects of spiritual and ethical leadership are often given scant attention. Despite the transformative potential of these principles in guiding leaders toward exercising a more profound impact, the prevailing focus fixates more on pragmatic outcomes than on the values necessary to underpin good leadership practices. This imbalance points to the dearth of due consideration presently being given to the moral and spiritual dimensions of leadership within the broader conversation.

While some may argue that the spiritual and ethical facets of leadership are paramount in importance, this view is only partially accurate. The pursuit of productive, positive, and significant outcomes is equally as vital to successful leadership as is striving for spiritual well-being and ethical conduct. Then again, it must be remembered that although effectiveness is intricately connected to spiritual and ethical considerations, its importance should in no way overshadow those considerations. Essentially, this chapter argues for a holistic approach, asserting that cultivating impactful and enduring leadership requires a balance between the focus on effectiveness as an end and the due attention to the spiritual and ethical aspects of leadership.

Many years ago, my eldest brother, Anatoliy, an experienced engineer, was involved in reconstructing a church building in the sweltering hot climate of southern Ukraine. Each morning, he would meet with the construction crew, which consisted mainly of volunteers. Before launching into the day's work assignments, these volunteers would typically engage in lengthy discussions on how best to go about carrying out those assignments. While it is true that meticulous planning holds undeniable importance in any engagement, my brother was acutely aware that, nonetheless, certain principles on a work project like this were beyond debate. In the interest of increasing efficiency and saving time, it was in my brother's way of thinking, more advantageous to commence the day's work promptly. At times, then, he would quietly leave the planning sessions and begin working. Why? It's because he identified the most needed steps and then implemented them before the scorching temperatures became prohibitive to the project.

In an organizational leadership workshop that I conducted, there were both older and younger managers. I encouraged all participants to share what they would consider to be the factors influencing leadership effectiveness in an organizational setting. Notably, the older managers present had received their training and subsequent experience in a much different political and social context compared to that of their younger counterparts. Not surprisingly, these more established leaders contended that leadership effectiveness is associated with control and strict regulations. They also emphasized what, in their opinion, it was important to have a powerful, persuasive, and brilliant leader in command. According to this older age group, a strong central figure was crucial for organizational success. On the other hand, the younger managers expressed a different viewpoint. They expressed, in general, a preference for a more horizontal style of leadership, as opposed to the top-down hierarchical approach favored by the older managers. Behind this preference was their stated belief that leadership effectiveness within an organization is closely tied to the psychological climate existing among the workers under that leadership. Thus, to be truly effective, an organization's leadership must engage in cultivating a culture of trust and creativity among the team members whom it oversees. This, rather than relying solely on so-called experts who possess comprehensive knowledge but lack a willingness to collaborate. To state it otherwise, the consensus among the younger managers at the workshop was that organizational effectiveness is contingent on an environment that fosters participation, trust, a sense of belonging, and an accountability among team members.

Questions for Reflection
- What do you think about effective leadership from the context of these stories?
- What are your takeaways from these two stories?

Personal Comment
I believe that these stories emphasize that effective leadership is not a one-size-fits-all concept. It can be viewed from various perspectives. Effectiveness can be achieved by promptly identifying and implementing critical components of organizational operation and well-being. Effective leadership demands adaptability, an understanding of the context in which it operates, and the ability to balance planning with action, all the while considering the ever-changing needs and perspectives of team members. As for me, I belong to a generation that argues that the psychological climate existing within a team and the aptness of the leadership style overseeing that team can significantly influence effectiveness.

2. THE COMPLEXITY OF EFFECTIVE LEADERSHIP

As a human phenomenon, leadership has been studied for decades, over which time various theoretical models have arisen to explain both its existence and its effectiveness when exercised in certain ways. Leadership is a deeply complex matter, so much so that it is nearly impossible to define it in any way as to satisfy all concerned. It is just too complex to invite simplistic conceptions. Leadership's complexities are also highlighted by the fact that fixed rules as to how it should be practiced effectively are decidedly few in number.

When theorists posit their ideas on leadership effectiveness, they are naturally guided by their suppositions as to what they think leadership is and what they consider to be the most important factors governing how it should be practiced. Those suppositions, of course, are not constant; they change, and thus the perception of how effective leadership is achieved also changes. For example, analysis of developments within leadership studies over the years clearly shows that in recent decades, two primary shifts have taken place in the way leadership is conceptualized: (1) from the personal (individualistic) characteristics of the solo-leader, to the role that a leader plays in the personal interactions within his or her social or organizational context, and (2) from leadership concentrated in the individual perched at the top of the administrative structure to leadership as a social process that involves all the participants in pursuing a common task.

For those who have not made this shift, the effectiveness of leadership in their thinking is still connected to the more or less doctrinaire traits of the leader. Those who, on the other hand, have embraced this shift in emphasis see leadership effectiveness as connected to cooperation and interrelationships within the team, organization, or community where such leadership is being played out.

Leadership is an ever-moving target, often paradoxical and always perplexing. Because of this somewhat abstruse quality within its nature, scholars in leadership studies suggest that executing successful leadership is not only a science, but also a finely tuned art. Roger Gill, for example, says that leadership "is an art in terms of the imitative, or imaginative skills needed to achieve form, function and meaning. It is a science in terms of the systematic cognitive processes and formulated knowledge that effective leaders use in the forming and testing of ideas and practices."[1] Effective leadership, therefore, hinges on a delicate balance between intuition and imaginative insight on the one hand and scientific know-how and precision on the other hand, enabling leaders to navigate the ever-shifting landscape of team or organizational dynamics with agility and insight.

Because of its multifaceted and complex character, effective leadership cannot be confined to a single theoretical framework. Rather, it must be understood as encompassing a holistic approach that integrates different theoretical insights into practical applications. In his ninth edition of *Leadership: Theory and Practice*, Peter Northouse provides an overview of primary leadership approaches suggested over the years. He emphasizes that there is no singular model or theory of leadership, but instead, numerous theoretical perspectives that can enrich the understanding and practice of leadership. According to Northouse, some theories interpret leadership through the lens of (1) the leader and his or her behavior, (2) the follower and the context in which that follower navigates, (3) the interaction between leaders and followers, and (4) a process that changes and transforms people. Integrating these concepts, Northouse himself then defines leadership as "a process whereby an individual influences a group of individuals to achieve a common goal."[2] Effectiveness in leadership, as elucidated by Northouse's insights, rides on a nuanced understanding of the leader's role, the context in which that role is exercised, the dynamics between leaders and followers, and the transformative processes at play.

The complexity of leadership within team or organizational settings is further highlighted when leadership takes on designated formal and informal roles within those settings. An aspect of leadership involving a socially dynamic process where individuals assume various positions and responsibilities within an organizational structure. Part of the complexity here has to do with individuals temporarily or interchangeably adopting the roles of leaders, followers, or both.

Decision-making, too, is another central component of leadership that lends to its complexity. Decisions can be either effective or ineffective. To make timely, informed choices, effective leaders carefully weigh pros and cons, seeking input when necessary. The success of this process, of course, is closely intertwined with strategic planning and its execution toward achieving clearly defined goals. For leadership to successfully shoulder these tasks, however, it is vitally important that it possesses foresight and astute decision-making ability in order to adapt strategies and approaches to address diverse challenges or pursue new opportunities.

No discussion regarding the complexities involved in effective leadership would be complete without pointing out the connection between effectiveness and quality or excellence. The quality of leadership outcomes relies on both initial supportive conditions and the practices followed by the leader(s). It must be emphasized, however, that effective leadership results deemed to be quality are so only because they have been shaped by top quality input and the high quality of the processes employed to achieve the outcomes. Recognizing this interdependence is essential.

As stated above, effective leadership is a multifaceted and highly complex aspect of any collective endeavor. It goes without question, however, that effectiveness in leadership, as also discussed above, extends beyond the tangible aspects of team or organizational success. Effective leadership encompasses such values as integrity, accountability, continuous learning, and others that one might associate with the spiritual and ethical. All of which is to say in conclusion to this section's study, effective spiritual leaders are leaders who will prioritize the well-being of their team members, recognizing the significance of their holistic development and fulfillment.

3. EFFECTIVE LEADING AND FOLLOWING

In my view, effective leadership is comprised of three essential factors:

1. **The effectiveness of those who lead (leaders):** Effective leadership begins with leaders themselves. Leaders who embody and uphold strong spiritual and ethical values set a positive example for their teams. Their actions and decisions are guided by a moral compass, fostering trust and respect among their followers.

2. **The effectiveness of those who follow (followers):** Leadership is a two-way relationship. Followers, too, play a crucial role in the overall effectiveness of leadership.

When followers also embrace spiritual and ethical values, they contribute to a harmonious and purpose-driven work environment. Their alignment with these values helps maintain the practice of integrity within a team environment.

3. **The effectiveness of processes followed for achieving common goals by leaders and followers:** Effective leadership hinges on the collaboration between leaders and followers to achieve common goals. Leaders should also employ ethical and spiritual values as a foundation for decision-making and goal-setting. In this way, the entire process, from planning to execution, is underpinned by a commitment to ethical and meaningful outcomes.

By recognizing the interplay of these three factors, organizations and teams can foster a leadership culture that not only achieves objectives but also upholds values that contribute to a positive and purposeful atmosphere. Leadership and followership stand as inseparable pillars for effective teams and organizations. Leadership and followership represent the dual facets of critical synergy. The intricate dance between leaders and followers stands as a pivotal factor in this equation, captured by the nuanced concepts of "ways of leading" and "ways of following."

Delving deeper into the relationship between leaders and followers unveils a dynamic interchange of diverse styles, approaches, and perspectives. The desired reality of spiritual, ethical, and effective leadership unfolds as a mosaic shaped by the amalgamation of various and nuanced interactions. The art of leadership and followership transcends mere competency; it hinges upon the willingness and capacity of both leaders and followers to grasp the intricacies involved in their mutual relationship with each other, to choose the best options to fulfill their respective roles, and to harmonize their efforts toward a shared objective.

4. COMMUNICATION, LISTENING, AND FEEDBACK

Effective leadership as a subject of inquiry is all the more imperative when we think of how leadership itself spans such diverse organizational settings as hospitals, universities, business corporations, government agencies, non-government organizations, etc. What then, it might be asked, could be a set of general principles that could transform the mere presence of leadership, in whatever venue it may appear? Actually, effective leadership relies on many factors, one of them is to be identified by the way in which members of the group communicate, listen, and provide feedback. These elements, among others, ensure the continuous improvement of any organization as well as the personal welfare of its members.

Gary Yukl, the author of several books, including the highly influential text *Leadership in Organizations*, defines leadership as "the process of influencing others to understand and agree about what needs to be done and how to do it, and the process of facilitating individual and collective efforts to accomplish shared objectives."[3] As Yukl's definition suggests, effective leadership is a dynamic process that requires the ability to inspire, guide, and coordinate efforts toward a common purpose. Effective organizational leadership involves not only directing others, but also facilitating a collective commitment to shared goals. In essence, the effectiveness of leadership is deeply intertwined with the capacity to navigate and harmonize the diverse elements inherent within team or organizational contexts.

If effectiveness in leadership, as Yukl contends, is all about inspiring others to work toward meaningful goals, then certainly the well-being of those working together to achieve those goals must be as paramount in importance as the goals themselves. That sense of well-being, is a very important aspect of effective leadership!

Open communication and purposeful listening shape organizational culture in a positive way, building trust, reducing misunderstandings, and allowing the free expression of thought and emotion. It is vital for collaborative problem-solving and encourages idea-sharing. Active listening fosters a sense of connection, prevents conflicts, promotes empathy, and supports emotional well-being.

Both effective communication and effective listening acknowledge individual contributions and ensure an understanding of the shared mission, vision, values, and strategy of the organization. Both are vital to develop the engagement necessary for determining and implementing shared efforts.

Transparent dialogue is essential when trying to share ideas in a straightforward and brief manner. It is positive in the sense that it focuses on open, inclusive, constructive, and optimistic language. And, not the least of benefits, good communication is adaptable, that is, you can adjust the style to suit any given audience or situation.

Effective and conscientious listening, the other half of the communication equation here, is characterized by an attentive and heedful spirit. Always respectful and considerate, it entertains the thoughts and opinions of others as valuable input into the life and operation of the organization or team. Effective listeners are patient and focused; they listen with undivided attention and avoid being sidetracked. Effectiveness in listening, it might be added, obviously depends on a willingness not only to show genuine interest in what others are saying, but also to avoid any immediate criticism or premature conclusions.

If effective communication and listening are crucial to the growth and general welfare of an organization and its teams, the presence of feedback mechanisms within the organizational structure becomes an absolute must! They are the vehicles that make effective communicating and listening possible. In practical operation, these processes are built around previously defined goals and expected outcomes, measuring and evaluating achieved results, changing ineffective behavior, and so on. While feedback to team members may be aimed at correcting or improving immediate performance, it is at the same time also targeted at positively encouraging overall individual development. Ideally, the goal is not to criticize or humiliate but to help individuals grow and improve. Feedback should never be overwhelmingly negative to the person receiving it.

Administering effective feedback depends on at least two conditions: (1) the presence of an established feedback process, and (2) a willingness to participate in the dialogue. That being said, several factors can still hinder the provision of quality feedback:

- Lack of interest in others' opinions,
- Absence of trust among colleagues, and
- Inexperience, thus hindering the exchange of opinions beneficial to both the individual and, consequently, the group.

Administering quality feedback (from a leader to an employee or from an employee to a leader) is marked by three steps:

1. Highlight some specific achievements that you can celebrate.
2. Suggest, if necessary, what needs to be changed.
3. In addition to any recommendations, prompt the individual to think independently about what can or should be undertaken going forward. Here, the appeal is for reflection and exploration on what needs to be changed in one's practice, what needs further work, and what to build future success on.

Effective leadership in diverse organizational contexts is a multifaceted endeavor based on key elements that include communication, active listening, and feedback mechanisms. Good communication, respectful dialogues, and constructive feedback positively shape organizational culture, providing impetus for achieving organizational goals and, even more importantly, fostering an environment that assures the overall well-being of those who work cooperatively within it.

5. LEADERSHIP STYLES FOR EFFECTIVENESS

The effectiveness of leadership and followership is often tied to the wisdom individuals exercise in applying their personal styles and life experiences to different organizational situations. Since leadership is dynamic, you will almost always adapt in a manner that reflects the way one should lead or follow.

Leadership styles exist on a spectrum rather than in distinct categories. In practice, those who lead or follow exhibit a blend of different styles based on circumstances, context, or the individual/organizational needs confronting them.

A continuum of leadership approaches extends across a range covering three general styles:

1. **Autocratic.** This style focuses on tasks and the centralization of decision-making authority.

2. **Democratic.** This style emphasizes collaboration and the involvement of team members in both task-related activities and the social dynamics at play within a group.

3. **Laissez-faire** (French: "allow to do"). This style exercises minimal interference and direction, permitting team members significant freedom and autonomy.

In addition to the three general styles of leadership, there exist numerous nuanced approaches, each characterized by its own specific tendencies or convictions. These nuanced approaches carry with them their own sets of principles and strategies. Recognizing and understanding these nuanced styles adds depth to the dynamic landscape of effective leadership.

Effective leadership is of a multifaceted nature. It involves a leader's level of knowledge and skills, natural abilities and talents, and a recognition of past experience, as well the intangible items such as personality, character, and general leadership style. Another key factor in all of this is the experience and cohesive nature of the team, coupled with the way it interrelates with the leader. In fact, within the broad range of leadership literature and practice, today's discussion on the key concepts and practices of effective leadership narrows down more directly to the specifics applicable to teams and organizations than they do upon the individual leader directing them.

In the following sections, I present an assortment of selected themes that I have set up in pairs, as dichotomies, highlighting varying levels of similarity or variance between them. (*some themes have been adopted from *Key Concepts in Leadership*[4]). Each section focuses upon what team or organizational leaders assume and ask in their efforts to attain effectiveness. Besides the explanatory material I also include practical recommendations and questions for reflection.

Power vs. Reputation

During my tenure as an academic dean at a Christian university, we hired a relatively young lecturer who was assigned both teaching and administrative responsibilities. After a few months, he insisted on changing his job title, arguing that a more impressive title would earn him more respect from students and colleagues. Now let me ask you: if you were in an executive role, how would you handle this situation, and how would you respond? What thoughts might you have regarding the request?

The exercise of power is how things are accomplished, the pathway to achieving goals. Some people possess more power than others. Should we actively seek power, and if so, what kind? Do we lead spiritually, ethically, and effectively from a position of formal power or from a positive reputation, or perhaps both? Furthermore, what types of power are specifically linked to Christian spirituality? There are different forms of power.

- **Power of service:** Service is an integral aspect of a servant-leadership mindset. It enables us to identify the needs of others and provide care with sincerity and excellence.

- **Power of wisdom:** Effective leadership relies on wisdom, a kind which stems from reverence for God and practical wisdom.
- **Power of humility:** Humility grants the freedom to seek advice, ask for assistance, and acknowledge and rectify mistakes. It enables us to recognize and respect the value and talents of others.
- **Power of forgiveness:** Forgiveness has a healing and transformative effect. It liberates individuals, allowing them to move beyond failures, mistakes, or hurts, even those that were intentionally inflicted.
- **Expert power:** This type of power is established by demonstrating great knowledge and extraordinary proficiency of skills.
- **Positional, legitimate power:** Such power enables assigning tasks, making decisions, and monitoring performance.
- **Regulatory power:** This power authorizes the establishment of rules, policies, and protocols.
- **Coercive Power:** Coercive power employs force to compel compliance with procedures and to achieve tasks.

In any organization, authority that is linked to positional and/or regulatory powers is undoubtedly necessary. However, the exercise of these powers also implies a responsibility for the ethical use of them. Abusing this power can lead to autocratic leadership, which promotes mere compliance rather than encouraging individuals to exceed minimal requirements. Abuse of power often leads to an unsavory moral or professional reputation, which in turn can only lead to further erosion of authority. Organizational leaders who lack professional excellence, moral authority, and a commendable reputation may be tempted to rely excessively on the exercise of formal power, adopting a tough, demanding, micromanaging, threatening, pressuring, or even manipulative leadership style.

True leaders are followed not as a result of coercion but by the voluntary and conscious choice of their followers. Spiritual leaders provide a type of leadership that is rooted in love and trust, not in fear or force. The biblical teachings foundational to Christian leadership are explicit in that genuine human leadership is not exerted through formal power alone but through obedience to God and through a reputation associated with a righteous character. A reputation built patiently, founded on effectiveness, integrity, and a deep connection to God, represents leadership that transcends any positional power or job title.

Key Recommendations
1. Strive for a balance between formal power and a positive reputation. While formal power is essential, it should be complemented by a reputation for integrity, competence, efficiency, and ethical conduct.
2. Recognize the importance of humility in leadership. Humility enables you to acknowledge the talents of others, seek help, and admit and rectify your mistakes. It fosters a culture of openness and collaboration.
3. Embrace forgiveness as a powerful leadership tool. Forgiveness can transform and heal, leading to improved relationships and increased trust.

> **Questions for Reflection**
> - What will help balance the use of formal power and the cultivation of a positive reputation to live and lead well?
> - What role does humility play in leadership and followership, and how can it be developed and encouraged within a team or organization?
> - What promotes trust, collaboration, and personal growth within a team or institution?

Monopolization vs. Participation

The choice of leadership style significantly shapes the dynamics within a team or organization. Contrasting approaches to leadership do exist, ranging from the rigid and often heavy-handed ways of an "authoritarian" and "directive" approach to the collaborative and inclusive style embodied by "collaborative," "participative," and "democratic" leadership. These distinct terms encapsulate the fundamental but disparate concepts of monopolization and participation in leadership. On one end of the spectrum, some leaders assert their authority, making decisions independently and minimizing the involvement of others – a phenomenon I refer to as monopolization. On the opposite end, some leaders embrace participatory approaches and seek collaboration, involving team members in decision-making processes to foster a sense of collective ownership and shared responsibility.

Participatory leadership within organizations can be explained as an attitude toward leadership that welcomes team members or colleagues to participate in critical organizational processes and procedures like planning, execution, evaluation, feedback, etc.

Highly motivational, it is an organizational approach that optimizes and improves the quality of decision-making.

Within the participatory model, leaders see themselves as first among equals, instilling within the teams with which they work an understanding of the value of each member. It is important to note here, however, that the effectiveness of a participative leader is not necessarily guaranteed simply by involving team members in the leadership process. Also necessary is the presence of expertise and maturity within the team's ranks, as well as mutual respect and a commitment to a common goal.

If involving team members at the highest levels of organizational procedures and decisions, there is nonetheless an attendant danger against which leaders must be on guard. That danger lies in the temptation to ease back on or perhaps even to abdicate altogether their responsibilities as leaders, especially in the area of decision-making. On one level, the leader may be just another fellow team member, but as "first among the equals," he or she still has the special responsibilities to the group of mobilizing, organizing, directing, motivating, empowering, and a host of other expectations that exist on a different plane than that of any other team member. Any shrinking away from those responsibilities is bound to negatively impact the morale, sense of common purpose, and commitment to shared goals among the group's membership. The result will be a weakening or failure to realize organizational vision, purpose, and goals.

Authoritarian leadership is observed in those leaders who retain for themselves the exclusive right to initiate actions, make decisions, evaluate the performance of others, and other functions normally associated with the leadership office. Authoritarian leaders see themselves as indispensable individuals who have the abilities and experience necessary for the team or organization to succeed. They think that they do not need advisors, that their decisions are not subject to discussion, and that they hold all the wisdom and strategies needed for success. Such leaders do not spend time entertaining the views or opinions of others. They set tasks and compel others to execute those tasks, demanding a controlled timeline and nothing short of excellence.

Monopolization is not always necessarily negative. In conditions where members of an organization or team are inexperienced, general confusion is prevalent within the group, or an acute crisis has arisen, a strong hand at the helm can be decidedly effective in dealing with the problems involved. In such situations, the leader's ability to lead is strengthened, of course, by the hierarchical structure of authority already in place. That hierarchical order, by its very nature, lends a strong underpinning of support when the one at the top requires it. It should be remembered, however, that beneath that self-sufficient front that the authoritarian leader may project, there may also exist – as is often the case – the setbacks of self-doubt, fear of losing power, suspicion, and/or the literal inability to work as a part of a team.

Key Recommendations
Leadership effectiveness sometimes requires monopolization and at other times a participative approach. We should keep in mind that these styles are not mutually exclusive; it is important to weigh how much of each approach should be employed when addressing the needs of a team or organization.

Questions for Reflection
- Can you provide examples of authoritarian and participative leaders you have encountered?
- With whom did you find it more comfortable to interact? With whom was your work more effective?
- Which leadership style is characteristic of you personally?

Distance vs. Involvement

If individuals understand their responsibilities, they can control their commitment level accordingly, choosing either full engagement or minimum effort. The choice varies depending on various factors and goals. Some leaders aim to grant their team members autonomy, fostering independent work toward desired outcomes. This approach values empowering colleagues to achieve results without interfering with team or organizational processes. In contrast, other leaders tend to exercise direct control over every aspect of organizational life, a behavior often labelled as micromanagement. This inclination is common among inexperienced leaders, perfectionists, or those guided by authoritarian leanings.

While it is rare for leaders to entirely distance themselves from collective matters, some leaders do limit contact and participation in key processes where perhaps they *should* be actively involved. This avoidance trait can manifest itself in various ways, such as going on frequent business trips, attending an inordinate number of external events, or taking unplanned leaves, for example. Here, distance may be defined as shirking responsibilities, opposite perhaps to authoritarian interference, but hardly explainable as the type of leadership that practices a hands-off approach as a means of empowering team members to maximize their contributions to the organization's goals.

Although direct personal involvement can be beneficial in discharging small-scale tasks which require clear oversight from a superior, an overly intrusive leader may inadvertently fall into an authoritarian stance. This often results in mistakes due to an inability to attend to every detail. Excessive incursion from a leader into the space of the team or the organization turns that team or organization into something like an orchestra where, the conductor (the leader) finds him or herself trying to direct a host of multiple tasks and responsibilities without losing count or falling apart. However, unlike the conductor who orchestrates beautiful and harmonious music from a group of finely tuned musicians, the micromanaging, authoritarian leader may find him or herself in a total breakdown—a failure to make it to the last bar of music.

The level of a leader's involvement or detachment is no more apparent than when seen in the presence of conflict resolution, strategic planning, summarizing results, or direct management of work activities. Here weak leaders will typically behave in one or the other of two predictable ways. If they see positive collective efforts transpiring within the organization, they may move to involve themselves more diligently, seeking to position themselves at the center of what really is a commonly produced success. Conversely, when faced with the hard but responsible tasks of leadership, weak leaders often display detachment issues. They delay important decisions, find reasons not to participate in meetings or conflict resolution, and ignore the achievements (or failures) of colleagues or the organization at large. When an organization experiences such a withdrawal of leadership, all involved are disadvantaged.

Key Recommendations

Effective leadership means focusing on those responsibilities that truly require personal attention at the top leadership level. It is vital for leaders to avoid engaging in tasks that would be better delegated to others.

In some situations, a greater measure of involvement may be necessary on the part of a leader; while in other circumstances, tasks and authority should be delegated to others within the organization or team. Healthy distancing will afford team members the freedom to take risks and act independently. It not only fosters a sense of ownership but also provides them opportunities for learning and maturing on their leadership journey.

While delegating tasks and responsibilities, and at the same time empowering those to whom the tasks have been committed, leaders need to ensure that they neither distance themselves from their team nor attempt to evade accountability.

Questions for Reflection
- Have you ever felt a desire to distance yourself from your current tasks at work? If so, what prompted this inclination, and what exactly were you hoping to achieve?
- From your perspective, what would be the optimal way to allocate responsibilities and tasks in order to prevent burnout from work overload while still maintaining a strong connection to your

> team and the overall work processes in which all are involved?
> - How much involvement in an organization's overall venture do you believe is essential for effectively carrying out your Christian mission in the workplace?

Visibility vs. Invisibility

Some individuals lead visibly, taking center stage and directing from the forefront, while others prefer an invisible role, orchestrating actions from behind the scenes. The motivating factors and perceptions surrounding each of these choices is critical, for they possess the power to influence both visible and invisible leadership, making it either constructive or destructive.

On the positive side, visible leaders, those who function comfortably in the limelight or refuse to hide behind others, deserve respect for their boldness, confidence, and inspiration. Their clear voice and open profile deserve recognition. These leaders possess vision and are often gifted with oratorical skills. Their settling into the spotlight can be directed toward the greater good.

On the negative side, visible leadership may be employed as a vehicle through which self-centered leaders draw much-desired attention to themselves and the power which they wield. An extensive number of speeches, frequent meetings, or one-sided planning sessions can be the manifestations of such negative visibility.

Invisible leaders who embrace quiet, behind-the-scenes leadership are a less conspicuous group. Given no formal authority, they function away from the glare of the spotlight. Even so, they often exert more positive influence within an organization than those in official positions. Instrumental in the development of others, these leaders make their impact through quietly offered suggestions, ideas, and encouragement, all the while seeking no recognition for the contributions they make. Because they don't seek credit for their contributions, they often do not receive it.

On the flip side, invisible leadership can also be characterized by an adverse negativity. A malicious streak within a leader can express itself in covert actions aimed at destabilizing, sabotaging, or creating discord within a team. Leaders who actively withdraw or distance themselves from the overall operations of the organization or team(s) they lead often avoid personal interaction, particularly during challenging times. They may struggle with bad news, and as a result, seek refuge in seclusion. Not surprisingly, such invisible leaders are perpetually out of reach when they are most needed. Conversely, when all is going well and success is being experienced on all fronts, such individuals may desire to make their leadership more visible.

> **Key Recommendations**
> Leaders should recognize that their actions, whether visible or invisible, exercise a profound impact on team dynamics and organizational culture. Striking a balance between visibility and invisibility contributes to a healthy leadership dynamic. It is not always necessary to be in the spotlight; balance is what is needed. Am I stepping into the limelight primarily to attract attention to myself and expand my sphere of influence, or is it a move to advance

the greater good and performance of the team or the organization I lead? Am I shunning the stage to shirk my responsibilities, or am I doing so to exert a positive influence that can be more effectively exercised while remaining in the background?

Questions for Reflection
- Have you encountered so-called invisible leaders? What factors contributed to their effectiveness or ineffectiveness?
- Which type of leader do you find easier to trust - those who are constantly in the spotlight, or those who operate quietly behind the scenes?
- In which setting would you feel more comfortable influencing others, onstage as the center of attention or offstage drawing little or no attention to yourself?

Product vs. People

In the professional world, every team or organization represents a collective effort to create a product or service. Churches, non-profits, business companies, and governmental agencies are invariably committed to various objectives that are accomplished by their staff, employees, and/or volunteers working together. Within these organizations, the leadership approach can lean either to a "product-focused leadership" where the emphasis is placed on the quality of the product produced or the service rendered, or to a "people-focused leadership" where the concern is for the well-being of those involved in the creation of the product or delivery of the service.

In ideal conditions, we can focus on the achievement of product or service excellence and the attention we give to the personal welfare and development of those in our care. Unfortunately, leaders who concentrate less on caring for those under their watch than they do in creating strategic plans, programs, or projects do exist. To such leaders, team members are regarded as a resource whose function it is to serve for the betterment of the organization.

Leaders who are in tune with their personnel are interested in benefitting from the team's diverse life experiences. They pay attention to people beyond their organizational and team roles and are especially willing to work with those who are young and promising but lack basic knowledge and skills. They attempt to build relationships within their teams, care about their team's personal welfare, and promote the growth and development of the talents and abilities of those team members.

Leadership that is oriented toward developing people can sometimes conflict with service and production or the need to achieve quality results. Striking a balance in such cases is essential. Excessive focus on product and team/organizational goals may devalue the worth of the individuals, while excessive emphasis on staff/employee interests can negatively impact the performance of a team or organization.

> **Key Recommendations**
> British leadership scholar, John Adair, correctly observes that effective leadership occurs at the intersection of three spheres: the team, the tasks, and the individuals.[5]

Effective leadership entails achieving organizational goals, developing a cohesive team, and caring for each individual within the team. The focus should be on both the quality of the product or service and the well-being and professionalism of those who are creating the product. Sustainability in any organization depends on producing quality products or delivering hallmark service; thus, a professional team with satisfied needs and motivated members is critical.

A higher purpose of leadership exists beyond that of creating excellent products or amassing financial gain. In addition to the quality of a product, effective leadership should be marked by taking responsibility for the personal interests and development of those in the group.

Questions for Reflection
- With which type of leader do you find it more comfortable to work: one who is primarily goal-oriented or one who is primarily focused on the well-being of the individuals on the team?
- In your opinion, what needs to be done to strike a healthy balance between the quality of a product or service and the care extended to the team members who produced or delivered that output?
- Imagine a situation where a Christian family owns and operates a restaurant. What is their Christian mission at work:
  a. Caring for the well-being of family members and employees
  b. Improving the restaurant's overall service

> c. Increasing the restaurant's profits
> d. Demonstrating social responsibility, such as providing free meals to the elderly.
> e. Reducing the restuaurant's environmental impact?

Self-Development vs. Developing Others

Consider the leadership of Jesus Christ. The Gospels depict Jesus as growing in wisdom and stature (Luke 2:52), specifying moments of solitude and prayer in his life. These moments are often presented as times of spiritual reflection and communion with God. Jesus's life reveals a healthy equilibrium: while faithfully attending to his own spiritual well-being, he also nurtured his disciples with needed care, teachings, assignments, and feedback. We could say that Jesus' effectiveness could be seen, on one hand, in cultivating and drawing upon his relationship with God the Father for personal renewal and empowerment while, on the other hand, pouring himself into the training and personal growth of his small band of disciples.

Self-development is a leadership style centered on one's own personal growth, while coaching or mentoring involves actively guiding and supporting others in their individual paths of development. Both styles can coexist within effective leadership. Leaders must balance the attention they devote to their own personal betterment with the attention they devote to the development of their team members.

Some leaders, regrettably, focus more on enhancing their own individual performance than they do on equipping their team members to progress and thrive. The faults that might be cited against such leaders are many. Some seek only the opportunities that make themselves more effective in *their* roles, overlooking other opportunities that might benefit the growth of their followers. In this vein, they strategically leverage the skills, resources, and efforts of team members to primarily serve their own success and interests. Considering themselves key experts, they believe that their assumed expertise is the major (or only) legitimate factor applicable to team and organizational success. Accordingly, they take much more immediate and up-close control on how they direct those operating under them. Hindering the growth of all involved, this style of leadership makes achieving distributed or shared leadership very challenging!

If a leader's concern is solely fixed on his or her own personal development to the exclusion of training, coaching and/or mentoring others, it can be concluded that that leader may not be fully committed at all to the overall well-being and development of the team or organization. Such leadership is associated with a more transactional or exploitative approach.

A contrast to the adverse style of leadership just described is when coaching and mentoring others is of prime concern. This approach to leadership focuses on caring for and developing others. Mentors support individuals under their guidance, providing advice, sharing experience, and helping mentees navigate their career paths. At the heart of the mentoring process is the formation of collaborative relationships that center on shared success and effectiveness.

> **Key Recommendations**
> Encourage a culture of coaching or mentorship within leadership. It is crucial that a leadership style be adopted

that transcends personal gain and actively fosters the growth and development of the entire team.

To avoid falling into complete dependency on a self-directed and autonomous form of leadership, leaders should go beyond the time-tested method of issuing direct instructions to direct reports. Delegating responsibilities and providing team members with the tools necessary for independent task completion is essential for cultivating a more empowered and sustainable collaboration.

While there may be situations where self-development and solo performance may seem compelling, it must be remembered that the long-term efficiency of a team and/or organization is most enhanced by prioritizing the development of others. Focusing on helping others to act independently contributes to sustained, shared success.

Questions for Reflection
- Who has helped you develop personally in your field of work? How did this person do it? How can you help others acquire or enhance their qualifications? How can you assist others in their personal development?
- Personally, do you find it more comfortable to receive direct and detailed instructions from someone over you, or to have the freedom to act independently in completing a task?

Unity vs. Diversity

Allow me to recall two brief memories as a way to approach the sensitive topic of unity and diversity in our quest to define effective leadership.

1. While I was pursuing my Ph.D. at the University of Pretoria in South Africa, my perspective on biblical studies and higher education was profoundly influenced by my doctoral supervisor, Prof. Jan van der Watt. His inspiration motivated me to cultivate a teaching approach that not only preserves the roots of important theological and cultural traditions but also encourages students to appreciate new perspectives, approaches, and traditions. In essence, he instilled in me the importance of a style of leadership that values and balances both unity and diversity.

2. Some years ago, I had the privilege of attending a lecture on child-rearing delivered by an Ukrainian philosopher. Speaking to a diverse audience of educators and young parents, he emphasized the importance of raising and educating children in a manner that equips them to earn a livelihood, collaborate effectively with individuals from diverse backgrounds, and cultivate a strong sense of integrity. While all three points were noteworthy, the notion of forming a mindset and acquiring skills to live and collaborate with people of varying perspectives struck me as particularly profound and has stayed with me to this day.

Unity and diversity are ideas that often evoke tension and edginess. These topics are responsible for many debates and arguments, but dealing constructively with the emotional strains created by the diversity and unity is what makes a leader effective. The debate requires both intentionality and wisdom. Effective leaders model their wisdom through nuanced approaches in achieving that balancing act. Such approaches foster unity, collaboration, and shared goals while also recognizing the critical importance of embracing and nurturing diversity and inclusion.

Most contemporary organizations, regardless of size and goals, consist of people with diverse backgrounds all working together. Teams (crews, departments, divisions, etc.), guided by shared and understood values, are formed to accomplish common objectives and internal tasks. Interactions within these teams are often influenced by the reality that employees share a diversity of life experiences, hold different worldviews, and vary in age and nationality. Some value this diversity and see its benefits. Others prefer to work in a homogeneous environment, seeking to form teams with colleagues who share a similar background and outlook upon the world.

Diversity of people, perspectives, approaches, and experiences is extremely valuable. Cultural and professional diversity expands the horizons on how team members are able to understand themselves as well as the environment around them, an environment that includes clients, partners, and competitors. Diversity also creates many opportunities for enhancing skills in dialogue, negotiating, and appreciating people. Without diversity, there is always the risk of bringing only limited perspectives, stifled innovation, and a lack of adaptability to bear upon the rapidly changing environments that arise to test an organization. Confronted with such challenges, a leadership style that ignores diversity misses a prime opportunity to tap into a wide range of talents and experience, significantly diminishing the potential for optimal performance and output on the part of a team or organization as a whole.

A shared similarity within a leadership team is not without its benefits. It is much easier to interact with those who share similar life experiences, or with those who possess an equivalent level of education, or with those who happen to work in one's own specialty field. Likenesses in at least some essential characteristics pertaining to vocation and life in general contributes to unity among work colleagues.

> **Key Recommendations**
>
> Avoid creating artificial barriers to diversity. If the individuals within a leadership team are possessed of similar know-how and experience but do not interact with others of dissimilar backgrounds and different types of expertise, the result can easily lead to organizational stagnation. In diverse environments, flexibility is essential. Team members, and especially leaders, should be sensitive to cultural, national, age, and other differences, remain aware of variations in individuals' values, and understand which leadership approaches are suitable to meet the needs of diverse individuals.
>
> **Questions for Reflection**
> - How does your Christian faith help you appreciate unity and diversity in life?
> - What aspects of diversity do you find acceptable and desirable within a collective?
> - If leadership focuses on achieving homogeneity, what negative consequences might arise for the leader and the organization as a whole?
> - What can be said about leaders who surround themselves with individuals who think just like them? What issues and dangers are associated with such a leadership approach?

Analysis vs. Intuition

The contemporary era, defined as it is by constant change, confronts individuals with decisions on every hand, ranging all the way from those that regularly fall into the daily routines of life to those of life-changing significance. The question arises: before determining a course of action, should one meticulously analyze every factor related to a decision, particularly focusing on the dissecting of possible outcomes stemming from that decision? Or, alternatively, is there merit in an intuitive approach where decisions, especially those that need to be made immediately, rely on personal instincts?

Analytical leaders prioritize an understanding of both the past and present, while simultaneously advocating for a thoughtful and well-planned movement forward. They scrutinize factors impeding or contributing to organizational or team success. Incorporating such tools as analytical reports and strategic planning into an organization's *modus operandi*, however, may sometimes lead to resistance from those averse to such an approach.

In contrast to methodic and logically oriented leaders are those who prefer to navigate situations on the fly. They contend that thinking through every detail pertaining to a decision is impractical, and thus advocate for relying on intuition as a more fitting solution. These leaders argue that a sole dependence on logic can lead to conventional and outdated approaches, as well as cause information overload, doubts, time delays—and ultimately, mistakes.

> **Key Recommendation**
> Try to strike a balance between analytical thinking and intuitive decision-making. Recognize that each approach

has its own particular merit, and depending on the nature of an impending decision as well as the context in which that decision is to be made, it can be applied with equal effectiveness. Value research and analysis. Demonstrate the importance of staying informed about industry trends and evolving best practices. But in an environment of constant change and uncertainty, remember that detailed, slow-paced analysis often proves to be less effective than quick-thinking but well-informed intuitive decisions.

Questions for Reflection
- Have you encountered individuals who practice one of the described approaches to leadership? How did their methods affect you?
- What type of leadership do you personally lean toward – analytical or intuitive?

Skills vs. Personality

Leadership effectiveness is intricately tied to whether certain individuals are well suited for the specific roles and tasks related to the role. While some argue that professional responsibilities demand specific skills and experiences, others highlight that effectiveness is contingent on the personalities of the individuals involved.

The individual personality traits of the leader versus the background training, experience, and natural aptitude for specific professional tasks gives rise to two distinct leadership styles. When teams or organizations seek candidates to fill vacancies, they will carefully weigh which of the two styles is better suited to meet the immediate and long-term responsibilities and tasks that naturally go along with the leadership position.

The task-oriented leadership style is grounded in the belief that recruiting for a specific task and providing particular skill training and practice will enhance a leader's effectiveness across various domains. Alternatively, those who underscore the importance of a consistent temperament and an interactive style when relating to colleagues and team members prioritize recruiting and developing individuals with the following traits:

- **Extroversion.** Such effectiveness is invariably associated with leaders who are outgoing, energetic, and excelling in social interactions.
- **Agreeableness.** An agreeable nature demonstrates trustworthiness, straightforwardness, appreciation, and generosity.
- **Conscientiousness.** Individuals instilled with this character trait display competence, orderliness, self-discipline, and responsibility. In their professional capacities, they emphasize strategic planning and goal attainment.
- **Openness.** It is vital to embrace imagination, innovation, and a creative and experimental environment.
- **Effectiveness** depends on a low level of neuroticism (or, conversely, on a high level of emotional stability). In an organizational or relational context, it is important to remain calm, self-assured, and emotionally resilient under pressure and during crises.

Key Recommendation

As a leader, consider incorporating personality assessments to identify individuals with skills and traits aligned with specific tasks or roles. Invest in training and professional development programs that focus on enhancing both technical/professional skills and personality traits. Foster a culture that supports individuals with various personality traits. Establish mechanisms for continuous feedback and evaluation. Regularly assess the alignment between individuals' personalities, skills, and the tasks to which they are assigned, making adjustments as needed.

Questions for Reflection

- In your opinion, do you consider yourself primarily an extrovert, an introvert, or an ambivert (someone who displays characteristics of both)? Taking into account your personality traits, reflect on the leadership challenges you have encountered.
- Do you see any principles in the Christian faith or teachings from biblical texts that help you recognize individual differences in temperament and behavioral types?
- How can a thoughtful understanding of personality differences enhance your ability to serve others effectively? (Consider specific instances where adjusting your approach according to individual temperaments might lead to more impactful leadership.)

Cognition vs. Emotion

There is an opinion, held by many, that the only requirement for effective leadership is the presence of a high level of cognitive ability, functioning successfully in such areas as acquiring knowledge, analyzing information, planning strategically, and understanding the big picture of leadership. Cognition itself is a broad term that includes various mental processes such as learning, reasoning, and problem-solving; and although those cognitive proficiencies are undoubtedly important for effective leadership, they are not the sole requirement.

Effective leadership is also significantly influenced by emotional intelligence. As a formal designation, "emotional intelligence" refers to possessing the ability to recognize and manage emotions, regularly sensing and interpreting the emotional state of others. Applied to leadership, the skill translates into effective, emotionally intelligent leaders who display empathy and establish relationships primarily on the basis of positive feelings and emotions. Emotionally intelligent leadership focuses on monitoring the emotional climate within a team environment. Here, the understanding is that emotional reactions among individuals may vary, in fact, vary widely to whatever may be happening in the environment around them. Leaders attuned to this reality will be careful to have mechanisms in place to manage an elevated stress level, no matter what is causing it.

Key Recommendations

It should not be assumed, as some believe, that there is no need to develop mental and/or emotional sensitivities for an individual to achieve success. It is important to learn how to be more attuned to the emotions and feelings of both self and others. Leaders should establish systems that regularly assess and monitor the emotional climate within their teams.

Questions for Reflection
- Would you say that you are sensitive to your own emotions as well as the emotions of others?
- Have you encountered leaders with an apparent low emotional intelligence? If so, what, in your view, should they do to enhance their capacity to perceive and interpret emotions within themselves and within the team?

Inspiration vs. Implementation

Whether instilling a shared vision or executing a meticulously developed strategic plan, effective leadership ultimately relies on a wise sagacity to balance inspiration and implementation. Within certain teams or organizations, leaders often serve as motivators, inspiring and encouraging others to follow a certain course or to act in a specific way. They are skilled and persuasive communicators who articulate goals and strategies to foster a collective sense of purpose. These leaders are effective if their followers internalize their inspiring words. That's because intrinsic motivation is by far a more powerful impulse than a mere external inspirational prompting, however stimulating it may be at the time.

The implementation-style of leadership, on the other hand, is characterized by a steadfast commitment to translating ideas into tangible outcomes. Leaders that apply this style display a lower inclination toward the usefulness of positive verbal inspirations. They are quick to initiate the practical aspects of a project and, not surprisingly, they work more effectively with individuals who do not require constant inspiration. However, their focus on implementation and process may overshadow the need for the emotional support needed by their teams. This is something to watch out for with this style of leadership.

Those who turn ideas into reality are those who are generally revered and admired. That is why we underscore the importance of implementation over the poignant declaration of big ideas. While many talk about inspirational goals, not everyone achieves them. We tend to value those most who actually do translate inspired ideas into concrete reality. Yet, implementing good and complex ideas does demand willpower, teamwork, belief in a project's goal, and more. And so, in the end, the priority for implementation does not in any way diminish the benefit of the inspiration that sustains enthusiasm. It plays an important role in preventing people from working in isolation from one another or becoming dispirited in heart.

> **Key Recommendation**
> Leadership should be oriented toward implementing vision **and** achieving results. This is not possible, however, without first creating a team or help fulfill that vision and the goals that go along with it. It is important to build positive relationships within the team, knowing how to inspire them. Inspiring leaders recognize the diverse needs represented among team members and seek to understand the variations in their levels of intrinsic motivation. In short, strive for a balance between goal-oriented execution and fostering positive team dynamics.

> **Questions for Reflection**
> - Reflect on your own personal experiences and consider which type of leader you would find more comfortable to work with – the motivator who inspires or the implementer focused on execution?
> - Are you inclined toward motivating and inspiring, or do you resonate more with the implementation-oriented approach?
> - In your opinion, how crucial is it for leaders to strike a balance between goal-oriented execution and a well-cared-for team? How might an imbalance in either direction affect collaboration and overall team performance?

Stability vs. Change

It is commonly accepted that leadership is needed for change and transformation. In contrast to this generally held opinion is the question of whether effective leadership might not be better interpreted as the desire to preserve what has been achieved and to solidify what is currently working.

Those leaders who gravitate toward a "stability leadership style" exhibit a preference for establishing enduring rules and formalizing procedures. They tend to be defensive when asked to revisit their beliefs and approaches, using for their alibi the importance of consistency and continuity. For them, effectiveness is defined by the ability to minimize risks, avoid unnecessary interventions, and limit change. Stability, in the context of this leadership style, is synonymous with an attained sense of safety, overall well-being, role clarity, and well-maintained order. Valuing the security and assurance that stability brings to both team and organization, these leaders prioritize creating structured and predictable working environments and believe that this is how they can best take care of their team(s).

If leaders who are oriented towards stability can be characterized as cautious and guarded in pursuing transformation or growth, then individuals who are oriented toward change can be characterized as risk-taking, resolute, innovative, and open to pursuing alternatives to the status quo. However, such leadership is at times liable to introducing chaos and instability into an organization, potentially undermining its existing order. The change-friendly leader usually has somewhat hurried decision-making and also creates the impression that when change is required, this kind of leadership embraces changing everything all at once, instantly and without question. This can be a downfall of this leadership style.

> **Key Recommendations**
> Today's rapid changes in so many different areas of life create a pressing need for leaders capable of realigning their teams and organizations to fit new realities into the existing framework. However, such leaders also need to understand which facets of organizational life should remain intact and where teams need a consistent level of internal continuity and stability.
>
> When initiating changes, it is essential to approach issues sensibly, considering such factors as the necessity for and speed of change, people's readiness for change, and the presence of an optimal and wise plan with which to implement the changes. Change for the sake of change cannot

be considered effective leadership. At times, it is necessary to preserve and nurture what has already been proven successful in practice. So, as the common saying goes, "If it ain't broke, don't fix it!" An excessive number and frequency of changes will only lead to disorientation and to the discrediting of new proposals.

Questions for Reflection
- Why change something if it is only for a short period?
- Have you ever had to react to abrupt changes on short notice? What steps did you take, and what did you change?
- In your field of activity, how do you maintain what has proven itself to be successful, while at the same time, making necessary changes due to changing circumstances?
- What are your thoughts on striving for a balance between embracing change and preserving stability? Do you perceive a tension between the two?
- Reflecting on the Christian notion of a kingdom marked by love, justice, peace, and order, how can leaders strike a balance between the pursuit of change and the preservation of stability within their teams and organizations?

Competition vs. Partnership

Often discussions on leadership revolve around the archetype of the leader as a warrior or champion. The dominant notion is that leadership success is linked to battling competitors and challenges in the market. In this vein, the successful leader is the one who emerges victorious in the battle or competition, the victory attributed to their individual strength, intelligence, toughness, and self-driven determination. This perspective suggests that leadership effectiveness can be reduced to something like a claim that success comes from simply outshining rival competitors through a combination of superior attributes and skills. In other words, leadership is first and foremost about gaining a competitive advantage.

However, leadership scholars and practitioners are increasingly exploring alternate ways to define leadership than the one focused on competitiveness and the leader's attributes. They seek a description of leadership which reflects shared vision, commitment, resources, and success. The growing sentiment is that we need an approach to leadership that fosters efficiency and success through collaborative effort and partnership. This shift in perspective underscores the value of shared goals, mutual commitment, and the optimization of resources.

Some years ago, I developed and led a leadership program for a group of small business companies owned by a former student of mine. This entrepreneur implemented a merit-based pay system to motivate employees to excel at their jobs. High performers were financially rewarded for their dedication and achievements. The goal was to inspire employees to consistently deliver their best. Overall, it was an honest and transparent system and seemed to result in higher job satisfaction and an increased morale. However, a significant challenge emerged. Some employees fell to the temptation to outperform their peers at any cost. Inexperienced employees began to experience discouragement and felt undervalued despite their best efforts. Collaboration and knowledge-sharing took a backseat as employees focused more on personal successes in order to secure the higher pay. A competitive environment had set in, hindering collaboration and teamwork.

The line between competitive and partnership-oriented leadership is a narrow one, as competitive approaches often do result in successes. Partnership-oriented leadership, akin to a more friendly contest or match, prioritizes joint practice and the creation of something new through collective action. It often takes more time to set up and is difficult to maintain if there is high employee turnover.

Effective leadership is usually achieved through commonly held values and goals, though, admittedly, satisfying all parties' interests may not always be possible. In a highly competitive environment, on the other hand, individuals assume either a radical, self-compromising approach, sacrificing their needs for the sake of others, or a radical competitive style that strives to win at any cost. These extremes, while not always effective, highlight the challenging balancing act between the surrendering of one's autonomy versus a relentless scrambling to be at the top.

Key Recommendations

Effective leadership requires balancing competition with partnership. Teams and organizations can create a competitive environment that promotes growth, collaboration, and positive individual development. Yet it is important to minimize negative aspects often associated with unhealthy competition. In most cases, it is wise to adopt a collaborative leadership style that prioritizes shared visions, commitment, and success. Valuing collective endeavors and the optimization of resources through partnership can help steer you away from an overly competitive mindset.

If the framework of partnership-oriented leadership is more appealing to you, try adopting an active listening approach. Be willing to listen and understand your employees and collaborate with them to achieve common goals. Demonstrate openness and an interest in mutual success along with the expectation of results.

Questions for Reflection
- Are you willing to compromise your individual interests for the sake of common goals? How about sacrificing your own interests for the benefit of others?
- If you align with common Christian principles in your work, which leadership style do you find more fitting: competition-oriented or partnership-oriented? Between these two styles, which one aligns more with your preferences? Do you find it easier to compromise (adapt) or stand your ground (compete)?

Domestic vs. International

In today's world, we interact with individuals from different cultures and backgrounds on a regular basis, often as part of our professional commitments. It follows, then, that understanding and bridging cultural differences will play a vital role in effective leadership in any organization. In fact, cross-cultural competence looms as a must for any organization that wishes to be effective either locally or globally, domestically or internationally.

Cross-cultural leadership, however, may be adversely impacted by two particularly pertinent types of bias:

1. Some leaders have a negative bias toward those of cultures other than one's own; an unhealthy ethnocentrism. With the relatively recent rise of so-called "identity politics," ethnocentrism as a phenomenon has assumed somewhat of a universal scale. Its potential danger lies in the belief that one's own particular racial, ethnic, linguistic, or cultural group serves as the banner by which all others are to be judged. Uncontrolled, however, toxic ethnocentrism hinders the ability to objectively assess the ideas and behaviors of team members from different cultural groupings or to recognize and appreciate the *distinctive* aspects that they bring with them to an organization due to their cultural traditions and practices.

2. Some leaders are typical representatives of their local culture, and within that local context, may be viewed as highly effective. They see the world around them as a single, uniform space. As a result, they choose the one seemingly tried-and-tested leadership style that they have found successful for themselves, and they apply it in all circumstances, disregarding any possible accommodation to ethnic or cultural differences. These myopic leaders seek to generalize their mode of interacting with all others beneath them. They are unusually strong advocates for universal standards, values, norms, and approaches to be observed by all team members.

In contrast to this brand of leader, are other leaders who understand that what works effectively in one situation with certain people may not necessarily work the same way in another setting with different people. These leaders acknowledge the existence of numerous culturally diverse societies within the workplace, and they take into account the distinct and unique characteristics of those local cultures and the various needs people might have in that particular global region.

Key Recommendations

It is naive to assume that we live in a relatively simple and uniform global society and that, accordingly, what works domestically (locally) is applicable internationally (globally). Give due attention to the similarities and differences that exist between various international and ethnic communities. Effective leadership devotes well-advised consideration to the values and traditions shared commonly within any given people group.

Leaders of international and multiethnic teams can enhance cross-cultural leadership effectiveness by emphasizing competence development, cultural sensitivity and understanding, bias mitigation, flexibility in leadership styles, avoiding generalizations, facilitating cross-cultural training, and celebrating diversity within a team environment.

Questions for Reflection
- How do your Christian beliefs influence your perception of people who hail from different cultures?
- Have you ever worked on a team consisting of individuals from various cultures? What challenges did you face?
- What did you learn from your experience of interacting with people from different cultures?
- Provide examples of local and global (international) leadership. Which of them demonstrated the effectiveness of one approach over another? Why?

Endnotes

1 Gill, Roger. *Theory and Practice of Leadership*. 2nd ed. Sage, 2011, p. 288.
2 Northouse, Peter G. *Leadership: Theory and Practice*. 9th ed. SAGE, 2022, p. 6.
3 Yukl, G. A. & William L. Gardner. *Leadership in Organizations*. 9th. ed., Pearson, 2020, p. 26.
4 Gosling, J., Sutherland, I., Jones, S., & Dijkstra, J. *Key Concepts in Leadership*. Sage, 2012.
5 Adair, J. *Action-centred Leadership*. McGraw-Hill, 1984; Adair, J. *Develop your leadership skills*. 5th ed. Kogan Page, 2022.

In tandem with their personal spiritual journey with God, our future leaders need environments that encourage participation, nurture diverse talents, and foster collaborative experiences.

CHAPTER 9

LEADERSHIP FORMATION AND LEADERSHIP DEVELOPMENT

1. ILLUMINATING THE PATH

The path to becoming a better leader – or better follower – is not a prescribed formula but rather an intricate interplay of self-discovery, determination for growth and change, and positive interaction with external events or opportunities for development.

In chapter 3, we talked about the profound influence that Andre L. Delbecq has had on my understanding of leadership formation and leadership development. Delbecq, a longstanding professor at Santa Clara University and Senior Fellow at the Ignatian Center for Jesuit Education, posits that leadership formation is rooted in spiritual wisdom, while leadership development is grounded empirically in the social and management sciences. He doesn't argue, however, that these two aspects of leadership are mutually exclusive of each other. There is, he emphasizes, within effective leadership, a definite interconnection between the two. Inspired by Delbecq and other mentors like Margaret Benefiel and Jody Fry,[1] I advocate for an integrative approach to leadership maturation. Such an approach encompasses acquiring leadership skills, cultivating character, and nurturing well-being and spiritual formation.

In this chapter, I examine at length both leadership formation and leadership development, two distinct but not separate concepts. I'll be guided in this investigation by the lessons I've learned from my personal research and leadership practice. As we venture into this exploration of leadership formation and leadership development, allow me to begin with three stories. Along with other case studies that will serve as signposts pointing the way in our growing understanding of these important concepts.

Factors Affecting Leadership Formation

If we're to make progress in leadership formation, we first need to ask what the main factors are that give rise to it. Some years ago, I had the privilege of undergoing training in the leadership program offered by the University of Cambridge Institute for Sustainability Leadership. Tailored for business leaders aiming to enhance their leadership skills and to drive sustainable change within their organizations, this program provided me with many valuable insights and perspectives.

During one online group chat with fellow learners, I immersed myself in discussing the roots of leadership success. At one point, the conversation took an unexpected turn to the relevance of the ethical teachings of Jesus as they might bear upon modern business practices. A European corporate executive ignited the discussion by putting forward a thought-provoking question: could following the principles taught by Jesus truly pave the way to success in today's world? His strong skepticism resonated deeply with the group, sparking a robust exchange of ideas. Some questioned the compatibility of Jesus's teachings with the relentless pursuits of modern business practices. In contrast, others emphasized that Jesus's prioritizing of compassion and humility doesn't necessarily entail passivity or lack of ambition. Somehow, our discussion ended with recognizing the importance of Jesus' ancient community as an important factor in the character formation of early Christians. In this regard, all agreed that in being part of a supportive community of like-minded individuals, we will cultivate the virtues necessary to lead with compassion, humility, and resilience. A supportive community provides emotional encouragement, strengthens accountability, offers diverse perspectives for problem-solving, and creates a sense of belonging that can help individuals in their journey of life.

My training at Cambridge coincided with a reflective reading of Eugene Peterson's *The Jesus Way*. In this book, Peterson stresses that following Jesus Christ and heeding his wisdom yields positive formative results. He writes, "I am interested in the ways Jesus leads because they are necessarily the ways by which I follow. I cannot follow Jesus any which way I like. My following must be consonant with his leading. The way Jesus leads and the way that I follow Jesus are symbiotic."[2] This statement made a profound impact on me. Knowing God, learning from Jesus, practicing the way of Jesus, and belonging to a healthy Christian community are all essential for forming spirituality and authentic leadership.

A Vision for Leadership Formation

During my inaugural year as the president of St. Petersburg Christian University, I immersed myself in the critical strategic planning process. Collaborating with a fellow colleague who expertly guided the endeavor, we navigated a series of thought-provoking questions designed to steer my team's journey in crafting our strategic vision, goals, and initiatives. Our overarching mission and vision were consolidated into a first draft of a strategic plan. Amid further inquiries into more detailed methodologies for developing a refined strategic plan, two questions resonated deeply with me: (1) What kind of people must we be to lead the university toward our strategic goals, and (2) What brand of leadership do we need to cultivate within the university? These questions underscored the undeniable interconnection between leadership development on the one hand and organizational development on the other. Remaining static as a leader isn't an option, for without personal evolution in this role, an institution's progress is also compromised.

Two important principles imprinted themselves upon me from this experience: (1) leaders must embrace personal growth and spiritual formation to effectively lead an organization or a team through changes necessary to growth; (2) leadership development should be an integral part of the strategic planning process.

Nurturing the Desire for Change

In June 2023 amid the ongoing war in Ukraine, the Hodos Institute in collaboration with Ukrainian partners, hosted a conference titled "Leadership Today and Tomorrow." This event centered on addressing leadership issues significant to the Ukrainian people, not only within the context of the ongoing war but also within the rebuilding process. During the conference, one participant expressed his view on the future of leadership development in the country by suggesting that Ukrainian colleges and universities need to "build" or "develop" a specific type of leader. In response to this view, Mihail Krikunov, a prominent leadership expert and dean of Kyiv Business School in Ukraine (and also a good friend of mine) offered a witty and insightful retort. He playfully emphasized that leaders cannot be developed or constructed like buildings. He debunked the notion that leaders can be manufactured or molded at will. Instead, he underscored the importance of facilitating leadership development or formation for those who genuinely *wish* to transform and enhance their leadership capabilities. I wholeheartedly concur with his viewpoint!

This account suggests at least two important insights: (1) Leadership development is not about creating leaders from scratch, but rather about facilitating the growth and enhancement of innate and existing leadership qualities; (2) Leadership development should be a process that supports and empowers individuals in their journey to become better leaders and followers, rather than creating leadership traits artificially.

2. THE KEY ELEMENTS

There are those who think leadership ability is a trait with which an individual is born, a personal quality endued by birth. Others think good leaders are fashioned through hard work and learned experience. Prevalent also among some is the idea that sometimes unexpected situations give rise to a leader even if that individual has had no previous leadership aspirations. Most leadership researchers and practitioners agree that genes are important factors in determining the likelihood of one becoming a leader; but they also point out that human beings are much more than the mere product of their genes. Childhood, social, and spiritual environments, combined with educational and work experiences are significant driving forces in a healthy leadership mindset and practice.

Spiritual, ethical, and effective leadership is modeled by distinctively different individuals and to varying degrees. The key to appreciating how such leaders emerge is the understanding that leaders, regardless of whatever background, personality, or level of development can progress. It is more than possible to mature in leadership if the mindset, attributes, and skills that are integral to success are nurtured and refined. If leadership potential exists, developing that potential is always possible.

How then is leadership potential developed? Roger Gill rightly says, "Developing leadership potential is a combination of the accidental, the incidental and the planned. All of us have the potential to improve our leadership effectiveness, some more than others for various reasons."[3]

Following are some of the more common and important understandings of what constitutes effective leadership formation:

1. Leadership formation is a response to knowing God and self. Christian spirituality stresses the importance of both knowing God and knowing oneself in relation to God. For its part, leadership formation originates as a response to God's grace that is active in one's life, a response that is subsequently characterized by faith, obedience, transformation, and alignment with God's will in every area of life and leadership. Over time, seeking an ever deeper and more meaningful relationship with God and engaging in an ongoing self-examination in light of God's truth and righteousness become the hallmarks of leadership formation.

This seeking of God and engagement in self-reflection, in turn, translates into a continuous process of spiritual growth and formation that is empowered by the Holy Spirit. We might say, then, that spiritual formation, and by extension, leadership formation, is a response to God's invitation to personal transformation. God achieves this transformation through conviction for sin, revealing truth, renewing minds, empowering change, producing fruit, and fostering community and fellowship within the body of Christ. And, to emphasize the point once again, followers of Jesus who develop a deep personal knowledge of God will also find themselves experiencing a profound understanding of themselves. As David Benner writes, "Paradoxically, we come to know God best not by looking at God exclusively, but by looking at God and then looking at ourselves – then looking at God, and then again looking at ourselves."[4]

2. Leadership formation is a process. Leadership formation (or development) is not an event or occurrence but rather an ongoing and dynamic progression that unfolds over time. It's a journey characterized by continuous growth, refinement, and adaptation. While a single book, course, or brief workshop may offer valuable insights and tools, true leadership formation requires a sustained and deliberate commitment. The journey, in all likelihood, will also encompass missteps and unexpected obstacles. Embracing, however, the notion that growth often emerges from setbacks can lead to a more resilient and adaptive leadership approach. Those setbacks become an integral part of nurturing well-rounded and effective leaders.

It's important to say that no one travels very far along the path into leadership formation without first observing and experiencing the following three spiritual requisites: encountering God, making space and time for contemplative reflections, and engaging with others who share the journey of following Jesus Christ.

3. Leadership formation is holistic. Leadership formation should be centered around not only professional growth, but also personal and spiritual growth. On the one hand, leadership formation entails enhancing professional leadership techniques and acquiring vital and meaningful leadership competencies. On the other hand, however, it's equally concerned with delving into the depths of self-awareness, emotional intelligence, and ethical principles. A balanced approach to leadership formation (or development) encourages leaders to adopt a holistic perspective that goes beyond the mere professional and career aspects of leadership to acknowledging the significance of reflecting on one's character, values, and life experiences.

Through this harmonious fusion, individuals nurture a form of leadership that transcends mere titles and positions. It's the holistic approach that extends beyond the bounds of professionalism, reaching into the personal and inner spheres of one's being (to be a better person), rather than simply doing (to become a better professional).

4. Leadership formation is collaborative. How well leadership formation works depends on the willingness of both individuals (and the groups or organizations to which they belong) to obligate themselves to growth and development of leadership skills. It is a collaborative journey that requires a synchronized effort, an alignment of objectives, and a shared commitment to growth. It's important to remember that if an individual is not actively interested in becoming a better leader, even the best of leadership programs will make little or no difference towards accomplishing that end.

5. Leadership formation involves a long-term strategy. The questions of "why" and "for what" hold greater significance in leadership formation than does the question of "how." Whether considering personal or organizational leadership, successful leadership formation is contingent upon the presence of a comprehensive, long-term strategy that outlines the reasons and methods for cultivating leadership. The dynamics of leadership formation are linked to the existence or absence of such an overarching strategy. When understood that positive outcomes of leadership formation (or development) are rooted in a clear framework of future aspirations, both individuals and the organizations with which they are affiliated are guided toward a trajectory of sustainable and purposeful growth.

6. Leadership formation is experiential. While mentally grasping leadership principles is crucial, the heartbeat of maturity lies in acting upon those principles. Genuine understanding and significant growth come not from passive observation, but in actively participating in the leadership process and in embracing the experience resulting from that participation. In James 1:22, there is a powerful message in this respect: "Be doers of the word, and not hearers only, deceiving yourselves." Here "the word" refers to instructions given by God. James is encouraging his readers to hear or understand these instructions not merely at the bare intellectual level, but in the interest of true growth and transformation. In the context of leadership formation, this verse serves as a reminder that true growth and improvement come from far more than just cognitive learning.

7. Leadership formation, similar to leadership development, requires and cultivates different intelligences. Ronald Riggio, professor of psychology and distinguished leadership scholar, says that while possession of a high IQ is important for good leadership, it's not the sole determinant. He points out that "emotional and social skills represent the basic "building blocks" for the "soft skills" that are needed for leaders to be successful."[5] Highly intelligent individuals may excel in certain areas such as verbal communication, analytical and problem-solving, or strategic planning, but it's nonetheless true that *bona fide* leadership also requires well-developed emotional, social, spiritual and other intelligences.

8. Leadership formation is empowered by constructive feedback. Essential to leadership formation is feedback provided by those who observe and are affected by the behaviors of the leadership under which they operate. Feedback serves as a mirror that reflects actions, decisions, and interactions, allowing those who lead to see themselves from an external and more objective perspective. This external appraising is invaluable as it unveils blind spots, illuminates strengths, and reveals areas for improvement. Constructive criticism not only helps in acknowledging missteps but also serves as a useful guide for those in leadership positions towards adopting meaningful course corrections. I think that having a spiritual guide or mentor can provide profound insight and wisdom, further enriching the process of self-discovery and leadership formation. Their guidance often helps leaders align their actions with deeper awareness of God and relationships with God, offering a unique perspective that complements feedback from other sources.

9. Leadership formation is about personal drive. Self-development and the desire to excel are pivotal factors in leadership maturity. When individuals lack this desire and the personal drive behind it, imposing upon them leadership development concepts and practices can actually be counterproductive. In *Hardwiring New*

Leadership Habits, author, Dick Daniels, emphasizes that effective leadership development should include three essential dimensions: performance, potential, and personal drive.[6] While it's logical to invest in individuals who demonstrate strong performance and high potential, Daniels highlights that personal drive is in fact the pivotal factor! It's the differentiator between those who merely settle for average outcomes and those who genuinely excel in their roles and leadership positions.

10. Leadership development and leadership formation require a diversity of pedagogical approaches. Successful leadership development combines various methods of instruction with different learning styles, successfully engaging participants at all levels of development. A ready mix of such leadership development approaches are available for today's churches, business firms, and nonprofits to facilitate their development programs. These include workshops and seminars, experiential learning, mentorship and coaching, project-based learning, self-assessment tools, e-learning, case studies, group discussions and peer learning, guest speakers, site visits, field trips, reading assignments, skill-building exercises, networking, peer interaction, and personal reflection.

11. Leadership development reaps what it sows. In the teachings of Jesus, there is the profound wisdom that echoes through the ages: "A good tree cannot bear bad fruit, and a bad tree cannot bear good fruit" (Matt. 7:18). This metaphor resonates far beyond its immediate agrarian wording. It's a reminder that the nature of a tree, its inner life and health, determines the quality of the fruit it produces. Followers often acquire the skills and traits of their leaders. Authoritarian, narcissistic leadership, recognized for its self-promoting and domineering nature, engenders an environment where authority and ego are paramount. In contrast, genuine servant leadership breeds a working environment rooted in humility, empathy, and a dedication to serving the needs of others. In the process of leadership development, it must always be remembered that individuals embrace the tenets of what they observe in their role models, whether good or bad.

3. CLIMBING LEADERSHIP MOUNTAIN

Leadership formation or development isn't confined to formal training but can also be cultivated through personal journeys, experiential learning, and authentic self-discovery. In this section, I'll link these ideas to the metaphor of climbing a mountain or traveling on a journey as a means of helping us to better understand the process of leadership development as a whole. I assume that you've done at least some traveling, and perhaps have even trekked through some challenging hills or mountains. Allow me, then, to begin this section with several probing questions:

- *Have you ever reflected on how your personal development is akin to a journey, and if so, what has this meant to you?*
- *What have you learned from this journey about yourself and others? How has this travel experience changed you?*

It's useful to think about leadership formation in terms of arduous travel, where individuals reflect on what they have learned. Traveling along on a journey offers valuable leadership insights, including the importance of vision and direction, adaptability and resilience, effective communication, trust and empowerment, continuous learning and growth, experiencing different leadership styles, and celebration and reflection. By applying these lessons, leaders learn to successfully navigate challenges, inspire their teams, and create a culture of achievement and growth.

Many books and articles have also been written to draw the parallel between scaling mountains and developing leadership, and there's a reason for this. Summiting a mountain is more than just conquering nature; it's a trial of resilience, adaptability, and strategic thinking. Additionally, it provides the opportunity to elevate self-awareness and to understand the value of serving and working with others. Whether traveling on a journey or climbing a mountain, the venture is often not a solitary one. Sharing information and providing/receiving support mirrors the art of communication in team leadership. Shared experiences in the midst of difficult moments bring forth character, virtuous behavior, and ethical fortitude. Perhaps the most profound lessons are found during those introspective moments experienced high on the mountain side. As climbers look inward, they discover their true selves and come into a more profound understanding of the need for personal growth in every area of life.

Rená A. Koesler, a former professor of Outdoor Education and Environmental Education at Longwood University, possesses a rich experience of climbing mountains. She notes that the untamed wilderness lays bare the inadequacy of measuring a leader's worth solely by his or her title, appearance, or academic credentials. The vast expanse of the wilderness serves instead as a setting for authentic leadership to shine. In her book, *Unflappable: Leadership Lessons from Climbing Mountains*, she says, "It is hard to be someone you are not in the wilderness, surrounded by daily uncertainties and the spontaneous adventures experienced along the way."[7] In other words, the mountainous wilderness strips away facades, pressing individuals to expose themselves as they truly are. It's in those moments that an open opportunity presents itself to the climber to embrace personal change and to take that next step along the way towards becoming a true and tested mountaineer. So it is also in the journey of developing into an effective, ethical, and spiritual leader.

Herta von Stiegel authored a book based on an expedition she led in July 2008 climbing Africa's Mount Kilimanjaro. She reveals that amid the expedition, she came to understand several principles that can be applied to organizational leadership:

- Not to stay too long at the mountain's summit (leaders who remain in power for extended periods tend to lose perspective and become consumed by power, status, and wealth)
- To value calling over skills (leaders who acknowledge having a calling report experiencing less job stress, longer tenures, and greater satisfaction in their endeavors)
- To appreciate the significance of authentic teamwork and feedback (leaders must adeptly handle criticism and esteem collaborative thinking over any sense of inflated self-importance).[8]

The Leadership Development Journey

As mentioned above, journeys, especially when arduous, provide opportunities for personal growth, learning, and expanding one's horizons. Being on a journey also provides the opportunity to consider the needs and well-being of others. Journeys are not only about resolutely pressing on, but also about finishing well. It's very exciting when a journey culminates in moments of celebration and thankful reflection. By way of imaginative comparison to a journey, leadership development, then, presupposes learning, growth, celebration of milestones and achievements, and the contributions of others toward one's development.

In his excellent work, *Leadership Development*, Ronald Riggio employs the journey metaphor to illustrate the gradual nature of leadership growth, a growth which overall he describes as requiring time, determination, and intentionality. Progress occurs in degrees, he argues, but actually takes place when individuals take personal charge over their own paths toward growth and excellence. Numerous avenues may exist to plan the long and winding journey of leadership development, select tools and resources may be readily available for the task, and various individuals such as friends, mentors, and supervisors may be there to aid in the process; however, the paramount factor, according to Riggio, still lies in "committing to the continuous journey of development."[9]

Riggio contends that within the leadership development journey, emphasis should be placed on cultivating self-identity,[10] gaining insights into personal traits, increasing self-awareness,[11] and monitoring shifts in leadership perceptions and practices. Such a journey parallels life's trajectory. For aspiring leaders, Riggio recommends serious reflection upon questions like "Where am I headed? What matters most? What lessons are unfolding?" These questions prove pivotal, especially when making critical decisions or otherwise facing moments of pressing concern. Should such self-deliberations unveil issues counterproductive to one's development, Riggio advocates for transforming such negativity into constructive action by taking positive steps towards improvement.

In the leadership development journey, it's important to review one's progress at various points along the way. As a guide to such reviews Riggio suggests a useful framework, one that emphasizes the importance of using multiple criteria for self-evaluation, and one which poses such reflective questions as the following:

- **Reaction Criteria** ("How do you feel about your development?"): On a scale of 1 to 10, how much do you believe you've improved your leadership since you began this journey?
- **Knowledge Criteria** ("What new knowledge have you retained?"): What have you learned about leadership? Name 3-5 key takeaways.
- **Behavioral Criteria** ("Are you behaving differently?"): Have others noticed positive changes in your behavior?
- **Results Criteria** ("Did you profit?"): Have your developmental efforts resulted in clear and positive outcomes?

4. A MULTIGENERATIONAL APPROACH

I define a multigenerational approach in leadership development as a strategy to create a lasting and positive impact on several generations. This approach recognizes the intricate interplay between different age groups and focuses on two primary objectives:

- Enhancing the leadership abilities of adults within a community or organization
- Shaping the development and growth of younger generations, including adolescents, young adults, and young professionals

In practice, this approach utilizes a dual strategy:

- A direct impact on both adults and youth
- An indirect influence on youth by empowering adults

I acknowledge the vital role of older generations in guiding and nurturing younger ones. Adults can and should learn the best practices on how to be most helpful to the youth of the day. One of the ways this learning could happen is through the creation of small groups where adults learn from young people themselves on how to be most effective in mentoring them. Small discussion groups and innovative leadership labs exclusive to adults could also serve as platforms to better equip them to transfer knowledge and experience from their generation to the next.

Leadership Development Extends Beyond Adults

The *hodos leadership* approach believes in leadership development beyond just simply adult-oriented paradigms. Leadership development should not be restricted to adults alone; rather, it should also be geared toward initiating and customizing such development for the younger generation as well.

When I was involved in launching a graduate program for leadership studies and training at St. Petersburg Christian University, I harbored some deep concerns. Foremost among those concerns was the reality that many students enrolled in the program were primarily preoccupied with how their training would benefit their personal lives and careers. Seldom did any of them explicitly express that their interest in leadership studies and development represented a step toward equipping themselves for growth among the younger generation.

It was my view, however, that leadership development is primarily about empowering the next generation. We **must** have a genuine interest and determination in implementing wise and creative approaches to leadership development among teens and youth. I think there are two main compelling reasons for this:

1. **Preparing for the present.** Within leadership development among youth, the focus shouldn't be restricted to just preparing for the distant horizon of adulthood. Instead, it's essential to recognize the significance of equipping young people to become better individuals and leaders now, given that their impact is already unfolding. They're active participants among their peers, within their families, and amid their social groups.

   By advancing the ideals of effective, ethical, and spiritual leadership among teens and young people, a ripple effect is set in motion that extends far beyond their immediate circles. The training in the ideals and practices of good leadership provides the much-needed attributes of discernment, resilience, courage, flexibility, humility, and service to others—all vital for facing the tests that confront today's youth. Many of today's challenges, such as social division, moral corruption, and technological ethics, require prudent perspectives and approaches. Engaging young people in leadership development equips them to tackle these complex issues with a sense of mission and responsibility.

2. **Preparing for the future.** Engaging young people in leadership development helps create a bridge between generations. Teens and young people represent the next generation of individuals who will impact the world either for good or bad. By investing in their leadership development early on, a continuous cycle of effective, ethical, and spiritual leadership is set in motion, the result being good leadership in the future.

Christian adults can and should play a pivotal role in nurturing essential character and leadership qualities among teens and youth, qualities such as:

- Appreciation for spiritual guidance: cultivating the habit of seeking wisdom through various Christian practices such as daily prayer and regular Bible study. Such practices foster a desire to follow Jesus' example by integrating his teachings into day-to-day activities.
- Wise discernment: making decisions in alignment with Christian values through thoughtful consideration.
- Altruistic love and service: practicing placing the needs of others before one's own.
- Humility and receptiveness: cultivating a receptive attitude to learning from others.
- Faith and hope: demonstrating trust in a higher purpose; and fostering willpower and optimism.
- Visionary thinking: exercising the ability to conceive a vision and to work toward a brighter future.
- A collaborative spirit: working harmoniously in partnership with others to achieve shared goals.
- Truthfulness, integrity, and ethicalness: upholding honesty, uprightness, and ethical conduct.
- Self-awareness: recognizing one's strengths and talents.
- Stewardship: taking responsibility for the care of God's creation (environmental responsibility).
- Justice and compassion: advocating fairness and assisting marginalized individuals.
- Appreciation and gratitude: valuing and acknowledging the contributions and service of others.
- Forgiveness: letting go of resentments and embracing the power of forgiveness.

- Critical thinking: engaging in independent and analytical thought processes.
- Discipline: skillfully managing time, tasks, and responsibilities.

Case Study: Leadership Formation Among Christian Youth

Between 2015 and 2017, along with a research team under my supervision, I conducted a study on leadership formation among young Evangelical Christians in Ukraine and several Eurasian countries. The objective of our study was to identify the principles and best practices for forming leadership among young people.

During the first phase of research (from January 2015 to February 2016) 500 individuals participated in our individual and focus group interviews, including (1) high-ranking Christian leaders, comprised of senior pastors and presidents of seminaries and mission organizations, (2) youth pastors and youth workers, and (3) Christian young people themselves. Thirteen open-ended questions helped participants to generate and express their views free from any undue constraints.

Among other items in our interviews and focus groups, we asked these questions:

- How do you understand leadership and leadership potential?
- How do your youth understand leadership? Give examples of leadership in their lives.
- How do your youth distinguish between positive and negative leaders?
- How is a leadership culture formed among your youth?

- Are there any leadership formation programs for youth in your church, organization, or school? By what criteria do you determine if those programs are effective?
- What do you think is necessary for the formation of leadership among your youth?

After analyzing the transcripts of these interviews, we developed an online questionnaire to dive deeper and collect information from a younger generation of Evangelicals. About 2,500 young Christians, aged 13 to 29, completed our questionnaire. We concluded our study by organizing several small conferences, during which we shared our findings with youth pastors from whom we also leveraged input into formulating principles and recommendations based on our collective research.

The following paragraphs both summarize the findings from our research and highlight practical insights that were gained.

Perceptions of Leadership

Some participants, especially those in conservative congregations, were cautious and suspicious about the use of the terms "leader" and "leadership." They considered these words to be "foreign," strange, unclear, and alien to their Christian faith. They felt that, as Christians, we are called upon to *serve* rather than to *lead*. To *lead* negatively suggested ruling, commanding, being first, or standing above others in a high-handed and authoritarian manner. Those respondents who demonstrated a negative attitude toward the words "leadership" or "leader" also tended to associate these words with greed, envy, unrestrained ambition, favoritism, financial dishonesty, the quest for power, and the pursuit of selfish aims. Such perceptions are nothing new: St. Paul, some 2,000 years ago, found them to be present among the citizens of Corinth, even after the recent introduction of Christianity into the city (read 1 Cor.). In our interviews, not surprisingly, respondents often reduced the concept of leadership to a particular leader whom they held in low esteem. They saw the role and views of followers (team members) as usually discounted or even ignored by this figure.

Most respondents from Eastern Europe and Central Asia tended to view leadership as not involving collaboration or teamwork that entailed interaction between leaders, and they viewed followers as being just as important as that of leaders. With the exception of Ukraine, a predominant view among our respondents was that transformation, change, and successfully meeting crises depended specifically on the few individuals who run organizations, parties, movements, churches, companies, and even countries.

The notion of leadership development prevailing among these youth boiled down to that of developing a few "great" *leaders* rather than developing good *leadership* and, more particularly, educating and promoting effective, ethical, and spiritual leadership among young people in general.

Generational Perspectives on Leadership

In Eastern Europe and Central Asia, as is probably the case everywhere, we can observe discrepancies between the values of the older generation and the ideals of the younger generation. However, the rapid economic, political, and social changes in the world over the last thirty years have led to a generation gap that today is much more obvious and deeper than in the past. Our study showed that many older people assume that, like themselves, young people also perceive leadership as "celebrity" or "popularity." However, fewer than 1% of young respondents in our study expressed such a view, a vivid example of the generation gap that currently exists in our understanding of how different generations view leadership.

Addressing this generational gap one respected church leader made this comment:

> *Instead of dialoguing with young people, the older generation pressures them. Young people are always considered wicked and wrong. There are few attempts to establish continuity, dialogue, and common language with our young people.*

Surprisingly, the older generation tended to have an optimistic view of the leadership potential of young people. Yet young people themselves tended not to estimate their own potential with any degree of positiveness at all. One student from Moldova, for example, unambiguously stated it this way:

> *My peers have potential. But it seems to me that they don't realize how great it [their potential] is. They need a push in order to see what direction to go. I need it too. The problem is that we are not even 80% sure of our true direction in life.*

Many young people whom we interviewed indicated that they had no concrete goals for the upcoming years. It appears that they needed the help of parents and mentors to identify their life goals. In this regard, they emphasized that such help would be most effective when provided within a relationship of trust and friendship rather than from "directives" and "orders."

In our conversations with established church leaders, we found a tendency on their part to focus on how to use or involve young people in church activities rather than on how to serve or help them grow. As one respondent said:

> *We are not forming them; we use them... and this is a tragedy.*

Among the older people surveyed, leadership was often seen merely as an exercise in inspiring people, motivating them, or calling them to action, but disregarding, however, other such important aspects of leadership as providing an appealing vision, mission, purpose, or setting an example of ethical behavior.

Another important finding from our research was that the younger people felt little or no prominence when it came to training their age brackets for leadership, and that it wasn't even understood that effective and ethical leadership depends on both leaders and followers. Young people also felt that taking or performing non-leader roles or positions didn't necessarily imply irresponsibility, blind obedience, or ineffective passivity.

Makeover From Bad to Good Leadership

Leadership development primarily arises out of the desire and necessity to grow a leader in the task of guiding and inspiring others. A second reason for leadership development is linked to the need to remedy ineffective or undesirable leadership behaviors, thereby assisting individuals in their desire to transform into a more skillful, moral, and spiritually effective leader. The need for such leadership development along these lines was all too evident in our research findings.

Most Protestant Evangelical Christians who participated in our study acknowledged that, alongside good leadership, "negative" leadership also existed within their communities. They characterized "bad leadership" as the pursuit of control, promotion of selfish interests, pride, dictatorship, lies, and greed—all problems standing in need of correction.

Many Christian young people indicated that within their churches, leadership excellence predominantly revolves around just one focus, such as knowing the Bible, actively engaging in church activities. At the same time, they felt organizational leadership and the moral integrity of church leaders was very important. Some young Christians also pointed out a systemic lack of interest among top Christian leaders in seeking proper feedback and in conducting regular evaluations of their own and other leaders' behavior.

Principles and Recommendations

Our research project encompassed not only the collection and analysis of data but also subsequent discussions of our findings with key youth pastors. Collaborating with them, our team formulated the following principles and recommendations that we believe hold significance, not only to Eastern Europe and Central Asia, but also far beyond.

- Developing leadership among youth requires adopting a holistic approach that places a premium on inner maturation. This necessitates consistent and structured engagement, not only on the acquisition and expansion of knowledge and skills but also on the cultivation of spiritual and character growth.

- Introducing all young believers to the idea that principles underlying team leadership are far more important than the attempt to develop a few "great" leaders among them.
- Helping young people identify their potential both as leaders and as followers, in and outside the church, and then assisting them in converting that potential into reality is a must.
- Learning and understanding leadership is better acquired and mastered within a group setting than it is in isolation. Collaborative work can help turn abstract concepts about leadership into effective and ethical applications at the practical level.
- Forming leadership through a mentoring process is one of the most important means by which young leaders and followers can be effectively trained. It is important to remember that today's younger generation isn't looking for mentoring that's reduced to the proverbial list of "dos and don'ts," incorporating a string of prohibitions, restrictions, or diktats from "the top down," but rather, they're looking for mentoring that comes by way of a good example, a relationship built on trust, and a demonstrated capacity and willingness for teamwork.
- Stating *what* needs to be done isn't merely enough when working with youth; it's also critical to explain *why* it needs to be done.
- Including young people in the formation and achievement of shared visions and goals is another necessity. The older generation must involve young adults in these processes rather than imposing their own visions and goals.
- Bestowing praise and appreciation are vitally important. Young people, like all of us, crave and need approval,

gratitude, and sincere acknowledgement of their efforts and achievements.
- Engaging in reflection and critical self-evaluation are crucial elements in the process of leadership formation. It's important to analyze both the process and the results of one's own personal performance and growth, as well as those of other team members with whom a leader or follower has been working.

5. LEADERSHIP FORMATION AND YOUTH

From research studies focused on leadership, a key factor identified in its development is that the seeds of leadership are often sown in our early years. Looking back and reflecting upon the formative influences and experiences that shaped us during our youth can prove very helpful. Such reflection can be facilitated by working through the following three questions. Thinking about them should shed valuable light on how those early encounters contributed to our personal leadership journey:

- Who impacted you when you were young? And how did they impact you?
- What do you think about leadership formation among adolescents?
- What in your opinion is essential in helping adolescents to team up and lead well?

Who, and how the "who" impacted us during our youth holds the key to understanding the foundation of our leadership inclinations. Perhaps it was a teacher who encouraged us to take charge in a group project, a family member who emphasized assuming responsibility, or a mentor who sparked our interest in guiding others. Recognizing our leadership influencers will help us trace the origins behind our frame of mind toward leadership.

Adolescence is a time of self-discovery, experimentation, and values shaping. It's during this period that the basic principles of how to communicate, engage in teamwork, show empathy, and practice decision-making begin to take root. Pondering what is essential in helping adolescents team up and lead well highlights the importance of providing the right environment in which they can accomplish these skills. Our future leaders need spaces that encourage participation, nurture diverse talents, and foster collaborative experiences. Instilling values like integrity, resilience, and adaptability at this stage of life lays a solid foundation for future leadership roles.

Research Insights from an Ukrainian Study

Several years ago, along with my colleagues at Hodos Institute, I studied how Ukrainian churches and other Christian organizations contribute to leadership formation among adolescents. We conducted interviews with 350 individuals and subsequently developed an online questionnaire. More than 1,300 Ukrainian adolescents participated in the survey. After several months of analyzing the collected data, we identified seven interconnected themes and practices that contribute to effective leadership formation among adolescents.

We organized these themes and practices into a model we call the "Pro 7." While they can be implemented individually, their true impact is realized when they are combined, for only then do they represent the most fruitful and well-organized approach to leadership formation.

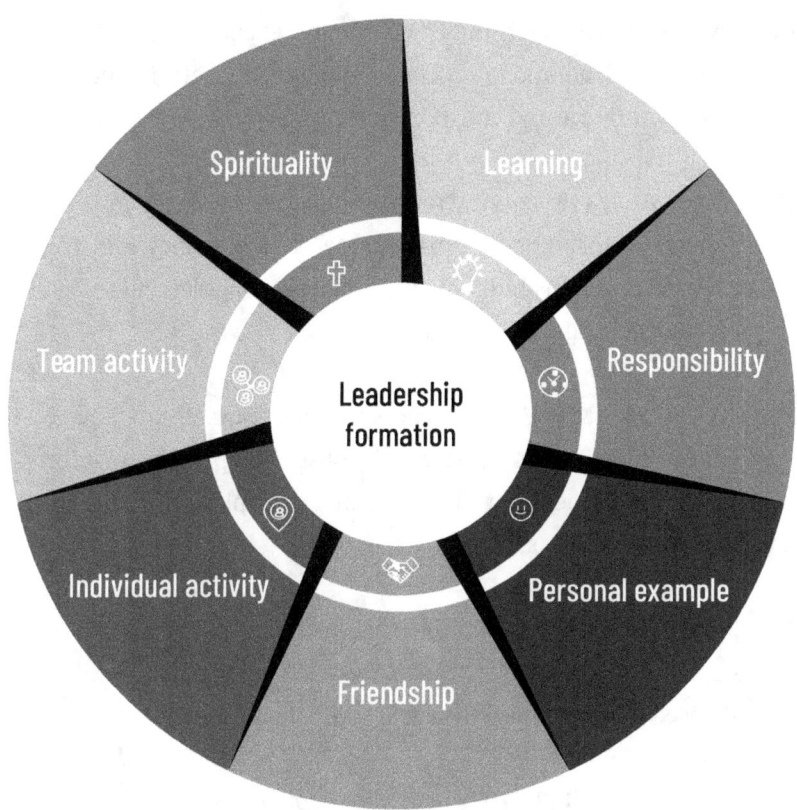

The Leadership Formation Model – "Pro7"

Following is a breakdown of the "Pro7" model into its seven themes, accompanied by a brief description of the mentoring attitude and practice that should attend that particular theme.

SPIRITUALITY: Spirituality forms the cornerstone of Christian leadership development. Guiding young individuals in seeking God, understanding his care for humanity, and recognizing his many and various revelations are essential aspects of leadership training.

LEARNING: Holistic learning is paramount, encompassing spiritual, intellectual, emotional, social, and physical facets, including hands-on experience and collaboration on practical projects.

RESPONSIBILITY: Mastering responsibility is crucial for youth. Observing such role models as parents, teachers, coaches, and others who exemplify responsibility plays a vital role in adolescents learning this important quality of character.

PERSONAL EXAMPLE: Adolescents emulate traits like personal discipline, diligence, and dedication by observing parents, mentors, and peers. The influence of these personal examples often surpasses that exercised by words.

FRIENDSHIP: A friendly environment fostered by mentors and peers cultivates trust and facilitates feedback and exchange, allowing adolescents to give and receive in equal measure.

INDIVIDUAL ACTIVITY: True maturity for adolescents stems from opportunities to independently tackle diverse tasks. Essential qualities like self-confidence and sense of responsibility are forged through such individual endeavors.

TEAM ACTIVITY: An adolescent's leadership development necessitates improving teamwork skills and fostering a sense of community. Engaging in collaborative efforts nurtures accountability, communication, mutual respect, personal and shared responsibility, and a desire to uplift others.

Moving the Focus from Youth to Adults

Our study on how Ukrainian churches and other Christian organizations contribute to leadership formation among adolescents also highlighted five principles that are as relevant and adaptable to adults as they are to adolescents:

1. **Acceptance, trust, and respect:** Like adults, adolescents also thrive in environments where they feel accepted, trusted, and respected. Creating a culture of respect and acceptance fosters a positive atmosphere and enhances collaboration among adults.

2. **Self-identity awareness:** Adults grapple with self-identity issues at various life stages. Encouraging self-reflection and understanding helps people navigate their own identities and enhance their self-awareness during these difficult moments.

3. **Talent discovery:** Adults, regardless of age, have untapped talents and abilities. Encouraging them to explore and utilize those talents can lead to personal growth and contribution within both their professional and personal lives.

4. **Project development:** Just as it is crucial to align projects with adolescents' needs, the same applies to adults. Tailoring projects to match adults' skills and aspirations can enhance engagement and productivity.

5. **Teamwork and collaboration:** Leadership development is equally relevant to adults as it is to young people, and fostering a culture of teamwork and collaboration remains pivotal to that development. Effective leaders, regardless of age, understand the value of collaboration and teamwork in achieving common goals.

6. LEADERSHIP DEVELOPMENT AND ORGANIZATIONAL CULTURE

Within any organization, leadership development is about nurturing leaders who reflect the organization's values, lead by example, and perpetuate a culture of authenticity. It acts as a catalyst for continual organizational success and sustainability. For those who focus on leadership development within an organizational culture, leadership signifies more than the mere accumulation of hard or soft skills; it embodies a comprehensive way of thinking on how leadership is perceived, practiced, and ingrained at all levels.

I have worked in various organizations, including an industrial plant, an institution of higher education, a local church, and a nonprofit. From these experiences, I can affirm that within leadership development exists an essential paradigm—one that is deeply intertwined in the culture of any given organization.

What is that paradigm? Let me ask you the following questions:

1. What is the prevailing culture functioning within your team, community, or organization?
2. How does this culture motivate and support leaders and followers to excel in their roles?

Pursuing our topic further, let me draw insights from a case study that exemplifies the fusion of culture, leadership, and faith-driven initiatives (the paradigm we just discussed). It's a case study that sheds light on the best practices for nurturing leaders within any specific organizational context.

Case Study: Christian Substance Abuse Rehabilitation Centers

The growing challenge of drug trafficking and substance abuse represents a global concern, prompting new efforts toward effective prevention, treatment, and harm reduction. Amid these challenges, numerous faith-driven initiatives and rehabilitation centers have emerged. These centers use a combination of conventional rehabilitation practices and spiritual guidance, prayer, biblical teachings, and faith-centered healing. The case study that follows delves into leadership formation and practices within these Christian rehab centers, exploring their strategies for nurturing effective leaders within an instilled culture of faith-based recovery.

Research Background

In 2017-2018, the Hodos Institute undertook a comprehensive study of leadership formation and practices within Christian rehab centers across Ukraine, Moldova, Kazakhstan, Russia and Israel. The study's aim was to identify optimal approaches for fostering leadership and mission development within these faith-based rehabilitation institutions. The study encompassed interviews with over sixty prominent leaders from these centers and further involved an online questionnaire completed by more than 500 respondents, including current and former staff members as well as clients. The majority of participants were in their 30s and 40s, with a quarter representing women. The respondents in this study shared valuable leadership insights.

Leadership Insights Emerging from the Study

1. The importance of spiritual transformation: Christian rehab centers emphasized that healing from addiction necessitates inner spiritual transformation rather than sole dependence upon medical or clinical interventions.

2. Leading through service: Leadership was understood as encouraging and guiding others to follow, with service being a vital component. Leaders within these centers were thus seen as servants who exhibited maturity, accountability, and a clear understanding of personal and organizational goals.

3. The tasks of organizational leaders: Key tasks for leaders in these centers encompassed facilitating spiritual formation, sharing the Gospel, acquiring resources, maintaining discipline, and grooming new leaders.

4. Love as a leading principle: Love emerged as the most influential and endearing quality for leaders. Individualized approaches, friendships, and mentorships built on love pave the way to freedom from addiction.

Leadership Formation Recommendations
- Embrace love as a foundation, aligning it with biblical teachings and contemporary theories of leadership.
- Prioritize spiritual formation to maintain a God-centered approach to leadership.
- Cultivate mentorship, accountability, and partnerships.
- Invest in personal and team development.
- Lead by example, combining sincerity with discipline.
- Implement an individualized approach while maintaining general order.
- Regularly evaluate outcomes, focusing on strengths.
- Extend leadership formation beyond rehab centers, equipping individuals for broader leadership roles.

Questions for Reflection
1. How can we integrate spiritual values to promote authenticity and growth within our own organization?
2. In what ways can we lead through service, fostering accountability and humility across all levels of our organization?
3. Based on the case study of rehab centers, what key leadership tasks can we effectively implement within our organization, irrespective of the economic, political, or social structure in which we may find ourselves?
4. How can we establish love as the cornerstone of our leadership approach, thereby nurturing trust and fostering strong relationships within our organization?
5. Drawing from the insights gleaned from the rehab centers study, how might we tailor and apply these leadership principles so as to excel within our organization, regardless of the specific sector of general society within which the organization may be located?

7. LEADERSHIP DEVELOPMENT IN NONPROFIT ORGANIZATIONS

Many are familiar with the somewhat lengthy, yet highly popular book by American author Jim Collins, *Good to Great: Why Some Companies Make the Leap and Others Don't*, published in 2001.[12] Together with a group of researchers, Collins unraveled the secrets of leadership existing among twenty-eight of the largest companies listed in the Fortune 500. Upon the basis of those secrets, Collins then formulated a development model to serve as a blueprint on how to transform a "good company" into a "great" one. The book has been translated into dozens of languages and to this day, is a must read for all those interested in leadership development.

Few know, however, that in 2005 Collins wrote a much shorter book titled *Good to Great in the Social Sector*.[13] This book, only thirty-five pages long (nearly ten times shorter) than the previous one, was originally conceived as a chapter for a larger upcoming book. Collins chose to publish it separately, noting that both books (the 2001 and the 2005 publications) could (and should) be read together.

Central to Collins' thesis in his two books is his belief that leadership knowledge and management skills in business don't provide answers for the needs of modern society. Although business, he argues, unquestionably acts as a vehicle in enhancing the world's standard of living, it doesn't, however, in any way act as one of society's moral torchbearers. According to Collins, the non-profit sector must turn to find the moral and spiritual purpose – the reason we live - that should characterize leadership in every sector of life.

According to Collins, the greatness of leadership in the best non-profit companies lies in the fact that they demonstrate the epitome of conscious moral choices and organizational discipline. This is what he calls ethical and effective leadership.

In my view, exploring how non-profits focus on leadership development holds significant importance for several reasons:

1. The success or failure in cultivating effective leadership within these entities directly influences their ability to address societal challenges.

2. In today's rapidly changing world, adaptability is invaluable. By delving into how nonprofit leaders navigate change and growth, adaptable leadership skills that are universally applicable across diverse contexts can be learned.

3. Nonprofits heavily rely on the dedication of motivated volunteers and employees. Studying how these organizations effectively motivate their teams provides valuable insights into how to engage talent, foster loyalty, and cultivate a culture of continuous learning and contribution.

4. Nonprofits often operate with limited resources. Learning from their resource management approaches not only inspires effective decision-making but also leads to the optimization of available resources and how to ultimately maximize their impact.

5. Nonprofits excel in creating environments that foster collaboration and innovation.

Case Study: Leadership Development and Corporate Governance

In 2019, I initiated a small-scale study with the aim of exploring the intricacies of board governance within non-profit organizations in Ukraine and its neighboring countries. The primary objective of this study was twofold: (1) to uncover effective governance practices; and (2) to identify areas of concern. To achieve this goal, interviews were conducted with seasoned board members from nearly twenty non-profit entities.

- Amid a range of open-ended questions, several probes were focused on leadership development:
- What are your thoughts on leadership development within your organization?
- What strategies do you employ to foster the leadership capabilities of your board and its individual members?
- How does your board assess its leadership and effectiveness?
- What factors have contributed to your personal growth as an effective team player? What obstacles have hindered your development?

The results revealed a surprising revelation: only three participants in the study indicated that their respective non-profit organizations intentionally emphasized leadership development for their board members. The absence of deliberate training and assessment, as reported by other participants, suggests a missed opportunity for non-profit boards to attain higher levels of effectiveness. The following two replies are typical of the responses we received:

> *Our board has never talked about evaluating our leadership. This question is interesting. Honestly, there is no self-assessment. It is something that should be done, but it never happened.* – **interviewee from Ukraine**

> *I have been on the board for a long time. I have never seen our board members learn about how the board should lead or function. This is a big drawback.* – **interviewee from undisclosed country**

Final Thoughts

Our research aligns with the commonly observed trend among non-profit organizations that more often than not, they are guilty of negligence when it comes to paying conscious attention to leadership development. A strategic commitment to leadership, however, could potentially enhance governance and overall organizational outcomes. The insights garnered from this case study underscore the need for distinct improvement in how non-profit entities approach their leadership development and governance strategies. However, this potential for improvement can only be realized if executive leaders begin to actively seek feedback and initiate self-assessment processes.

> **Questions for Reflection**
>
> After reviewing the case study cited above, take a moment to think about what leadership development in organizations should look like. In your reflections, consider the following questions:
> - What valuable lessons have you learned about leadership development with respect to teams or organizations?
> - How have these insights highlighted potential paths for enhancing leadership growth within your team or organization?
> - What strategies can you implement to foster leadership within your team, community, or organization?
> - How do you assess your own progress? How do you identify positive or negative shifts in your own leadership, as well as those within the individuals around you?

Case Study: Mentoring Among Christians Professionals

In 2017–2018, together with my research team from the Hodos Institute, I conducted a study on mentorship among Christians whose occupational status would clearly be categorized as professional. The study was conducted in Ukraine and its neighboring countries. We interviewed over 100 middle-aged professionals, with 30 percent of participants coming from the healthcare sector and the remaining individuals representing such various fields as education, technical specialties, creative professions (advertising, fashion, design, music, etc.), business entrepreneurship, psychology, economics, law, IT specialists, and so on. In this study, we gathered two main conclusions.

Deficit of Mentors

According to our research, the practice of mentorship among Christians, wherein older and more experienced Christians assist younger believers both spiritually and in their professional endeavors, is a rarity. Some respondents indicated that other Christians do guide them in spiritual matters (such as Bible reading and prayer, for example), but that this mentorship is not necessarily connected to their work and professional lives. An educator expressed it this way: "*Non-Christians form professional groups to support each other. We Christians don't engage in that. It's unfortunate. We're missing the opportunity to grow together, both spiritually and professionally.*"

Among our participants, around 30 percent revealed that they'd never experienced being mentored in their spiritual and professional journeys. Many of them stressed that they were navigating these journeys on their own. Another approximately 30 percent of participants disclosed that they'd never served as mentors or disciples to others. Pertinent to these findings and representative of medical doctors from the central part of Russia, for example, was the following comment:

> *"The situation with mentors is quite bleak. There's little interest in mentoring. I had to learn everything independently, both within the Church and at my workplace."*

Typical of many responses, a businessman poignantly shared,

> *"Coaching and mentorship are extremely valuable, and unfortunately, they've been lacking in my life. If I had a mentor with whom I could be open and honest, someone who wouldn't judge me or label things as 'good' or 'bad,' but rather help me grapple with my questions, I could have avoided numerous mistakes. I would have saved my time, nerves, and money."*

Search for Models

Our survey participants shared their expectations for effective, ethical, and spiritual mentors, outlining what they considered to be several desirable qualities.

They indicated that mentors should ideally be:
- followers of Christ (to provide support in the mentee's faith journey),
- experienced in both spiritual and professional aspects (with emphasis on the spiritual),
- admirable examples of professional and spiritual life,
- active listeners,
- sensitive to individual needs and interests (using flexible approaches),
- patient with mentees,

- skilled at asking insightful questions (recognizing the value of questions in the mentoring process),
- ready to build genuine and trustworthy relationships,
- open to mutual accountability and feedback,
- goal-oriented,
- dedicated to others' development,
- holistic in their approach (addressing spirituality, family, work, and other areas of life without arbitrarily segregating them into separate compartments), and
- attuned to emotions and feelings.

Remarks and Lessons Learned

Our research shows that mentoring should cover both faith and occupation. Experienced Christians in these areas should be encouraged to guide younger ones in their spiritual and professional journeys. If non-Christians support each other in the workplace, why should Christians not do the same? The church should help create such networks for learning and growing together!

The number of people mentoring or being mentored within the larger body of Christ is far below the level of what is needed. The cross-generational shortage in sharing wisdom relative to faith and career can only be rectified as churches encourage increased interaction and dialogue among different age brackets. It's only when such a cross-generational dynamic comes into play that the wealth of knowledge and experience possessed by the older generation can be effectively passed on to and benefit the younger generation.

If we recognize that good mentoring and coaching help form future church leaders, we must, then, learn to mentor and coach well. I believe the observations highlighted by our research naturally point to several recommendations that Christian communities can put into practice to do just that.

Here are three such recommendations:
1. Encourage Christian communities to embrace mentorship that encompasses both faith and career, recognizing the interconnectedness of spiritual and professional growth.

2. Foster the creation of mentorship groups and networks where experienced individuals can guide and support younger members in spiritual and professional matters. Promote intergenerational dialogue and learning.

3. Encourage Christians in the professional world to develop coaching skills so that they can provide support to other professionals in their spiritual and professional journeys.

8. SHOWING THE WAY: THE ROLE OF MENTORING AND COACHING

In referring to human development systems in various fields, psychologists and leadership specialists use different terms to denote specific forms of support and guidance—terms such as "mentoring," "coaching," and "facilitating." Coaching and mentoring share a lot in common, yet they are distinct and separate practices. It's often said that coaching is always a part of mentoring, but coaching doesn't always encompass mentoring. Many fine books have been written about mentoring and coaching. Two I highly recommend is, *Mentoring: How to Find a Mentor and How to Become One* by Bobb Biehl[14] and *The Coach Model for Christian Leaders* by Keith Webb.[15] Both are excellent reads.

Within the literature addressed to the topic of leadership development, the term "mentor" is often used to refer to advice-givers, those whose function involves acting as consultants relative to a specific situation or practice. The "mentee" is sometimes referred to as a protégé (from the French word that means "protected or sheltered"). A mentee is a person who receives a specific form of guidance or support from another. Both terms (mentor and mentee) typically refer to the interaction between two or more individuals with the aim of transmitting knowledge, professional skills, values, behavioral culture, and life wisdom from one to the other. Simply put, the mentor fosters the personal and professional growth of the mentee. It's an altruistic, selfless process; it's an interpersonal, voluntary partnership between two individuals, crafted for personal or organizational development. From a Christian perspective, Bobb Biehl's definition of the process is appropriate: "Mentoring is a long-term relationship in which a mentor assists the protégé in realizing the God-given potential within them."[16]

Coaches, like mentors, also initiate purposeful conversations and establish meaningful relationships. However, in their relationships with clients, coaches, unlike mentors, don't provide information, give advice, or issue specific directions. Instead of formulating tasks and specific solutions, coaches help clients explore and discover their own solutions by steering them in the right direction, rather than prescribing exact tasks or answers. The role here is to assist individuals in reaching an awareness of their responsibilities and then to guide them in fulfilling those responsibilities on their own initiative. This strategy is much more effective than burdening someone with "must do" and "how to do it right" statements. In terms of a Christian theological paradigm, one might say that "the coach seeks to help the coachee clarify what God is saying to him or her and assist them in discerning what it means to live that out."[17]

Dick Daniels in his book, *Leadership Briefs*, writes that communication in leadership development has more to do with the asking side of communication than with the telling side. In his view, sustainable leadership geared to leadership development follows the 25-25-50 rule: talking 25 percent of the time, saying what is useful for others to hear; asking 25 percent of the time, formulating penetrating questions to identify useful insights on the way to reaching important answers; and listening 50 percent of the time.[18]

Effective coaches conscientiously learn and cultivate this process, a process of combining wise instruction with thoughtful and perceptive questions in guiding their client's progress. Perfected, such coaching aids clients to independently determine what the next appropriate steps should be in fulfilling their leadership aspirations and assuming responsibility for the decisions and actions they take to fulfill those steps.

In both mentoring and coaching the process and outcome alike are essential. They prove to be effective when such factors as the following are considered:

- Mentors and/or coaches are well-trained and equipped.
- The mentoring and/or coaching process is well-designed.
- A direct link is established between the coaching and/or mentoring task at the input level and the outcome at the output level.
- Continuous assessment of the mentoring and/or coaching process is closely adhered to.

Mentoring and coaching are complex processes subject to a host of contributing factors. Some of those factors work towards positive outcomes, other factors not so much. Some mentoring, for example, might involve "bosses" mentoring through issuing orders; but this approach proves effective only for a short time. Later, new issues arise that mentees find they can't handle on their own, forcing them to resort to outside help. Independence and creativity haven't been adequately fostered to equip them to deal with these issues.

Assertive and dominant personalities that approach coaching primarily through doling out directives will invariably discover such a coaching style to be largely unsuccessful. More successful coaches focus on assisting their clients in learning how to independently seek and apply relevant know-how, formulate goals and strategies, and implement self-initiated tasks.

Mentoring and coaching that have a limited purview to that of just solving a specific problem or issue also operate on a misguided understanding of what these two concepts mean. Cultivating and supporting the spiritual, personal, and work-related facets of a mentee or coachee's life is what truly defines these terms. Such a process is only accomplished through a unique relationship in which each party interacts with the other on the highest levels of respect and trust.

Generally, mentoring and coaching are regarded as undertakings directed from adults to youths or from the more experienced and knowledgeable to the inexperienced. Mentoring and coaching can as easily and understandably occur between peers, old or young, as they can between those with similar backgrounds. Peer monitoring, in fact, is often much more productive than the more conventional hierarchical type, conducted as it frequently is in more informal and relaxed settings in which the conversation is more casual and the feedback between the participants equally mutual. The atmosphere created in such contexts is that of fellow companions journeying together along an adventurous path of growth.

What then, in conclusion, is the Christian perspective on mentoring and coaching? It's simply this: that mentors and coaches can achieve remarkable results by nurturing within themselves and those they tutor such virtues as integrity, trust, respect, sincerity, as well as humility, other-centeredness, service, and faith in God. They address more than just professional development with their clients; they strive also to facilitate the moral and spiritual transformation that produces ethically and spiritually motivated leaders. The concepts of mentoring and coaching are understood in the light of the most crucial aspect of life for all concerned in those processes, namely, the growth and maturing in one's relationship to God.

Endnotes

1. Benefiel, M. *Soul at Work: Spiritual Leadership in Organizations.* Seabury, 2005; Benefiel, M. *The Soul of a Leader: Finding Your Path to Fulfillment and Success.* Crossroad Pub. Co., 2008; Benefiel, M., and Michelle Abbott. "Spirituality and Leadership." *The Routledge International Handbook of Spirituality in Society and the Professions,* 1st ed., Routledge, 2019, p. 274-79; Fry, L. and Mark Kriger. "Towards a Theory of Being-Centered Leadership: Multiple Levels of Being as Context for Effective Leadership." *Human Relations* 62(11), 2009: 1667-96; Fry, L.W., and Melissa Sadler Nisiewicz. *Maximizing the Triple Bottom Line through Spiritual Leadership.* Stanford Business Books, an imprint of Stanford University Press, 2013.
2. Peterson, E. *The Jesus Way: A Conversation on the Ways that Jesus Is the Way.* Eerdmans, 2007, p. 8.
3. Gill, Roger. *Theory and Practice of Leadership.* 2nd ed. Sage, 2011, p. 324.
4. Benner, David. *The Gift of Being Yourselves: The Sacred Call to Self-Discovery.* InterVarsity Press, 2015, p. 27.
5. Riggio, Ronald. *Daily Leadership Development.* RiggioLeadership.org Press, 2020. p. 74.
6. Daniels, D. *Hardwiring New Leadership Habits.* Leadership Development Group, 2023, p. 52-53.
7. Rená A. Koesler. *Unflappable: Leadership Lessons from Climbing Mountains.* Summit Press, 2022, p. 4.
8. Herta von Stiegel. *The Mountain Within: Leadership Lessons and Inspiration for Your Climb to the Top.* McGraw-Hill, 2011.
9. Riggio, Ronald. *Daily Leadership Development.* p. 508.
10. Ibid., p. 15.
11. Ibid., p. 408
12. Collins, J. *Good to Great.* Harper Collins Publishers, 2001.
13. Collins, J. *Good to Great and the Social Sector.* Elements Design Group. 2005.
14. Biehl, B. *Mentoring. How to Find a Mentor and How to Become One.* Aylen Publishing, 2007.
15. Webb, K. *The Coach Model for Christian Leaders.* Morgan James Publishing, 2019.
16. Biehl, B. *Mentoring,* p. 19.
17. Webb, K. *The Coach Model for Christian Leaders.* Morgan James Publishing, 2019, p. 15.
18. Daniels, D. *Leadership Briefs.* Beavers Pond Press, 2015, p. 197-198.

In responding to this call and aligning yourself with divine purpose, you participate in the transformative work that brings glory to God's Kingdom.

THE NOW AND THE NEXT

Arriving here at this final section, you've stuck with me on this rather lengthy discussion on the *hodos* journey of leadership. I'm profoundly grateful to you for doing so. Thank you for your time and thoughtful engagement. I also hope that the book, with its emphasis on the journey-oriented metaphor of "showing the way," hasn't only opened your understanding to many different aspects of leadership, but has also encouraged you to advance good leadership in the different spheres in which you have influence.

Within the preceding chapters, I've addressed and explored with you various ideas and practices inextricably tied to leadership. They are meant for your reflection. So are the many thought-provoking questions and recommendations in connection with those notions. I trust you've found them to be helpful. Now, before you take leave, permit me to issue one final charge, a list of attitudes and ways of thinking you'll need to carry with you to be fruitful in all your future leadership endeavors.

Leadership's Ongoing Quest

What we understand about leadership today may not suffice for tomorrow and beyond. That being true, embracing continuous learning is absolutely crucial in preparing for the challenges that might arise tomorrow. Those challenges may well require that current convictions will need to be reshaped upon arriving at the next frontier. Today's understandings of leadership might be considered as "insights in transition" from "the now to the next."

Let me illustrate. The notion of servant leadership is well-known and widespread. For many years, I myself have advocated it as an excellent concept. In recent years, however, the whole philosophy of servant leadership has come under serious review. Researchers have demonstrated several pitfalls. Followers, for example, can exploit such leadership. Servant leaders themselves may struggle with role ambiguity, prove manipulative in how they use their leadership, be ineffective in dealing with crises, or perhaps not even be genuine in their servanthood. I highlight these research findings not to discuss the pros and cons of servant leadership but to point out, as this example so well demonstrates, the necessity of remaining open to continuous learning and inquiry. What we take for granted today may well be what is hotly contested tomorrow, requiring forward thinking leadership to meet the challenge.

Caring for Your Soul

Many of my wise friends and mentors often repeat phrases like "Care for your soul", "Keep your soul pure," and "Nurture your inner life" underscoring the importance of nurturing and protecting one's inner spiritual and emotional well-being. I too believe that looking after one's soul or inner self is necessary. Just as you would tend to your physical health, these suggestions advocate for actively caring for the deeper aspects of yourself.

Once, I had the privilege of speaking with Dr. Jene Maynard, the author of *Trekking: A Guidebook to Spiritual Transformation*. He advocates for nurturing an intimate relationship with God through various spiritual practices, which ultimately enrich our soul and transform our mind. Dr. Maynard rightly argues that soul health is essential, not optional, and poses a powerful question: "Who is the keeper of your soul?"[1] He then provides an answer: it is we, individually, who bear the responsibility for the well-being of our soul. Our well-being depends on how we invite and allow God to heal and renew our soul.

Our leadership journey "from the now and to the next" relies on our commitment to pursuing soul-deep healing and transformation. We must remain attentive to the well-being of our inner life, ensuring that we care for our own spiritual health before seeking to spiritually shepherd others.

Spiritual Detachment

Some modern influencers in personal development and psychologists suggest that making deep connections with others or pursuits to which we may attach ourselves should be balanced with a kind of emotional withdrawal or letting go from them. This withdrawal they refer to as spiritual detachment. Indeed, spiritual detachment is very important, particularly in a context calling for it. For instance, it's crucial not to overly attach oneself to the pursuit of material possessions, social status, or untrammeled pleasure in life. A countless number of other self-centered fixations could be added here, none of which could be said to pay any significant spiritual dividends.

Recently, I've read several books by David Benner, a well-known, Canadian-born psychotherapist whose insights on spiritual detachment I sincerely appreciate. He teaches that detachment, properly understood, is a philosophy of life that involves learning to hold onto things lightly. That is, not latching onto anything in life so tightly that we can't let go of it. From a spiritual perspective, observing this principle results in a heart so detached from everything else that it's then free to devote itself wholly to God, embracing him rather than something other as a substitute. When we're spiritually detached as described in this manner, from self, from others, or from whatever else, then we are all the more attached to God. Spiritual detachment always translates into spiritual growth - a growth that may be described as a shift and movement, typically *from* self-absorption *to* self-transcendence and *from* idolatry *to* worshiping the true God. God then transforms us to live and lead well.

Suffering

Certain types of suffering or contexts in which suffering may occur are not necessarily indicative of the kind of hardships that frequently befall spiritual, ethical, and effective leaders. Not all suffering inherently creates leadership, yet good leadership cannot be exercised without suffering. Actually, good leadership is a magnet for pain, and we all know how terribly painful change can be. Suffering is an integral part of life and thus, by extension, an integral part of leadership. Navigating through uncertainty, moving forward without adequate resources, facing adversaries, and charting unknown territories are just some of the prices to be paid in advancing the kind of leadership we've talked about in this book.

During the ongoing war of aggression that Russia has been inflicting upon Ukraine, the Ukrainian people have exemplified such character traits as duty, courage, responsibility, service, and strength in the face of great adversity. They've also shown profound compassion, evident in their tears of suffering. To be Ukrainian during these times, or otherwise to stand in solidarity with them, means to share in this suffering. For me, it's my home country, and it's personal. Compassionately suffering with others, especially the victims of unjustified violence, is the epitome of exemplary leadership.[2]

Vulnerability

Discussing leadership often revolves around attributes like courage, determination, resilience in the face of adversity, and securing noteworthy achievements. This narrative is all too pervasive, spawning a leadership culture synonymous with unwavering strength, remarkable success, and the archetype of the self-made individual. Such perspectives dominate our understanding of what it means to lead, shaping the aspirations and behaviors of emerging leaders who strive to embody these supposedly ideal traits. However, we need to remember that this conventional portrayal overlooks a critical leadership dimension that is deeply rooted in our human experience. That is: vulnerability.

To accept one's vulnerability is not a liability; it's part of our human nature. I strongly agree with such an affirmation! To be vulnerable is to be open about one's weaknesses, failings, and the unending human experience of not having all the answers. It's about pulling off the facade of invincibility and in its place, embracing the authenticity of one's true self with imperfections and all.

Resilience

Resilient individuals adapt to changing circumstances and unforeseen challenges, withstanding and bouncing back from the various difficulties that can easily derail the less resilient. A resilient leader serves as a positive role model, demonstrating how to cope with difficulties, handle pressures, and overcome the temptation to self-pity and capitulation.

For many years my wife Zena has been living with a diagnosis of multiple sclerosis. We're deeply grateful to God that the disease is currently in remission and not progressing. Zena is a testament to incredible spiritual strength and resilience. It's this resilience that's empowered her to navigate the emotional and physical complexities associated with her health condition. She faces each day with courage, purpose, responsibleness, service, and a sense of hope, in spite of her challenges and uncertain future. There's a daily example of resilience in my own home!

Thankfulness

Thankfulness should play a significant role in our lives. One of my mentors stated that in leadership, it's essential to understand where you currently stand, what you aspire to be, and how you remain grateful for everything in between. I concur!

By thanking the people we live or work with, we celebrate our mutual relationships and shared experiences, our interdependence, and a common sense of belonging. Expressing gratitude further cultivates an atmosphere of positive reinforcement, reciprocal respect, and mutual growth. Focusing on gratitude for others signifies a transformed and fulfilling life.

Knowing Goodness

As I conclude this book, I'm drawn back to the profound wisdom imparted by my grandfather, Oleksii Chumak. In recalling his words, "The most important thing in life is to know goodness," I'm reminded of the fundamental importance of all that goodness represents in my own life. It's a concept that requires deep spiritual contemplation. Yet, knowing goodness is not merely passive contemplation; it's a call to action. In responding to this call, aligning your leadership with divine purpose, you participate in the transformative work that brings glory to God's Kingdom.

As we navigate the complexities of leadership in an ever-changing world, let's hold fast to the timeless wisdom of seeking and knowing goodness. May it guide our decisions, inspire our endeavors, and illuminate the path forward as we strive to live and lead well.

What's Next?

This question addresses something more than the direction set by some action-oriented plan or another. It takes us back to the idea that *being* transcends *doing*. For Christians, a strong inner desire for Christlikeness should always be the priority. It's a blessing to every sphere of society, to the church, and to ourselves when Christians want to explicitly identify with Christ and be the people God intends them to be. It's truly exciting to be counted among those whom Dallas Willard calls *fortunate and blessed*: "those who are able to find or are given a path of life that will form their spirit and inner world in a way that is truly strong and good and directed Godward."[3]

Where Are We Going?

My prayer is that God will continue to guide us. May we see in our past actions leading to the present, and in our present actions pointing to the future, that the wise and judicious hand of God pilots us in the direction we should go. Yes, we can be confident that God will show us "the way." Philippians 1:6 says, "He who has begun a good work in you will carry it on to completion until the day of Christ Jesus."

As we conclude our exploration of leadership in this book, it's important to remember that **true leadership—rooted in spirituality, ethics, and effectiveness, and conscious of mindset, model, and maturity—flows from a deep relationship with God.**

Richard Foster emphasizes God's deep desire to commune with us in ever-growing intimacy. In his book on prayer, he writes: "Today the heart of God is an open wound of love. He aches over our distance and preoccupation. He mourns that we do not draw near to him. He grieves that we have forgotten him. He weeps over our obsession with muchness and manyness. He longs for our presence.... And he is inviting you—and me—to come home, to come home to where we belong.... His arms are stretched out wide to receive us. His heart is enlarged to take us in."[4]

Thank you for reading! If you enjoyed this book and found it valuable, I would greatly appreciate it if you could take a moment to leave a review on Amazon. Your feedback not only helps me as an author but also helps other readers discover this book. Thank you for your support!

Endnotes

1 Maynard, Jene. *Trekking: A Guidebook to Spiritual Transformation*. J. Maynard (self-publishing), 2023, p. 87.
2 See Negrov, Alexander and Ronald E. Riggio. *Leadership in Ukraine: Studies During Wartime*. Edward Elgar Publishing, 2025.
3 Willard, Dallas. *Renovation of the Heart*. NavPress, 2002, p. 20.
4 Foster, Richard J. *Prayer: The Heart's True Home*. Harper, 1992, p. 1.

ABOUT THE AUTHOR

ALEXANDER NEGROV, Ph.D., is a forward-thinking theologian and leadership researcher with over thirty years of teaching and leadership experience. As the founder and President of Hodos Institute, he leads efforts to impact leadership practices in the United States and his country of birth, Ukraine. He is deeply passionate about advancing spiritual, ethical, and effective leadership, as well as spiritual coaching and guidance. Dr. Negrov integrates all these practices into his broader leadership philosophy.

He holds two master's degrees, an M.A. in Old Testament and an M.A. in New Testament from Briercrest Biblical Seminary (Canada), and a Ph.D. in New Testament Studies from the University of Pretoria (South Africa). He has also studied leadership at the University of Durham, the University of Cambridge, and the University of Oxford (UK).

Alexander has served as President of Saint Petersburg Christian University and held visiting fellowships and adjunct teaching positions at several universities in the United States. He has been a member of the Society of Biblical Literature and the International Leadership Association. Dr. Negrov has presented at numerous academic conferences, published a range of academic books and articles in peer-review journals, and edited many volumes on theology and leadership.

Currently, he is actively engaged in research focusing on spiritual leadership and leadership development in both wartime and postwar contexts. He is the co-author of *Leadership in Ukraine: Studies During Wartime* and *Spiritual Leadership in Times of War and Peace*.

In addition to his passion for leadership and spirituality, Alexander enjoys hiking, reading good books, playing with his grandchildren, listening to jazz music, savoring great food, and engaging in meaningful, soulful conversations. He is a speaker, teacher, and workshop leader, bringing both expertise and personal warmth to his sessions and audiences.

Alexander is currently serving as one of the elders at Woodmark Church in Kirkland, WA.

Connect with Dr. Negrov
Email: alexander@negrov.com

LinkedIn: www.linkedin.com/in/anegrov/

ACKNOWLEDGMENTS

Gratitude pours from the depths of my heart to those who have walked beside me on this extraordinary journey called life, with a special acknowledgment of appreciation to my beloved family.

To my cherished wife, Zena, and our precious children and grandchildren, your steadfast love and boundless grace have been the foundation of my strength and resilience. I am very grateful to my Ukrainian heritage and my extended family, especially my parents and grandparents, who modeled for me how to live and lead well.

I am profoundly thankful to all current and past esteemed members of both the Governing Board and the Advisory Council of the Hodos Institute. They have graciously enabled me to focus on research and writing. While each member deserves individual recognition, I offer special acknowledgments to Mike Anderson, Dr. Bob Andringa, Allyn Beekman, Dr. Sharyl Corrado, Dr. Dick Daniels, Dr. Mark Elliott, Dr. Jason Ferenczi, Dr. Rich Gathro, Dr. Kathleen Mays, Dr. Patrick Mays, Dr. Anna Krull, Julie Peterson, Viktor Prozapas, Dr. Viktor Roudkovskii, Vladimir Shevchenko, Dr. Myron Steeves, Dr. Tim Watson, Dr. Michael Whyte, and Phil Young. Their intellectual and spiritual contributions have been indispensable.

I have had the privilege of delving into the realm of leadership alongside esteemed colleagues who have approached it from diverse perspectives. In this regard, I am particularly grateful to four distinguished scholars who serve on the Advisory Council of the Hodos Institute:

- Prof. Roger Gill, visiting Leadership Professor at Durham Business School, Durham University in the United Kingdom and a very dear friend and mentor, who has consistently encouraged me to adopt a holistic perspective on leadership and introduced me to the concept of leadership as "showing the way."
- Prof. Ronald E. Riggio, Claremont McKenna College, who has shared with me his invaluable knowledge on leadership scholarship, development, and the theory of transformational leadership.
- Prof. Louis W. (Jody) Fry at Texas A&M University-Central Texas, who has guided me in embracing an academic approach to spiritual leadership.
- Prof. Jean Lipman-Blumen, Claremont University, whose insights have illuminated my thought in the areas of connective leadership, followership, and toxic leadership.

I have also had the privilege of conducting research in biblical studies and hermeneutics under the guidance of Prof. Dr. Jan Gabriël Van der Watt, a prominent New Testament scholar from South Africa. Through his mentorship, I have gained insights into the importance of universal metaphors in comprehending what I refer to in chapter two as the realities and experiences (leadership being one of them) common to all human experience. Prof. Jan Van der Watt is widely acclaimed for his monograph *Family of the King: Dynamics of Metaphor in the Gospel According to John*, solidifying his international reputation in the field of New Testament scholarship. I extend my heartfelt gratitude to Prof. Jan for decades of friendship and exemplary leadership!

I initiated work on this book during the 2012-2013 academic year at California Baptist University (CBU). I owe special gratitude to Dr.

Ronald L. Ellis, who continues to effectively serve as the president of CBU. Dr. Ellis facilitated my sabbatical for me and my family and imparted numerous invaluable leadership lessons during our regular one-on-one conversations.

Throughout my Christian journey, I have been blessed with spiritual guidance from remarkable pastors and spiritual guides. I would like to extend special appreciation to the late Rev. Buddy Ellis (Wenatchee Valley Baptist Church, Wenatchee, WA), Pastor Russell Korets (Woodmark Church, Kirkland, WA), Dr. Tom Lance (The Grove Community Church, Riverside, CA), Dr. Margaret Benefiel (Shalem Institute), and Dr. Vicki Scheib (Sustainable Faith School of Spiritual Direction).

Deep gratitude resonates within me for my students, colleagues, and clients who continuously engage with my work, probing it with thoughtful questions and pushing me to new horizons. Their invaluable feedback illuminates the path forward, guiding me toward refining my leadership theory and practice.

I am deeply grateful to the hundreds of organizational leaders across various sectors in the United States and Ukraine (and other countries) who have generously shared their time and insights during interviews that drew upon their leadership wisdom and recommendations. Their willingness to impart their expertise has enriched my understanding immensely, and I am sincerely thankful for the invaluable lessons learned from these practitioners.

The realization of this book would not have been possible without the multi-year collaboration with my esteemed colleagues, particularly Dina Polishchuk (formerly Prokopchuk), Oleksandr Malov, and

Alexey Belov. Their invaluable insights and research support have been instrumental in bringing this project to fruition.

I am very grateful to my special and lifelong friend, Andy Brewer, who read and edited the entire first draft of the book with the task of improving my English. I also appreciate Heidi Sheard for editing the final draft, making the text more readable, and Kendal Marsh for designing the cover and interior layout.

I am truly blessed! To believe in Jesus Christ—the Way, the Truth, and the Life—and thereby to know God is to be blessed beyond all measure. I thank God for his love, a love that encompasses all creation, including you and me!

INDEX

A

abuse of power, 142, 214
acceptance, 72, 130, 158, 186, 281
accountability, 16, 47, 57, 64, 79, 120–21, 137, 142, 158, 166, 185, 187, 202, 206, 221, 253, 280, 284–85, 292
achievement, 71, 138, 179, 211, 220, 225, 243, 263–64, 276–77, 305
adaptability, 33, 137, 202, 231, 262–63, 278, 287
adult development, 266–67, 281
adult learning, 267
agreeableness, 235
alignment, 46, 57, 207, 236, 257–58, 269
analysis, 85, 97–98, 203, 233–34, 275
application, 67, 77, 96, 102, 204, 276, 319
appreciation, 10, 26, 187, 230–32, 235, 246, 256, 264, 269, 276, 304, 312, 314–15
arrogance, 13, 96, 114, 118, 139, 141, 174–76, 185
aspiration, xxxi, 17, 114, 132–33, 147, 256, 259, 281, 295, 305
assistance, 5, 10, 214
attitudes, 9, 41–42, 72, 80, 94, 130, 137, 141, 155, 161, 179–80, 216, 269, 271, 279, 302
authenticity, 3, 45, 123, 136–37, 187, 194, 282, 285, 305
authoritarian leadership, 57, 78, 141, 216–17, 219, 222, 261, 271
authority, 9, 26, 31, 46, 61, 78, 83, 86, 91–92, 95, 111, 113, 140, 178, 186, 212, 214–16, 218, 221–22, 261
autocratic leadership, 70, 214
autonomy, 111, 142, 182, 212, 219, 244
awareness, xxvi, xxviii, 8, 60, 68, 73, 119, 128, 137, 162, 168, 260, 281, 294

B

bad leadership, xxx, 13–14, 34, 48, 61, 74, 170, 173, 181, 196, 268, 274–75
balance, 57, 60, 70–71, 73, 83, 126, 142, 152, 158–59, 161, 164, 169, 172, 187, 192, 200, 202, 204, 215–16, 223, 225–27, 230, 233, 238–40, 242, 258, 303
beauty, 32–33, 187
behavior, 9, 13–14, 25, 37, 40–41, 49, 51, 54, 58, 61–62, 99, 103, 110, 127, 131, 137–40, 142, 159–60, 162, 165–69, 173–77, 182, 184–85, 187, 196, 204, 210, 219–20, 246, 260, 263, 266, 274–75, 305
belonging, 10, 101, 117, 130, 202, 253–54, 258, 306, 308
Bible, 26–27, 36, 48, 58, 61, 68, 72, 78–80, 86, 94–100, 102, 112, 116, 118, 138, 164, 179, 184, 190, 194, 269, 275, 290, 319
biblical teaching, xxviii, 4, 39, 79, 96, 102, 130, 178, 184, 189, 191, 215, 236, 283–84
biblical theology, 3, 52, 79–80

brand of leadership, 12, 170, 254
building relationship, 33, 56
building trust, 47, 56, 209
burnout, 162, 221

C

calling, xxix, 6, 67, 86, 88, 101, 117, 130, 132, 138, 147–48, 154, 184, 264, 274, 304
calling from God, 101
celebration, 130, 211, 247, 262, 264, 306
challenges, xxvi, xxx, 7, 33, 38, 50–51, 56, 98, 131, 133, 135, 138, 146, 149, 151, 156–59, 161, 168, 185, 205, 231, 236, 242–43, 247, 263, 268, 283, 286, 302, 306
change management, 74
character, xxvii, 6–7, 43, 60, 64–66, 68, 72, 78–79, 86, 89, 91–95, 98, 112, 124, 131, 138, 161, 166, 189, 204, 212, 215, 235, 252–53, 258, 263, 269, 275, 280, 286, 305
Christian mission, xxx, 102, 146–49, 153, 222, 226, 270
Christian professionals, xxix, 6, 129, 135, 151, 153, 159–60, 181, 184, 194, 319
Christian spirituality, 3, 40, 68, 74, 112–14, 116–17, 119–20, 124, 126, 131–32, 137, 143, 171, 176–78, 184, 189, 213, 254, 256, 279
Christian worldview, 101–2, 104, 126
Christlikeness, 8, 112, 124, 307
Church leaders, xxix, 101–2, 145, 148
coaching, 6, 17, 56, 74, 81, 183, 227–28, 261, 291–93, 295–97, 310
code of ethics, 182–83
cognition in leadership, 125, 237
collaboration, xxix, 15, 17, 26, 33, 35, 47, 49, 51, 56–57, 64, 81, 83, 101, 103, 137–38, 141, 160–61, 176, 178, 192, 202, 207, 209, 212, 215–16, 228–31, 240, 243–45, 250, 254, 258, 264, 269, 272, 275–76, 278, 280–81, 287, 314
commitment, xxxi, 1, 17, 26, 47, 58, 146, 156, 161–62, 168, 171, 177, 180, 182, 184–85, 187, 193–95, 207–8, 217, 219, 238, 243–45, 257–58, 289, 303
common goals, 12, 15, 26, 33, 48, 56, 169, 207, 217, 244–45, 281
communication, 12, 25, 33, 47–48, 87, 90–91, 95, 99, 119, 125, 158, 181, 188, 208–11, 238, 260, 262–63, 278, 280, 295
community, xxviii–xxix, 7, 10, 39–40, 43, 45, 50, 67, 78, 80–81, 87, 90, 94–95, 100, 111–12, 117, 121, 127, 130, 135–36, 138–42, 146, 152, 161, 166, 169–70, 180–81, 184, 189, 191, 204, 247, 253–54, 257, 266, 275, 280, 282, 289, 293, 314
companionship, 120, 122–24
compassion, xxviii, 43, 45, 48, 58, 61–62, 68, 78, 109–11, 120, 130, 132, 136, 138–40, 159, 167, 171–72, 178, 185, 191, 193, 206, 253, 269, 305
competence, 60, 64–65, 99, 161, 168, 182–83, 207, 215, 235, 245, 247, 258
competition, 41, 57, 158, 160, 231, 242–45
complacency, 179
complexity of leadership, 205, 307
confidence, 131, 222

conflicts, 69, 84, 140, 159, 161, 175, 183, 209
conscience, 172
consistency, 45, 175, 179, 194, 240
contemplation, 4, 8, 68, 73, 82, 110, 112, 122, 124, 129, 146, 258, 307
core themes and practices of leadership, 89
core values, 136, 157, 159
corporate governance, 287
courage, 35, 57, 64, 67, 78, 109, 132, 171–72, 268, 305–6
Creator (God), 87, 90–91, 95, 116, 186
crisis leadership, 92
critical thinking, 57, 141, 264, 270
cross-cultural leadership, 245, 247
cultural intelligence, 125–26
cultural sensitivity, 43, 178, 247
culture in organizations, 45, 201, 207, 282

D

death and resurrection of Jesus, 111
decision-making, 45–46, 49, 63–64, 87, 122, 142, 157, 172, 178, 182, 205, 207, 212, 216–17, 233, 241, 278, 287
dedication, 3, 68, 96, 146–47, 159, 177, 185, 194, 243, 262, 280, 287, 292
delegation, 50, 221, 229
democratic leadership, 57, 70, 216
desire in leadership, xxix–xxx, 2, 191, 223, 240, 260, 274
detachment, 220, 303–4
developing others, 64, 227–28
development of leadership, 60, 258
differences, 108, 110–11, 129, 161, 175, 232, 236, 245–47, 259
dignity, 67, 133, 138, 172, 178, 188
discernment, 63–64, 67–68, 113, 118–19, 122, 151, 158–59, 268–69
discipline, 8, 37, 68, 96, 118, 127, 132, 136, 168, 172, 177, 270, 280, 284, 286
distance, 219, 221, 223, 308
distributed leadership, 33, 228
diversity, 78, 88, 90, 109, 130, 142, 158, 161, 230–32, 247, 261
division, 34, 142, 231, 268
domestic, 245
drive in leadership, xxix, 29, 96, 103, 252, 260
dynamics in leadership, 11, 46, 80, 85, 138, 160, 167, 185, 216, 239, 259

E

effective following, xxx, 16, 19, 58, 89, 206–7, 238, 256, 274, 276, 295
effective leadership, xxiii–xxiv, xxix–xxxi, 1–4, 14–16, 25, 44–45, 47–51, 55–56, 58–62, 64, 70, 74, 76, 89, 91, 94–96, 100, 102, 125–26, 131, 157, 160–61, 170, 176, 181, 186, 199–209, 211–12,

214, 221, 225–27, 230, 237–38, 240, 242, 244–45, 247, 252, 254, 256–57, 261, 267–68, 272, 274, 276, 278, 285–86, 298, 304, 310, 319
effectiveness, 51, 60–61, 65, 68, 87, 170, 198–209, 211, 213, 215, 217–18, 224, 227–28, 234–35, 240, 243, 247, 256, 288, 308
egocentrism, 69, 82, 120, 126, 130, 137, 139, 141, 175
egoism, 188
emotional intelligence, 64, 125, 181, 237–38, 258, 260
emotions, 8, 128, 131, 209, 237–38, 292
empathy, 35, 48, 68–69, 78–79, 101, 111, 120, 130, 136, 142, 169, 171–72, 178, 209, 237, 262, 278
empowerment, 26, 60, 78, 100, 157, 227, 262
engagement, 26, 60, 100, 113, 124, 135, 152, 157–58, 167, 183, 188, 201, 209, 219, 257, 275, 281, 301
ethical considerations, 167, 170, 172–73, 181, 195, 200
ethical development, 95, 125, 168, 181, 183, 196, 258, 268, 319
ethical dilemmas, 159, 181, 188
ethicality, 166, 168–69, 177–78, 180–81, 187–89, 192, 213, 269, 297
ethical leadership, xxiii, xxix, 1–4, 14–15, 44, 47, 55, 58, 61–62, 89, 95–96, 100, 125, 160–61, 164–73, 176–81, 184–96, 200, 206–7, 214, 253, 256, 258, 268, 272, 274, 276, 286, 304, 308, 310, 319
ethical leadership checklists, 187
ethical principles, 40, 58, 165, 168, 170–71, 176–79, 181–82, 184, 186, 188–90, 200, 258
ethics, 44, 169, 176–78, 180–83, 185, 189, 268, 308
evaluation, 10–11, 57, 64, 90, 100, 151, 196, 210, 216–17, 236, 275, 284, 288
evil, 43, 82, 91–92, 114, 118, 138, 178
excellence, 35, 57, 78, 80, 96–97, 131, 136, 158, 185, 205, 214–15, 218, 225, 265, 275
expectations, 15, 51, 100, 140, 167, 177, 182, 217, 245, 291
experience, xxiv, xxviii, xxx–xxxi, 6, 9, 11–12, 33, 40, 49, 65–66, 68, 81, 84–85, 102–3, 108, 111, 114, 121–22, 127, 131, 136, 151–53, 158–59, 162–63, 170, 173–74, 178, 201, 211–12, 218, 220, 225, 228, 231–32, 234, 240, 243, 247, 250, 254–56, 258–59, 262–63, 267, 277–78, 280, 282, 292, 305–6, 310, 313, 319
exploration, 1, 64, 81, 88–89, 95, 108, 140, 211, 252, 308
extroversion, 235

F

fairness, 13, 58, 61, 79, 138, 158, 160, 167, 170, 172, 184–85, 187, 192–93, 269
faith, xxviii, 37, 39, 43–44, 58, 72, 77–79, 81–82, 84, 89, 92, 95, 102–3, 111, 114–15, 119, 122, 133, 137–40, 143, 145–47, 149–51, 153, 159, 171–72, 189, 194, 232, 236, 256, 269, 271, 282–83, 291–93, 297, 314
faithfulness, xxvii, 72, 120, 194–95
Fall (theological perspective), 92, 155
family, xxiv–xxvi, xxviii–xxix, 18, 33, 57, 84, 127, 129, 135, 148–50, 161–62, 166, 180, 187, 226, 268, 277, 292, 312–14
feedback, 4, 17–19, 49, 51, 56–57, 65, 127, 180, 208, 210–11, 216, 227, 236, 260, 264, 275, 280, 289, 292, 296, 314
fidelity, 182

flexibility, 137, 232, 247, 268

focus, xxvii, xxix–xxx, 17, 32–34, 47, 49, 51–52, 55–56, 62, 64–67, 70–73, 79–80, 82, 97, 100, 108, 111, 115, 122–23, 126, 129, 132, 135, 139, 148, 151, 154, 160, 172–73, 177, 181, 188, 200, 209, 212–13, 221, 225–29, 232–33, 236–37, 239–40, 243, 266, 268, 270, 273, 275, 277, 280, 282, 284, 286, 288, 296, 306, 311–12, 319

followers, xxx, 5–6, 9, 11–19, 21–23, 27, 29, 34–35, 37–39, 41–47, 49, 56–60, 62–64, 67, 79–80, 82–83, 85, 87–90, 93, 96–101, 103, 110–12, 114, 117–21, 123–24, 126–29, 132, 134–35, 138, 141–42, 146, 150–51, 157, 167–68, 171, 173, 175, 181, 189, 192–93, 195, 200, 204–7, 211, 213, 215–16, 228, 235, 238, 251, 253, 255–58, 261, 265, 269, 271–72, 274–77, 279, 282, 284, 288–91, 295, 302, 313

followership, 14–17, 19, 21, 39, 46, 83, 89, 103, 157, 167, 181, 207, 211, 216, 313

forgiveness, 24, 35, 39, 48, 58, 67, 92, 111, 114, 142, 178, 193–94, 214–15, 269

fostering culture, 16, 47, 142, 186, 207, 211, 215, 236, 281, 287, 294

fostering development, 147, 159, 184, 229, 280–81, 283

fostering relationships, 56, 176, 285

foundations, xxix, 3–5, 76, 81, 85, 89, 94, 102, 112, 135, 169–70, 177, 187, 189–90, 207, 277–78, 284, 312

freedom, 26, 34, 67, 84, 90, 113, 115, 130, 136, 188, 212, 214, 221, 229, 284

friendship, 117, 120, 122–23, 143, 273, 279–80, 284, 313

G

gap, xxx, 272–73

global, 6, 153, 245–47, 283

goals, 10–12, 15–17, 25–26, 33, 48–50, 56–57, 95, 99, 103, 131–33, 147, 153, 169, 175, 186, 192, 205, 207–11, 213, 217, 219, 225–26, 231, 238–39, 243–45, 254, 269, 273, 276, 281, 284, 296

God, xxiii, xxv–xxxi, 2, 4, 6–11, 14, 18–20, 26–27, 36–39, 41–42, 49, 54, 58, 61, 63–64, 66–68, 71–73, 76, 78–96, 98, 101–4, 110–24, 126–38, 143–46, 148, 150–56, 159, 162–63, 177–80, 184, 186–87, 189–94, 198, 214–15, 227, 250, 254, 256–60, 269, 279, 284, 294, 297, 300, 303–4, 306–8, 315

God's leadership, xxvii–xxviii, xxx–xxxi, 2, 4, 26, 72, 78–79, 86, 88–89, 92–94, 101, 103, 120, 133–34, 138, 186, 193, 256–57, 307

God's mission, xxvii, xxx, 83, 86, 150, 153

Golden Rule, 171

good leadership, xxiv–xxv, xxviii–xxxi, 3, 14–16, 23, 32, 34, 42, 47, 52, 59–62, 70–71, 80, 129, 133–35, 160, 165, 170–71, 173, 177, 185, 200, 223, 255, 260, 268, 272, 274–75, 285, 301, 304, 311

goodness, xxv–xxvi, 61, 72, 117, 192, 307

grace, xxix, xxxi, 58, 71–72, 95, 134, 139, 142, 179, 194, 256, 312

gratitude, 19, 36, 269, 277, 306, 312–14

group dynamics, 85, 212

growth, xxv, 2–8, 11, 17–20, 48, 50–51, 56–57, 60, 62–65, 68–70, 72–73, 80, 88–89, 108, 113, 119, 124, 127–28, 131, 133, 136, 139, 150, 158–60, 179, 210, 216, 225, 227–29, 241, 244, 251, 254–55, 257–59, 262–67, 275, 277, 281, 285, 287–89, 293–94, 296–97, 304, 306

guidance
  mentoring, 228, 293-94
  spiritual, 4, 8, 38, 41, 95, 102-3, 112, 116-18, 120, 122, 128, 131-32, 179, 269, 283, 310, 314
  trinitarian, 115

H

heart, xxvii-xxviii, 2, 6, 23, 27-28, 36-37, 58, 62-63, 85, 103, 109, 114-15, 118-21, 127, 131, 139, 143, 179, 184, 186, 189, 194, 228, 239, 304, 308-9, 312
hodos metaphor, 23, 31, 33-34
hodos terminology, 44-51
holistic approach, 102, 194, 200, 204, 258, 275, 292
Holy Spirit, 4, 6, 8, 41, 64, 78-79, 86-88, 90, 92-94, 102-3, 112-13, 116, 118-20, 122-23, 127-28, 144, 154, 163, 190, 257
honesty, 10, 46, 48, 58, 61, 79, 90, 120, 130, 136, 156, 159, 167, 169, 187, 192, 269, 288
hope, xxviii-xxix, 27, 35, 37, 43, 82, 103, 109, 126, 131, 146, 153, 161, 169, 171-72, 269, 301, 306
humanity, 26-27, 33, 42, 89-93, 95, 103, 108, 114, 117, 279
humility, 17, 41, 43, 45, 57-58, 61, 78, 83, 96, 113-14, 117-18, 121, 133, 161, 167, 178-79, 185, 191, 193, 214-16, 253, 262, 268-69, 285, 297
hypocrisy, 138, 140

I

identity, 39, 72, 78, 117, 146, 246, 281
impact, xxix, xxxi, 17, 45, 51, 60, 99-100, 113, 145-47, 161, 167, 172-73, 200, 217, 223, 225, 227, 245, 254, 266, 268, 277-78, 287, 310
implementation, 12, 25, 57, 64, 86, 90, 100, 157, 176, 201, 238-41, 243, 278, 284-85, 289, 296
individual approach, 6, 49, 151, 161, 228, 232, 234, 236, 244, 291
individualism, xxix-xxx, 6, 18-19, 26, 32, 45-47, 49, 56, 67-69, 80-81, 87-88, 95-96, 100, 103, 107-8, 111, 113-14, 116, 135-37, 139, 145-47, 150, 152-53, 156-57, 160-61, 167, 174, 180-82, 185, 188-89, 205, 210-11, 214, 218-19, 222-23, 225-26, 228, 230, 232-37, 239, 241, 244-45, 247, 253, 255-56, 258-63, 265, 268-70, 272, 274, 278-79, 284, 289-90, 293-94, 306
influence, 5, 7, 9, 14, 16, 19, 52, 63, 65-66, 77, 94-95, 100-101, 122, 125, 128, 142, 150, 168, 170, 190, 202, 205, 222-24, 230-31, 237, 247, 252, 266, 277-78, 280, 286, 301, 303
initiative, 134, 137, 140, 172, 180, 217, 239, 241, 254, 267, 282-83, 287, 289, 294, 313
inner life, 70, 122, 131-32, 261, 303, 307
inner peace, 71-72, 109
innovation, 4, 35, 49, 51, 57, 70, 160, 180, 231, 235, 241, 267, 287, 319
inspiration, 109, 117, 171, 222, 230, 238-39, 298
integrity, 3, 35, 43, 45, 48, 58, 64, 78-79, 113, 134, 136-38, 140, 159, 166-67, 170, 178, 182, 185, 192, 194, 198, 206-7, 215, 230, 269, 275, 278, 297
interconnectedness, 68-69, 91, 111, 115, 126, 128, 130, 151, 178, 252, 254, 278, 293
interests, xxiii, xxviii-xxix, 13, 44, 48, 74, 79, 82, 85, 88, 90, 94, 100, 115, 119, 125, 138-39, 141, 147-48, 151, 153, 162, 164, 167, 169, 174-75, 178, 180, 185, 187-88, 192-93, 201, 204, 207, 210,

219, 223, 225–26, 228, 231–32, 235, 238, 240, 244–45, 251, 259, 261, 266–67, 270–73, 275, 278, 283, 287–88, 290–92, 294, 296, 314
international, 52, 68, 74, 84, 140, 147, 183, 245, 247, 298, 311, 313, 319
intuition, 204, 233–34
invisibility, 222–23
involvement, 18–19, 103, 135, 152, 166, 212, 216, 219–22

J

jazz, 31–32, 52, 311
Jesus Christ, 39, 41, 78, 86–87, 92–93, 101, 103, 111–13, 115, 117, 120–21, 123, 153, 186, 227, 253, 257–58, 308, 315
journey of growth, 89
journey of leadership, 1, 265, 301
journey of leadership development, 265
journey of life, xxiv, 253
joy, xxvii, 6, 48, 72, 131
justice, xxvii, 79, 87, 90, 101, 109, 117, 120, 136, 169, 171–72, 178, 182, 188, 192–93, 242, 269

K

kindness, 41, 43, 48, 61, 72, 121, 159, 172, 191
knowing self, 65, 256
knowledge in leadership, 3, 11, 44, 59, 66, 80, 85, 90, 113, 212, 237, 266–67, 275, 286, 313, 319

L

laziness, 137, 155
leaders, xxiii–xxv, xxvii–xxxi, 1–27, 29, 31–35, 37, 39–107, 109, 111–13, 115, 117–21, 123–29, 131–43, 145–51, 153, 155–57, 159–61, 163–81, 183–209, 211–89, 291–95, 297–99, 301–19
leadership culture, xxx, 16, 57, 142, 170, 202, 207, 223, 228, 270, 281–82, 305
leadership defined, xxxi, 12, 23, 32, 66–67, 92–93, 109, 132, 139, 165, 203, 205, 208, 230, 243, 266
leadership development, 3, 5–8, 17–19, 45, 47, 56, 60, 62–66, 74, 82–84, 95, 125, 147–48, 196, 203, 226–28, 247, 251–52, 254–62, 264–68, 272, 274, 277, 279–83, 285–89, 293–95, 298, 311, 313, 319
leadership effectiveness, 51, 60–61, 65, 68, 199–206, 208–9, 211, 215, 218, 234, 243, 247, 256, 288, 308
leadership ethicality, 168, 177, 180–81, 187, 189
leadership formation, xxx, 8, 66–68, 129, 251–52, 254–62, 270–71, 277–80, 283–84
leadership in the Bible, 26, 79–80, 94–99, 102, 275
leadership maturity, 3, 17, 62–66, 69, 71–73, 95, 217, 259–60, 308
leadership metaphors, 23, 27, 31–35, 44, 51, 80, 117, 265, 301, 313
leadership mindset, 3, 45, 55–58, 83, 95, 102, 213, 256, 308
leadership model, xxiv–xxv, 3, 32–33, 45, 48, 58–61, 66, 78, 90, 95, 101–2, 104, 153, 161, 203–4, 256, 279, 285, 293, 298, 308
leadership potential, 6, 18, 56, 62, 92, 95, 161, 172, 186, 200, 241, 256, 261, 270, 273, 289

leadership skills, 18, 20, 60, 64–66, 79–80, 82, 95, 113, 204, 212, 243, 248, 252, 256, 258, 260–61, 275, 280, 282, 286–87

leadership styles, 11, 46, 50, 59, 161, 207, 211–12, 227, 234, 247, 261–62

leadership theories, xxiv, 83, 95, 141, 204, 284

learning, xxv, xxviii–xxix, 3–5, 57, 63, 65, 80, 96, 125, 127–29, 141, 157, 168, 176–77, 196, 206, 221, 237, 254, 259, 261–62, 264, 267, 269, 276, 279–80, 287, 292–93, 296, 302, 304

limitations, 68, 141, 158, 161

listening, 8, 14, 32–33, 45, 68, 123, 168–69, 208–11, 244–45, 291, 295, 311

love in leadership, xxxi, 43–44, 48, 52, 72, 82, 95–96, 103, 132, 134, 139–40, 172, 178, 186, 191, 215, 284–85, 315

M

management, 6, 66, 74, 90, 183, 220, 252, 286–87, 319

marketplace leadership, 135, 146

marketplace spirituality, 135

maturity in leadership, 3, 17, 62–66, 69, 71–73, 95, 217, 259–60, 308

meaning, xxiv, 10, 12, 31, 34–35, 39, 42, 52, 57, 62, 73, 84, 97–98, 108–10, 117, 126, 130–31, 136, 151–52, 154–56, 204

meaning of life, 110, 117, 130

mentoring, mentorship, 228, 261, 284, 290–91, 293, 313

metaphors, 23, 27–35, 41, 44, 51, 80, 117, 121, 131, 261–62, 265, 301, 313

metaphors of leadership, 32

mindfulness, 71, 109, 137

mindset in leadership, 3, 45, 55–58, 83, 95, 102, 213, 256, 308

mission (Christian), xxvi–xxvii, xxx, 25–26, 46–47, 57, 60, 67–68, 79, 82–83, 86, 91, 99, 102–3, 116, 119, 145–50, 153, 157, 163, 209, 222, 226, 254, 268, 270, 274, 283

missional professionals, 145, 153, 163

mission in leadership, xxvii, xxx, 68, 82–83, 102–3, 145–46, 148–49, 153, 157, 268, 274, 283

mission of God, 68, 146

mistakes, 65, 92, 130, 142, 160–61, 214–15, 220, 233, 291

model in leadership, xxiv–xxv, 3, 32–33, 45, 48, 58–61, 66, 78, 90, 95, 101–2, 104, 153, 161, 203–4, 256, 279, 285, 293, 298, 308

monopolization in leadership, 216, 218

morale, xxvi, 13, 43, 60–61, 166–67, 170, 185, 217, 243

morality, 60–61, 166–67, 185

moral principles, 140, 170, 179, 190

motivation, xxvi, xxix, 12, 16, 18–19, 26, 42, 48, 51, 65, 95, 103, 130–31, 135, 137, 142, 149, 155, 158, 161, 186, 217, 222, 226, 230, 238–40, 243, 274, 282, 287, 297

N

nonprofit organizations, 285

nurturing, 4, 73, 83, 108, 127, 135, 169, 176, 187, 227, 231, 242, 250, 252, 254, 256–58, 267, 269, 278, 280, 282–83, 285, 297, 303

O

objectiveness, 47, 50, 57, 161, 207–8, 224, 231, 258, 266

openness, 8, 57, 136, 215, 235, 245

organization, xxviii–xxx, 6, 9, 16, 19, 21, 45–51, 57, 59–60, 62, 64, 97, 108, 110, 129, 157, 161, 167, 169, 171, 178, 180, 182, 186, 188, 192, 194, 201, 204, 207–10, 213–26, 228–29, 231–34, 238, 241–42, 244–46, 248, 253–54, 258–59, 266, 270–72, 278, 280, 282, 285, 287–89, 298, 319

organizational culture, 16, 45, 57, 201, 207, 209, 211, 223, 282

organizational development, 47, 50, 60, 64, 66, 196, 223, 228–29, 254, 258–59, 282, 288–89, 294

organizational leadership, xxviii–xxx, 6, 21, 34, 44, 47–48, 51, 56–57, 59–62, 64, 66, 74, 79, 85, 96, 98, 104, 129, 135, 157, 161, 167, 171, 175, 178, 180, 186, 188, 192, 196, 201–8, 211, 213, 216–17, 219–20, 223–24, 226, 228, 231, 234, 241, 244–45, 248, 254, 258–59, 264, 266, 271, 275, 278, 280, 282, 285–86, 288–89, 298

organizational life, 3, 34, 61, 96, 98, 209, 211, 219, 225, 241

organizational values, 46, 48, 157, 185, 206, 209, 219, 282, 285

outcomes, xxxi, 46–48, 65, 68, 101, 132, 146, 200, 205–7, 210, 219, 233, 238, 259, 261, 266, 284, 289, 295

P

participative leadership, xxx, 33, 65, 101, 103–4, 216–18, 259, 307

passion, xxix, xxxi, 82, 311

peace, xxviii, 48, 62, 71–72, 109, 130–31, 140, 242, 311

peer learning, 65, 261

perceptions of leadership, 271

performance, xxx, 13, 26, 32, 50–51, 125, 159–60, 167, 169, 180, 183, 210, 214, 217, 224–25, 227, 229, 231, 240, 261, 277

perseverance, 43, 57, 78, 132–33

personal development, 3–4, 6, 8, 12, 17, 20, 60, 66, 70, 95, 117, 183–84, 225–29, 236, 254, 256, 260–62, 284, 288, 294, 303

personal drive, 260–61

personal example, 27, 185, 279–80

personal leadership, xxiv, xxix–xxx, 1, 3–4, 6–8, 12, 17, 27, 34, 44, 49, 51, 60, 66, 71–72, 77, 79–82, 85, 89, 95–96, 98–99, 113, 131–35, 137, 141–42, 155, 166, 177, 180, 184–85, 187, 192, 203, 211–12, 219, 221, 226–27, 234, 236, 252, 255–61, 263, 265, 267, 277, 319

perspective, xxiv, 3, 5, 17, 32, 44, 52, 57, 67, 74, 77–79, 89–90, 95, 100, 103–4, 110–11, 117, 119, 124, 131, 144, 146, 150–52, 154–55, 160, 170, 172, 181, 184–85, 196, 202, 204, 207, 221, 230–31, 243, 253, 258, 260, 264, 268, 272, 294, 297, 304–5, 312–13

planning, 64, 90, 100, 181, 201–2, 205, 207, 216, 220, 222, 233, 235, 237, 254, 260

plan of God, 79

power dynamics, 50, 80

powers, 214

present time, 227

priorities, xxvi, 48, 60–61, 70–71, 73, 95, 101, 133, 135, 139–42, 151, 160–61, 169, 174–75, 186, 188–89, 193, 200, 206, 229, 233, 235, 239, 241, 244, 253, 284, 307

problem solving, 45, 141, 296

processes, xxxi, 4–5, 8–9, 11, 16–17, 20, 45, 47, 49, 59, 63–65, 67, 81, 88, 97–98, 121–22, 124, 127–28, 154, 165, 196, 203–8, 210, 216–17, 219, 222, 228, 237, 239, 254–55, 257, 259–60, 262, 265, 270, 276–77, 289, 292, 294–97

professional development, 6, 62, 147, 158–59, 180–81, 183, 236, 258, 266, 297

professional ethics, 180, 182

professionalism, xxix, 6, 129, 135–36, 145, 147–48, 151, 153, 157, 159–60, 163, 174, 180–84, 188, 194–96, 226, 258, 266, 290, 293, 298, 319

prudence, 138, 171

purpose, xxvi–xxviii, 1, 3, 9–10, 14, 25–26, 46–47, 57, 65, 68, 72–73, 79, 84, 87, 89, 91, 98–99, 103, 108–9, 118, 121, 124, 126, 128, 131–34, 136, 145–46, 151–52, 154–57, 184, 191, 194, 207–9, 217, 226, 238, 259, 269, 274, 286, 294, 300, 306–7

Q

questions in leadership, xxiii, xxv, 5–7, 11, 14–15, 31, 56, 58, 83, 85, 126, 193, 195, 254, 259, 265, 288, 302, 319

R

reconciliation, 68–69, 194

recruitment, 167

redemption, 68, 79, 90, 92–93, 102–3, 111, 155–56

relationships, xxx, 8, 18–19, 26, 33, 38–41, 44, 46, 49–50, 56, 59, 63, 72, 82–83, 90, 93, 96, 103, 108, 112–17, 119–20, 122–24, 130, 135, 137, 146, 157, 166, 169, 176, 182–83, 190–91, 193–94, 206–8, 215, 225, 227–28, 237, 239, 257, 260, 273, 276, 285, 292, 294, 296–97, 303, 306, 308

religion, 85, 107–11, 113, 142

religious leadership, 81, 85, 95, 137, 139–42

religious spirituality, 107–11, 113, 115, 135

religious toxic leadership, 137, 139–42

renewal, 71, 93, 112, 156, 227, 257, 303

reputation, 198, 213–16, 313

research in leadership, xxix–xxx, 58, 85, 103, 125, 139, 147, 173, 252, 270, 274, 277, 302, 310–11, 319

resilience, 35, 253, 262–63, 268, 278, 305–6, 312

responsibility, 4–5, 37, 46, 50, 57, 61, 64–65, 67, 87–88, 90, 109, 117, 131–34, 136, 142, 154, 159, 161–62, 166, 170–71, 178, 181–87, 205, 213–14, 216–17, 219–21, 224, 226–27, 229, 234–35, 268–70, 277, 279–80, 294–95, 303, 305

results in leadership, xxxi, 206, 239, 319

revelation, 79, 86, 92, 102, 118–19, 279, 288

reward, 10, 155, 184, 243

righteousness, 34, 92, 96, 114–16, 120, 138, 257

role modeling, xxv, 180, 262, 280, 306

S

sacrifice, 39, 41, 71, 92, 103, 130
salvation, 92, 111, 113, 155
self-awareness, xxv, 7, 64–65, 71, 109, 130–31, 184, 258, 263, 265, 269, 281
self-control, 63, 72, 110, 172
self-denial, 41
self-development, 227, 229, 260
self-disciple, xxvii, 18–19, 235
self-inquiry, 8
self-transcendence, 68–69, 110–11, 304
servant leadership, 45, 57, 60, 171, 213, 261, 302
shepherding, 26, 29, 32, 38, 80, 116, 121, 303
showing the way, 11, 23–27, 33–37, 44, 46, 51, 117, 121, 131, 293, 301, 313
skills, 3, 17–18, 20, 26, 50, 57, 60, 64–66, 79–80, 82, 95, 99, 113, 131, 149, 158, 180, 204, 212, 214, 222, 225, 228, 230–31, 234, 236, 243, 248, 252, 256, 258, 260–61, 264, 275, 278, 280–82, 286–87, 293–94
soul, 2, 4, 36, 38, 115–16, 118–19, 150, 189, 298, 303
spiritual companionship, 120, 122–24
spiritual direction, 11, 120, 122–24, 127, 143, 314
spiritual disciplines, 8, 68, 127, 136, 284
spiritual intelligence in leadership, 124–26, 260
spirituality, 3, 6, 40, 44, 60–62, 66, 68, 74, 107–20, 124, 126, 129, 131–32, 135, 137–38, 143, 151, 171, 176–78, 184, 189, 213, 254, 256, 279, 292, 298, 308, 311
spiritual leadership theory, 52, 74
spiritual transformation, 8, 40, 63–64, 87, 90, 101, 110, 113, 115, 123, 128, 139, 158–59, 171, 200, 283, 297, 303, 309
stability, xxvii, 138, 179, 235, 240–42
standards, 12, 45, 87, 160, 166, 168, 176–78, 183, 185, 187–89, 246
stewardship, 61, 80, 133–34, 269
strategy, 13, 25–26, 46, 48, 50–51, 60, 65, 86, 91, 99, 157–58, 162, 175, 205, 209, 212, 218, 238, 259, 266, 283, 288–89, 294, 296, 319
stress, xxvii, 27, 40, 51, 136, 162, 181, 237, 253, 256, 264, 290
success, 1, 4, 11, 16, 24, 33, 50, 57, 69, 81, 94, 145, 158, 161, 167–68, 170, 173, 179, 192, 194, 201, 205–6, 211, 218, 220, 223, 228–29, 233, 237, 242–45, 253, 256, 282, 286, 298, 305
suffering, 69, 130, 181, 304–5
sustainability, 16, 61, 173, 226, 252, 282

T

team, teamwork, 280
thankfulness, 306
theocentric approach, 84–85
theological inquiry, xxix, 80–81, 83, 143

theological journey, 88
theology of leadership, 3, 52, 89
theology of work, 151–52, 154
tolerance, 172
toxic leadership, 13, 16, 56–57, 82, 137, 139–42, 165, 313
toxic religious leadership, 137, 139–42
transformational leadership, 3, 57, 60, 64, 69, 80, 87, 89, 101, 113, 138, 146, 171, 200, 240, 257, 259, 283, 307, 313, 319
transparency, 188
trinitarian guidance, 115
Trinity, 86, 94–95, 116, 120, 122–23, 143
trust, 13, 27, 37, 43, 45, 47–48, 56, 62, 78, 116–17, 119, 122, 136–38, 167, 169, 175–76, 182, 185, 194, 202, 206, 209–10, 215–16, 224, 262, 269, 273, 276, 280–81, 285, 296–97, 302

U

understanding in leadership, xxv, xxix–xxx, 3, 5–6, 11–12, 24, 31, 35, 50, 59, 66–67, 78, 80, 85–86, 89–91, 94–96, 100–103, 111, 138, 142, 161, 166, 176, 189, 193, 202, 204–5, 208, 212, 232, 237, 245, 247, 252, 256, 262, 264, 270, 272, 276–77, 279, 281, 301–2, 306, 314
unethical leadership, 48, 138, 160, 167, 170, 173, 175, 181, 185
unity, xxx–xxxi, 34, 41, 46, 68, 83, 86, 88, 90, 120, 190, 230–32, 310, 313–14

V

values in leadership, 25–26, 45, 48, 54, 57–58, 86, 108, 113, 136, 139–140, 157, 159, 165–194, 206–207, 244, 258, 269, 272, 278
veracity, 183
virtues, xxvii, 43, 45, 48, 67, 78–79, 90, 118, 145, 170–72, 253, 297
visibility, 222–23
vision, 12, 25–26, 46–48, 60, 79, 86, 91, 99, 132, 157, 172, 209, 217, 222, 238–39, 243–44, 254, 262, 269, 274, 276
VUCA (managerial framework), 63
vulnerability, 92, 305

W

war, 33, 140, 254–55, 305, 311
wisdom, xxv, xxvii–xxviii, 2, 4, 37, 42, 45, 54, 58, 63, 66, 73, 78, 80, 92, 94–95, 102, 109, 113, 116–17, 119, 122, 130, 143, 186, 211, 214, 218, 227, 230, 252–53, 260–61, 269, 292, 294, 307, 314, 319
work mindset, 56, 149, 152, 256
workplace, 7, 45, 128–29, 135–37, 145–46, 148–51, 153, 156–62, 172, 184–86, 194, 222, 246, 291–92
workplace realities, 156, 186

Y

youth leadership, 7, 267–72, 275, 277

NOTES

www.ingramcontent.com/pod-product-compliance
Lightning Source LLC
Chambersburg PA
CBHW052131070526
44585CB00017B/1780